The Constructivist Turn in Political Representation

In memory of Ernesto Laclau

THE CONSTRUCTIVIST TURN IN POLITICAL REPRESENTATION

Edited by
Lisa Disch,
Mathijs van de Sande and
Nadia Urbinati

EDINBURGH
University Press

Edinburgh University Press is one of the leading university presses in the UK. We publish academic books and journals in our selected subject areas across the humanities and social sciences, combining cutting-edge scholarship with high editorial and production values to produce academic works of lasting importance. For more information visit our website: edinburghuniversitypress.com

Edinburgh University Press Ltd
The Tun – Holyrood Road
12(2f) Jackson's Entry
Edinburgh EH8 8PJ

First published in hardback by Edinburgh University Press 2019

Typeset in 11/13 Adobe Sabon by
IDSUK (DataConnection) Ltd

A CIP record for this book is available from the British Library

ISBN 978 1 4744 4260 2 (hardback)
ISBN 978 1 4744 4261 9 (paperback)
ISBN 978 1 4744 4262 6 (webready PDF)
ISBN 978 1 4744 4263 3 (epub)

Contents

**Part III: Constructivist representation: critique and
reproduction of power**

Tables

Acknowledgements

Philosophical debates do not emerge spontaneously, and there is always a practical side to the meeting of different minds and perspectives. The inspiration for this volume came from a conference entitled 'Power and Representation', which was held at the Institute of Philosophy in Leuven between 4 and 6 June 2014. We would like to thank the organising committee of this conference: Toon Braeckman, Raf Geenens, Mathijs van de Sande – and in particular Marta Resmini, without whose tireless efforts that event would not have taken place. We would also like to express our gratitude to the other conference participants, whose critical questions and creative insights undoubtedly are reflected in several parts of this volume.

The editors are also indebted to several colleagues who helped to develop this volume at its various stages from a first idea to its point of completion. Lizzie Depentu has been of great practical assistance during the editorial process. Raf Geenens has lent some of his insights (and sentences) to the introductory chapter. Editions Belin has kindly offered us the right to publish an English translation of Claude Lefort's essay 'Démocratie et réprésentation', which was brilliantly translated by Greg Conti. Two anonymous reviewers have helped to improve the manuscript in several respects. The support and advice of Adela Rauchova, our commissioning editor at Edinburgh University Press, has been invaluable. Anna Stevenson's brisk and thoughtful copyediting greatly improved the final product.

Finally, the editors would like to thank all contributors to this volume. The breadth of subjects and problems addressed in this book, and the depth at which they are discussed, suggest that the philosophical debate on political representation is far from settled.

Introduction: the end of representative politics?

Lisa Disch

The 'end' of representative politics

For the past decade or so, citizens of the longstanding Western democracies have been quietly falling away from, visibly protesting and actively creating alternatives to the established institutions of political representation – establishment political parties in particular.[1] The litany of evidence is familiar. Membership in the major political parties is sharply declining. Popular support for challenger parties, protest candidacies and movements that circumvent parties altogether has taken establishment forces by surprise. These forms of 'subterranean politics' are no longer marginal but, rather, are 'striking a chord in the mainstream' as never before (Kaldor and Selchow 2013: 79).[2]

Europe has seen the eruption of M15 and Occupy movements, and the emergence of alternative parties and party alternatives to traditionally organised parties such as Podemos (Spain), Syriza (Greece), the Five Star Movement (Italy) and the Pirate Party movement (initially Sweden and Germany).[3] These movements are not motivated simply by economic circumstances and are not directed primarily at the politics of austerity. They are unique for giving voice to a new and distinctively democratic citizen anger. The media and the movements themselves coin new terms such as *Indignados* (Outraged) to signify that this protest targets the limitations and constraints of representative democracy as well as austerity economics (Kaldor and Selchow 2013: 81, 84–9). Political theorist Simon Tormey (2015) heralds this activity as the 'end of representative politics'. He takes these various movements to exemplify a 'horizontal' style of politics and to model an activism that 'seeks less to develop programmes and blueprints than to show directly the possibility of living in accordance with different values, a different ethos and a directly democratic mode of organizing communal life' (Tormey 2015: 9, 35; see also Sitrin and Azzellini 2014: 41).

We regard this democratic fervour not as the 'end' of representative politics *tout court* but as a protest against the peculiarly Anglo-Saxon idea of political representation as 'mandate representation' (Sintomer 2013: 22–3). Mandate representation – which German historian Hasso Hofmann defines as 'the people delegating power to a representative government' – is the dominant understanding of representative democracy today (Sintomer 2013: 23).[4] First conceived in the Middle Ages, it became 'politically hegemonic' in the seventeenth and eighteenth centuries with the 'rise of theories of natural law' and the emergence of republican ideas that privilege consent as the source of legitimate authority (Sintomer 2013: 22). Contemporary opposition to representative government takes aim at this core notion of democracy by electoral mandate – the 'transfer of juridical authority' from voters to legislators by means of a competitive election – in all of its aspects (Sintomer 2013: 23). These movements and alternative parties denounce legislatures as unrepresentative and unresponsive, condemn elections as distorted by mass media, money or both, and, above all, protest the reduction of political action to voting (Sintomer 2013: 23).

Even as they do so, they do not altogether renounce representation so much as practise it in a different mode (Gerbaudo 2017: 84). Take the signature declaration of Occupy ('We are the 99%'), which Sintomer (2013: 23) reads not as a 'performative contradiction' of their refusal to be 'considered as representatives' but as a rejection of mandate and embrace of identity representation: the protesters assert 'their ability to speak *like* the people rather than *for* them'. This is Hoffmann's 'identity representation', a part standing for a whole that it embodies, 'less "to act in the name of" than "to act as"' (Sintomer 2013: 23). Acting 'as' retains the symbolic core of representation ('99%' is no literal measure) but withholds the transfer of authority. It thereby refuses two defining principles of representative government, election and 'distinction' (Manin 1997: chs 2 and 3). The principle of election makes citizens 'primarily [. . .] the source of political legitimacy', as opposed to political actors in their own right. That of distinction justifies this reduced role by an 'aristocratic' premise: that election ensures representatives will be of 'higher social standing' than 'those who elected them' (Manin 1997: 95, 96, 94).

On par with these developments, political theory has made a 'constructivist turn' in the course of the past decades. This constructivist turn poses a conceptual challenge to the hegemony of mandate representation in Western academic scholarship. Its basic premise is that democratic politics requires at least some form of representation because constituencies or groups cohere as political agents only insofar as they are represented. Democracy, the implication goes, is impossible without representation.

We believe that this constructivist reconceptualisation of representation parallels the activist challenge to its practice in post-industrial democratic nations. How can that be so? Activists argue that representative government puts democracy into crisis. Scholars insist that representation – at least in the sense of representation *as* – is 'intrinsic' to democracy, not a fallback or supplement. These two positions, which may seem to be fundamentally at odds, share a radical premise: both reject the notion that social relations form the substrate of politics.

The social-as-substrate assumption formed the basis for post-World War II theories of representative democracy. As articulated by pluralists and social democrats alike, these theories held that politics manages relations of enmity and alliance that already exist outside of politics. Corporatists held these relations to be determined by the antagonism between capital and labour, whereas pluralists imagined that groups mobilise spontaneously when their political interests are threatened. Mid-century theorists of mandate representation did not believe that democratic political representation could 'mirror' society. They readily admitted that interests and opinions can and usually do undergo significant changes in the process of representation. They might be softened or sharpened, grow closer together or become more tensely opposed, and so on. Yet these scholars subordinated politics to social forces by assuming that political representatives echo, reproduce or track pre-existing social cleavages (Cameron 1974: 139).

Hanna Pitkin (1967: 140) gave normative expression to this assumption when she declared, 'As the "re" in "representation" seems to suggest, and as I have argued in rejecting the fascist theory of representation, the represented must be somehow logically prior; the representative must be responsive to him rather than the other way around' (Pitkin 1967: 140). Pitkin's pronouncement reads mandate representation off the 'etymological origins' of the term (Pitkin 1967: 8). She elevates a particular historically and culturally specific meaning of representation to the status of a general concept (Sintomer 2013: 15). She also fuses representation conceptually to democracy (Rehfeld 2006). On Pitkin's account, politicians not only should be responsive to the ideas and interests of their constituents, they *must* be responsive if they are to count as representatives at all. Even if constituent preferences do not make it into the winning policy option, they must be included and acknowledged in decision-making, and representatives must be prepared to justify their positions, particularly when a policy outcome conflicts with voters' views.

For those who accept Pitkin's account as standard, the constructivist turn poses a normative problem. It violates the basic assumption that 'public opinion on policy matters' ought to give democratic theory 'its starting point' (Achen 1975: 1220). How else to ensure that the people control their representatives and not vice versa? How is it possible for citizens or anyone else to judge when democratic representation is working well or badly if it cannot be assessed against the demands of the groups it is supposed to 'reflect'?

On one level, constructivists need not answer such questions. The claim that political representation, and democratic representation in particular, participates in creating that for which it claims only to stand is an observation. It is not a theoretical posture, resulting from a predilection for theorising representative democracy in one philosophical school rather than another, that constructivists are bound to defend. Yet, many scholars who subscribe to the constructivist approach recognise the normative problems it raises for democratic politics and are intrigued by them.

The 'constructivist turn': definitions and intellectual sources

The contributors to this volume argue that political representation in the advanced industrial democracies of today's globalised world works neither as its citizens imagine nor as the mid-century norm of mandate representation prescribes. For one thing, contemporary democracies have evolved to outgrow the mandate model (see Castiglione and Warren's chapter in this volume). With the emergence of supranational political institutions such as the European Union, the increasing political power of global corporations and global financial institutions such as the World Bank, and the urgency of global political issues 'such as migration, global trade, and environment', political representation takes place outside national parliaments and affects populations that are not formally organised as electorates (Urbinati and Warren 2008: 390). These structural changes place decision-making power in the hands of 'specialised and expert bodies' that are not authorised by electoral mandate and cannot be sanctioned by it (see p. 000 of this volume).

This new landscape of global interdependence provides opportunities for informal and 'self-appointed' representation by individuals and groups that 'make claims to represent others outside of electoral institutions or offices and apart from state authority' (Montanaro 2012: 1094). In these cases where there can be no electoral mandate, acts of representation do more than 're-present'. Constructivist scholars argue that they *solicit* their objects by engaging actively in 'making symbols or images of what is to be represented' (Saward 2010: 15).

This recognition and foregrounding of the symbolic and constitutive aspects of representation is one way to characterise the constructivist turn. Constructivist theorists regard political representation as a constitutive and mobilising force that 'does not simply allow the social to be translated into the political, but also *facilitates the formation of political groups and identities*' (Urbinati 2006: 37; emphasis added). As a consequence, representative functions are by no means restricted to particular mandated offices or institutions but can be fulfilled by a broad variety of social movements, organisations, individual citizens and media that 'mobilise, educate, and aggregate constituent perspectives and interests in the process of representing them' (Brown 2009: 8).

The constructivist turn can also be described in a different idiom as rejecting what Rogers Brubaker (2004: 8) terms the 'commonsense primordialism' that takes groups to be 'basic constituents of social life, chief protagonists of social conflicts, and fundamental units of social analysis'. Theorists of the constructivist turn understand power and representation to be intrinsically linked. They hold that analysts of democratic societies cannot take 'groups', their 'interests' or their 'demands' for granted as a starting place in studying relations of power and conflict because power is implicated in the very constitution of such groups and in their positioning in relations of conflict and cooperation (Laclau and Mouffe 1985).

The constructivist turn has several intellectual sources. One source is Swiss linguist Ferdinand de Saussure (2013), who proposed that language is a system of signs that creates meaning differentially, not referentially. Sense emerges from the oppositions and linkages among terms, not from the correspondence between words and things in the world. Saussurean semiotics emphasises that reality is symbolically mediated. Mediation does not mean that representations stand between subjects and the world like a filter. Instead, it accords agency to the subject who is no mere receiver of messages but an active participant in constituting the meaning of what they read, watch and listen (even if they experience themselves as merely taking it all in). The symbols they consume lend shape and intelligibility to their experience in turn.

Semiotics finds an unlikely counterpart in relatively recent empirical research findings on public opinion and political knowledge. Empirical research has demonstrated that individuals do not come to politics with fixed preferences that they have formed according to an instrumentally rational calculus; rather, they form preferences and opinions dynamically in response to the communications of electoral and policy campaigns (Carmines and Kuklinski 1990; Druckman 2004; Lupia 1992, 1994; Lupia and McCubbins 1998; Sniderman 2000).[5] These data confirm the theoretical shift that Gamson and Modligliani (1989) established from a rational individualist to an environmentalist account of the formation of beliefs, interests, and preferences.

This empirical research turns the classic model of democratic legitimacy on its head: citizens are responding to politicians rather than the other way around. Political learning and preference formation take place in the context of partisan combat as constituents learn from, not in spite of, the frames and cues that elites deploy to gain an edge in partisan contests. Not only has responsiveness turned the 'other way around' but, contrary to Pitkin, mass democracy needs it to do so for citizen learning to occur. Yet these findings do not make citizens pawns of elites, as Pitkin and others fear. Empirical researchers emphasise that individuals bring a multiplicity of considerations to bear on any given issue, and that an electoral or policy campaign inundates people with competing interpretive frames that aim to raise the salience of one consideration over another (Sniderman and Theriault 2004). In contexts of competitive messaging, scripting citizens' views is difficult, and office-holders who attempt it – even presidents – typically fail (Druckman and Jacobs 2015). Although individuals form preferences in response to issue framing, competition among frames invites political judgement, prompting people to consider which ones are most applicable and even to discount those that are most extreme (Chong and Druckman 2007).

The constructivist turn finds a third important source in work of Berger and Luckmann (1991: 27) whose 1966 classic aimed to raise the profile of sociology of knowledge by shifting its focus from 'theoretical thought' to 'common-sense "knowledge"'. They proposed the phrase 'social construction of reality' to signify the mutually constitutive relationship between the perceptions and material practices of human subjects and the 'objective facticit[y]' of the social world (Berger and Luckmann 1991: 30).[6] Constructivist analysis as they defined it neither debunks reality as merely social or patently ideological nor denies the materiality of the world. Instead, it aims to conceptualise the dynamic between human activity and social order in a way that does justice to a poignant paradox: that 'man is capable [. . .] of producing a reality that denies him' (Berger and Luckmann 1991: 70, 107). This tradition offers another way for constructivist approaches to arrive at understanding political representation as a mutually constitutive process that defines representative and represented alike.

Michael Saward's (2010, 2006) analysis of the 'representative claim' is the most systematic work to date to elaborate this process. Saward (2010: 51, 47) maintains that representing in politics, as in painting or theatre or literature, involves making claims that put forward 'verbal and visual images' of a constituency together with images of the would-be representative as a personality or symbol that must have 'a certain resonance' with those whom it aims to represent. Saward (2010: 36) maintains that claims-making constructs not a 'referent' but 'an idea of' the represented (see Disch 2015; Thompson 2012). Hacking (1999) uses the example of a scholarly work analysing the social construction of 'women refugees' (Moussa 1992) to illuminate the importance of drawing such a distinction, and to demonstrate that 'ideas' ought not be dismissed (by critics of social constructionism) as *mere* constructs. Hacking (1999: 11) emphasises that the term 'women refugees' does not 'refer directly to individual women' but to the classification ('women refugees') that can be granted to or withheld from 'women in flight' (Hacking 1999: 11). To analyse 'women refugees' as a construct is, first, to emphasise that there is nothing 'inevitable' in being assigned to the category 'refugees' and, second, to underscore that this idea has force (Hacking 1999: 11). It forms in a 'matrix', a 'complex of institutions, advocates, newspaper articles, lawyers, court decisions, immigration proceedings', that materialises an 'infrastructure, [of] barriers, passports, uniforms, counters at airports, detention centers, courthouses, holiday camps for refugee children' – all of which make a difference to women in flight (Hacking 1999: 10).

To cast Saward's argument in Hacking's terms, the representative claim constructs neither individual people nor groups directly but 'ideas' of constituencies that position them in the ideological and institutional 'matrices' of party politics. Rather than speak and act for a constituency ('represent' in the typical sense), claims-making solicits a constituency to recognise itself in a claim and to support the person who made it. The claim proposes a representative relationship that is not secured by formal institutions such as elections but, rather, sets in motion 'an ongoing process of making and receiving, accepting and rejecting claims' by the would-be representative and constituency alike (Saward 2010: 36). Saward's account brings 'constituency' in 'the active sense' (as a verb) to the foreground of the representation process as against the standard account which has featured constituency in its 'passive sense' (the noun), as 'a fixed territorial group of people or voters' (Saward 2010: 52). It exemplifies a constructivist turn that recasts Pitkin's (1967: 8–9; emphasis original) classic general definition (representation as the 'making present *in some sense* of something which is nevertheless *not* present literally or in fact') by insisting that specifically *political* representation puts the emphasis on the 'making' rather than the 'presence'.[7]

The 'claim-based focus' opposes Brubaker's 'commonsense primordialism' by refusing to take for granted the 'character of [a] constituency and the stability and ready knowability of its interests' (Saward 2006: 306). Many scholars find this approach enormously generative for studying political representation in practice. Judith Squires (2008: 190) proposes the concept 'constitutive representation of gender' to direct analysis away from issue congruence as a measure of women's representation to examining the ways that representatives of various kinds 'narrate' women's identities by making representative claims. Building on the work of Squires, Celis et al. (2014: 152) conducted an impressive multi-year, multi-national study of representative claims about 'women's interests' made by 'a broad range' of elected representatives and civil society actors. They found that such actors select and privilege 'particular portrayals of "women"' that will sell policy proposals to influential stakeholders and decision makers (Celis et al. 2014: 152).

The constructivist turn finds a final source in French poststructural philosophy, particularly its expression in the radical democratic theory of Ernesto Laclau and Chantal Mouffe.[8] Iris Young (2000: ch. 4) has demonstrated how French poststructuralism erodes the 'metaphysics of presence' that undergirded the mandate account of political representation. Young (2000) draws in particular on Jacques Derrida's philosophy of language and meaning. As is well known, Derrida (1973, 1982) argues that signs or 'representations' do not come after presence, but that the work of representation rather consists in making something present, through repetition and by referring to other signs. More generally, French poststructuralists are united around the claim that reality always comes to us through the mediation of language, discourse or a symbolic order. We are always caught up in a network of symbolic representations that constitute the reality we live in: these representations establish what elements are meaningful and determine how to act accordingly. Frank Ankersmit (1996: 45) argues that artistic practice is paradigmatic in this regard. As Geenens et al. (2015: 515) explain, 'when painting a picture or writing a book, artists or writers do not primarily intend to portray the world as it is' but to make it visible and intelligible in a particular way. Thus, far from reflecting reality, art discloses reality in a particular light.

Laclau and Mouffe emphasise the work of linkage (or 'articulation') that this mediation entails. They extrapolate from Saussure, arguing that not only language but society itself is a 'system of differences without positive terms' (Laclau and Mouffe 1985: 112). It follows that political representation can no more than linguistic representation be understood to reflect existing identities, commonalities or cleavages. The very concept of representation should be replaced 'with that of *articulation*', which conceives any unity between 'agents' to be the 'result of political construction and struggle' (Laclau and Mouffe 1985: 65). Laclau (1996: 98, 87) later elaborated that making non-necessary connections – or 'articulations' – between social actors is the activity of political representation (properly) understood in its 'essential impurity': not as 'the simple transmission of a pre-constituted interest' but as 'contribut[ing] to the identity of what is represented'.

It is important to distinguish between constructivism as theorists of representation have adapted it from these four sources and a radical linguistic constructivism that attributes to representation the 'power to make groups, to manipulate the objective structure of society' by the symbolic force of words (Bourdieu 1990: 138). Such a notion of constructivism may be conceivable in theory; it affords no purchase on politics.[9] Constructivist theorists do hold that representatives and constituencies are made – but not that they are made from scratch.[10] First, acts of representation take place within a context of beliefs and practices that constrain the kinds of appeals that are likely to be taken up. They exist in institutional and infrastructural 'matrices' that are fully material, not purely linguistic (Hacking 1999). Second, representation does not constitute the represented *tout court* but rather as a democratic political subject. Absent representation, there may be a population but there cannot be a people, constituency or group. The subject of democratic politics becomes recognisable as a unified and not merely aggregated entity only by means of representation. As Hans Lindahl (2003: 448) has put it, 'unity is necessarily a *represented* unity'. There can be no subject without an act or acts of representation that name the interest or principle or demand in virtue of which its various particulars can regard themselves as part of a larger whole. Their commonality is thoroughly political, existing by virtue of the array of allies and enemies that exist by the selection of one particular social cleavage over other possible lines of battle.

The constructivist turn: political and historical context

The 'constructivist turn' is not merely a theoretical posture. It is a political response motivated by a set of historical and political changes that we, following Bernard Manin (1997), understand as bringing about the metamorphosis of 'party democracy' into 'audience democracy'. Party democracy took shape with the emergence of mass political parties in the late nineteenth and early twentieth century. In the epoch of party democracy, mandate representation could, in fact, claim a social substrate. Party democracy exhibits a pronounced 'electoral stability' among voters, who inherit their party preference from their family, and a corresponding discipline among members in Parliament, who serve as 'spokesmen for [the] party' (Manin 1997: 211). In Europe especially, this stability derived from '*class divisions*', which made political representation 'primarily a reflection of the social structure', and rendered Parliament 'an instrument that measures and registers the relative forces of clashing interests' (Manin 1997: 209–10, 212). Parties dominated the expression of opinion as well. The partisan press ensured that citizens and opinion leaders '[were] little exposed to opposing views', and citizens had 'no voice other than that of the party and its affiliated organisations' (Manin 1997: 215). With its electoral stability and long-standing social cleavages, the terms of conflict '[were] a reflection of a social reality independent of the politicians' actions, [and] the electorate appear[ed] as the origin of the terms to which it responds in elections' (Manin 1997: 223).

Manin dates the metamorphosis of this form to the 1970s. With the emergence of a new social pluralism, characterised by a proliferation of 'social and cultural lines of cleavage', this period saw a notable breakdown in electoral stability that gave rise to representative government as 'audience democracy' (Manin 1997: 218). By contrast to party democracy, where voters cast their ballots for a party rather than for a person, audience democracy involves a 'personalisation of power', both in government and in the electorate (Manin 1997: 219). In government, this personalisation tends to concentrate power in the executive and either privilege presidential elections or (in parliamentary systems) focus attention on the party leader rather than the party platform. It can also lend momentum to charismatic politicians who rely for their organisational resources at least as much on pollsters, media consultants and image advisors as they do on traditional forms of voter education and outreach staffed by mass parties. Urbinati (2016: 25) has emphasised that this shift is consequential for changing the 'character' of the 'voting power' from an expression of democratic sovereignty – the choice of a party being an expression of support for and judgment about a particular set of policies – to 'an investiture or plebiscite of a leader'. In the electorate, politicians enjoy a new autonomy over the composition of conflict. Party identification becomes less constant as voters take their bearings from the 'terms of the electoral choice' which, no longer dictated by longstanding social cleavages (such as class), depend on 'perceptions of what is at stake in a particular election' (Manin 1997: 222).

The term 'audience democracy' has an undeniably pejorative connotation that seems to characterise voters as reactive spectators of representative politics who are ripe for elite manipulation.[11] Manin appeals to structural linguistics to block the manipulation move. Making reference to Saussure, Manin (1997: 227) proposes that 'an electoral campaign' neither reflects nor depicts a pre-existing field of conflict but, rather, 'creates a *system of differences*' that cannot be mastered by any single player. Elections put party elites, candidates, donors, political action committees and other organisations in competition against one another and in communication with voters to define what the election is about. In an election as in a language, the 'meaning of each term is a result of the coexistence of several terms distinguished from one another', which do not simply register on an audience but must be taken up by it (Manin 1997: 227).

Manipulation is a false concern because politicians cannot script electoral conflict however they please. To win elections, they must promote cleavages that mobilise voters to their side, and they 'do not know in advance' what these will be (Manin 1997: 223–4). Insofar as candidates compete against and in relation to one another to determine the stakes of the election, the 'choice that is finally presented [to the electorate] and the cleavage it activates are the result of the combination of the terms offered by each candidate' (Manin 1997: 224). Just as on the semiotic account of language no single speaker masters the meaning of speech without the participation of the addressee and competition from other speakers, so too in 'audience' democracy no single candidate masters the terms of electoral conflict.

In sum, Manin offers a historical account of the changes to representative government that make a constructivist turn in theories of democratic representation necessary. Although he introduces 'audience' democracy to characterise the transformation of representative politics, Manin does not pass judgment on it. He gives it a name and leaves the normative implications and consequences open to exploration. We carry the 'audience democracy' thesis beyond representative government to democratic representation broadly understood, as an activity not just of national political parties but of a host of informal, global and self-appointed representatives as well.

Overview of chapters

We divide the volume into an introduction and three parts. The first parts build the concept of the constructivist turn historically, by tracing its intellectual genealogy in a variety of ways. Contributors to the second part take up the challenge to explore how the normativity of representative democracy might be (re)conceived in light of the constructivist turn. Chapters in the third part take a critical approach to the constructivist turn from various vantage points.

Chapters in Part I trace the genealogy of the constructivist turn both in recent scholarship and in the history of Western political thought. The part begins with Dario Castiglione and Mark E. Warren's much-cited but heretofore unpublished chapter, 'Rethinking representation: eight theoretical issues and a postscript'. In this chapter, Castiglione and Warren frame many of the issues of this volume by making two important contributions. First, they situate democratic theorists' turn to political representation, and their specifically constructivist departure from the 'standard account' of political representation, in relation to the political changes that motivated it. They rightly observe that the principal-agent models of political representation that passed as general and typical accounts were specific to and limited by the territorially based politics of the democratic nation-state. The emergence of many transnational and subnational practices of representation displace this territorial model, together with the electorally based mechanisms of authorisation, accountability and responsiveness that held them consistent with democratic ideals. They bring to light the 'intrinsically dynamic' aspect of political representation that the standard account failed to track. Second, Castiglione and Warren pose the normative challenge that emerges from the transformation they describe. This is for democratic theorists to specify claims-making and activities of unelected claims-makers so as to make it possible to account for when they contribute (or not) to this 'basic norm of democracy': 'empowered inclusion of the community of those affected in collective decisions and actions' (see p. 24 of this volume).

In different ways, the chapters by Jan Biba, Bernard Flynn, Warren Breckman and Raf Geenens consider the relationship between representative democracy and conflict. Biba takes us back to the sixteenth century to the debate over the 'Venice myth'. There he finds, in the restricted republicanism of Francesco Guicciardini, a precursor to democratic elitism and, in Machiavelli's *Discourse on Remodelling the Government of Florence*, the design for a 'proto-democratic' republic that yokes together 'representation, conflict and inclusion' (see p. 54 of this volume). Flynn, Breckman and Geenens each elaborate the constructivist turn through the 'primacy of the symbolic' and the space that representation opens for contesting claims to political authority. For Flynn, the key thinker of this primacy is Claude Lefort, whose notion, 'quasi-representation', makes it possible to resist realism by emphasising society's tenuous identity and the contestability of any claim to rule (see p. 64 of this volume). Flynn juxtaposes Lefort's appreciation for the symbolic against the 'realism' of Michel Foucault, which amounts to a 'denegation' of the symbolic that manifests itself in Foucault's condoning the 'exercise of raw power outside of any lawful restraint' (see p. 73 of this volume). Breckman brings key theorists of radical democracy into the ambit of the constructivist turn and establishes a rival genealogy for their notion of the symbolic which, Breckman argues, they draw not exclusively from structuralism but from the romantics. Whereas structuralism does pose a normative problem for democracy, by raising the spectre of a 'ubiquitous ideological grid that always already inhabits our subjectivity', the romantics were the first to formulate the polyvalence of the symbolic that enables its disruptive character (see p. 77 of this volume). Like Flynn, Geenens also emphasises the genealogy of the constructivist turn in French philosophy, thereby amending Castiglione and Warren's account, which emphasises its roots in the tradition of deliberative democracy. He argues that the French genealogy, specifically the work of Claude Lefort, is consequential for disclosing the 'normative merit' of political representation which is that, by symbolically constituting society as a whole, representation enables individuals not only to position themselves as members of a community but to contest its organising principles (see p. 92 of this volume).

To conclude this part, we present the first English translation of a 1989 essay, 'Democracy and representation', that Claude Lefort delivered in Paris at the School of Advanced Studies in the Social Sciences (École des Hautes Études en Sciences Sociales) for a colloquium on Latin America organised by sociologist Daniel Pécaut. The chapter gives systematic expression to many of the themes of this section: the primacy of the symbolic, its relation to conflict and its generativity for a rich account of democratic representation beyond electoral politics. The chapter also offers rare insight into Lefort's practical vision for representative democracy, which he affirms should be understood as 'not merely the system in which *representatives* hold political authority in *the place of* citizens who have designated them' but 'also the system that assures to society "visibility"' (see p. 106 of this volume). Lefort draws explicit connections between his influential theorisation of modernity's 'disincorporation' of power and representative democracy, arguing that it provides the 'political stage' for the 'conflicts which play out in society' once its unity is no longer embodied in the sovereign, and 'a symbolic framework which prevents them from degenerating into civil war' (see p. 106 of this volume). On Lefort's account, political representation does not supplant the agency of citizens but fosters it, provided there exists a robust network of civil society associations that both manifest opposition to official institutions and propose new subjects of political representation.

The second part of the volume features chapters by Samuel Hayat, Oliver Marchart, Lasse Thomassen and Nadia Urbinati that wrestle with the normative challenges that follow from the constructivist turn from within the terms of the constructivist approach. Hayat's chapter explores the question of the agency of the represented by drawing on works of French sociologists Pierre Bourdieu and Luc Boltanski. He proposes an alternative normative criterion for democratic representation – representation as *proposition* – which claims that the represented acquires from the process of representation not just an identity but also the capacity to judge that identity. Marchart takes up the work of Frank Ankersmit and Ernesto Laclau to present a 'negative concept' of representation, as a relation of non-identity between representative and constituency, that attests to the ultimately ungroundable nature of the democratic regime. He exemplifies the argument with the case of Bosnia, after the Dayton Peace Agreement of 1995, which illustrates the disastrous consequences of a positive and identitarian notion of representation. Thomassen's chapter radicalises Michael Saward's formulation of the representative claim from a perspective informed by Jacques Derrida's concept of 'iterability'. He does so by showing that in a constructivist understanding of representation, the representative claim is an event, and, as such, ultimately impossible to pin down. The upshot is that the representative claim will always retain an element of opacity and instability. This has implications for technical aspects of Saward's theory of the representative claim (specifically the notions of referent and event) as well as the normative aspects of the theory, which remains within the horizon of a future in which we may one day be able to pin down the meaning of a representative claim. Urbinati's chapter focuses on the theory of representative claim-making as a celebration of the constructive power of ideology; it explores the implications of its affirmation of political realism and argues that it cannot avoid being tested by a claim of legitimacy, even when it proposes itself as only a creative event that is situated within the domain of opinion and factual consent.

The final part of the volume turns to contemporary politics. Chapters by Alessandro Mulieri, Mark Devenney and Mathijs van de Sande assess the role that constructivist practices of representation play in the critique and reproduction of power. Mulieri reconsiders the tendency among constructivist theorists of representation, most notably Saward, to propose the concept of claims making to direct attention to and legitimate democratic practices that fall outside formal institutions of government. Mulieri counters that constructivist theories of representation can function quite differently in global politics. Namely, they can lend democratic legitimacy to elite-dominant and expert-led practices of governance. Devenney argues that theorists of the constructivist turn raise a set of questions about the relationship between democracy, equality and representation that they cannot answer because they inadequately account for sedimented forms of inequality and the limitations that they impose on democratic equality. Failing to thematise the social and political conditions which make representative claims possible, these theorists neither address the ways that representative claims are over-determined by global forms of hegemonic order, nor attend to how they presuppose certain established notions about human beings. Devenney counters with a notion of democratic politics as improper that argues – counter to the constructivists – that representation is not intrinsic to democratic enactment. Van de Sande reconsiders a prominent criticism of new protest movements, such as Occupy or the *Indignados*, that have refused to address demands to representative institutions, refrained from claiming representative legitimacy for themselves and adopted direct democratic modes of organisation. When constructivists like Chantal Mouffe judge these refusals of representation to be politically naïve, they make two mistakes. First, they conflate representation as a symbolic and descriptive relation and representation as acting for others. Although these movements refused to practise and to speak of themselves in terms of representational politics, they vividly engaged symbolic representation in their slogans ('We are the 99%') and their names. Second, they get caught up in a 'constructivist paradox' by failing to apply precepts of constructivism to themselves: everything is discursively constructed, except for the underlying conception of how political change must be established.

Notes

1. I am grateful to Mathijs van de Sande and Nadia Urbinati for the many conversations that inspired this introduction and for their comments on multiple drafts, to Raf Geenens who contributed to the sections on poststructuralist theory and social constructivism, to Mark Brown for reading the penultimate version, and to two anonymous reviewers for the press who offered excellent advice on how to craft it.

2. Alongside this specifically democratic anger, there is also an undeniable strand of populist anti-establishmentarianism that citizens express through electoral channels. In Britain, this new anti-establishmentarianism is manifest by the election of Jeremy Corbyn to the leadership of the Labour Party, which announced a break with the party mainstream, and by the Brexit referendum, which renounced the European Union as an 'establishment' project. In the US, the rise of the Tea Party and the 2016 election to the US presidency of a real estate magnate who had made a fortune in reality television trumpet the disjuncture between *both* of the established political parties and their popular bases.

3. We leave out the National Front in France because it is a longstanding white nationalist party that is not part of this new wave even if it attempts to rebrand itself to take advantage of it. We also leave out *Wutbürger* (Angry Citizen), a term that the media coined to refer to supporters of right-wing populist parties or movements who protest not representation generally but their own *mis*-representation by liberal policies toward migration.

4. Sintomer (2013) and Mulieri (2016) are the only articles in English translation to offer a detailed account of Hasso Hofmann's 1974 classic in relation to contemporary debates about political representation (see also Mulieri in this volume). Despite its importance for a comparative political theoretic treatment of political representation, Hofmann's work has been only partially translated into French (see Hofmann 2013) and not at all into English.

5. As early as 1942, V. O. Key's influential studies on public opinion and pressure groups made it very clear that political and social elites have, maybe not a decisive, but certainly a formative influence on opinions held by the public (Key 1942).

6. In their words: 'the world of everyday life is not only taken for granted as reality by the ordinary members of society in the subjectively meaningful conduct of their lives. It is a world that originates in their thoughts and actions, and is maintained as real by these' (Berger and Luckmann 1991: 33).

7. The constructivist approach to representative politics bears a trace of Kantian moral constructivism in the insistence that acts of political representation do not simply derive their legitimacy and authority from institutions and electoral processes but must actively generate both of these, by the dynamic process of making and taking up political claims. Whereas the Kantian constructivist emphasises the need to prescribe normative standards for processes of argumentation and reasoned exchange so as to ensure that legitimacy functions as a context-independent standard, the constructivist approach to political representation treats legitimacy as a political and contextual achievement, not a universal regulatory ideal. That a particular audience in a particular place takes an act of representation or representative claim to be democratically legitimate neither ensures that it can stand the test of reasoning nor guarantees that it is not coercive (Disch 2015: 495–6).

8. Thank you to Raf Geenens for contributing to these next paragraphs.

9. It is doubtful that any self-avowed constructivist actually subscribes to radical linguistic constructivism. As Samuel A. Chambers (2003: ch. 1) has argued, the position nonetheless warrants refuting because it is frequently ascribed to constructivists by their critics.

10. In the context of sociology of science, Hacking (1992: 52) puts it this way: 'constructionalists hold that facts and phenomena are made, not observed, and that criteria for truth are produced, not preordained. They hold that scientific facts are real enough once the making has been done, but that scientific reality is not "retroactive"'.

11. Manin termed this form of representative government 'audience democracy' in the English translation of what was, in the French original, la démocratie du public. He chose this translation to avoid the distinctly positive connotation that 'public' confers in Anglo-American political contexts where liberal individualist ideologies predominate

as they do not in France. With the French term, he meant to convey that 'unlike in party democracy, the electorate and the society were no longer structured by a single preeminent cleavage, the class cleavage, but by multiple cleavages (*les publics*) that could be mobilised or not mobilised depending on circumstances' (Manin, pers. comm. 2016). The translation added a pejorative connotation that Manin neither intended nor foresaw. See for example Ursino and Cantaro (1993) who use 'audience democracy' to describe a surge of anti-party populist politics.

Part I

The constructivist turn: Anglo-American and Continental intellectual genealogies

2

Rethinking democratic representation: eight theoretical issues and a postscript[1]

Dario Castiglione and Mark E. Warren

Introduction

In countries we often term 'established democracies', the democratic concept evolved its familiar form based on elections of political representatives and a universal franchise. This form had two notable functions. First, the election of representatives enabled democracy to take root within large, integrated political units, producing mass democracy. Second, the electoral representative form established a viable if uneasy balance between the pressures of social and political democratisation and the rule of professional political elites. Owing to these functions, we have come to understand democratic representation as having three key characteristics:

1. Representation involves a principal-agent relationship (the representatives 'stood for' and 'acted on behalf of' the represented), mostly although not exclusively on a territorial basis, so that governments could be said to be responsive to the interests and opinions of the people constituted by territorial membership.
2. Representative roles have specified places within political decision-making structures, formalised in constitutional law. Representation identifies locations for political power to be exercised responsibly and with a degree of accountability, in large part by enabling citizens to have some influence upon and exercise some control over it.
3. The right to vote for representatives provides a simple means and measure of political equality, comprised as distributed empowerments to select and recall.

It has long been recognised, of course, that these representative relationships are complex both in meaning and in practice (Pitkin 1967).
They are enabled and mediated by many kinds of groups, including
mass political parties, interest groups and corporatist organisations.
In addition, public spheres and civil society organisations develop
and focus public opinion, so that mechanisms of representation have
never simply aggregated citizens' preferences, but also formed and
transformed them. Finally, the equality of representative relationships, while conceptually simple, is highly vulnerable to distortion
by everything from political institutions that exaggerate the powers
of majorities, pluralities or advantaged minorities, to the corruption
of representative relationships. Taken together, these propositions
and their related problematics define what we shall call the 'standard
account' of democratic representation. They describe, justify and
problematise large-scale, mass democratic institutions.

Yet contemporary democracies have evolved in ways that increasingly undermine the adequacy of the standard model. Two of these
involve the scale and complexity in processes of decision-making in
modern societies:

1. The emergence of transnational decision-making arenas, where
   new international and global players operate, tends to escape the
   reach of territorially democratic representation, as do the increasing number of issues that are non-territorial in nature (Rehfeld
   2005; Grant and Keohane 2005; Bohman 2007).
2. An increasing number of collective decision-making areas and
   issues, at both the national and supranational level, are now under
   the control of specialised and expert bodies, with only loose connections to the traditional institutions of political representation,
   and often lacking a place for the voice, influence and control of
   those affected (Zolo 1992; Beck 1997; Brown 2006).

Two other changes have to do with the ways people relate to their
political communities:

1. The simple political egalitarianism on which the institutions and
   mechanisms of modern representative democracy were established
   has given way to increasing demands for group recognition as well
   as for forms of equality related directly to people's needs, characteristics, identities and conditions (Taylor 1994; Phillips 1995;
   Williams 1998; Young 2000). These developments have produced

a more complex discourse of representation, for which simple egalitarian standards embedded in the standard model no longer seem adequate.

2. There has been a diffusion of more informal structures and opportunities for democratic representation and influence. This development partly reflects the diminished role of formal political structures in social decision-making, but also the increasing diversification of the forms of association in modern societies, post-material ideals and culture, as well as increasingly dense and complex forms of public discourse (Beck 1997; Offe 1996; Warren 2001).

In this chapter, we offer our reflections in the form of eight theoretical issues that, in our view, will help to focus an agenda for rethinking democratic representation that responds to these new circumstances of politics.

Eight theoretical issues

Historically, the practice of political representation emerged through two different processes: the establishment of the representative nature of the state and of its institutions, and the emergence of 'representative government'. The first process, often associated with Hobbes, is concerned with the act of authorisation. The second process identifies with the extent to which representatives can be made accountable to the represented. In the simplest terms, we can conceive of these two concepts emerging sequentially in the history of political thought, the first coinciding with the emergence of ideas of sovereign and absolute power in the sixteenth and seventeenth centuries, and the second taking root through the establishment of modern legislative institutions and constitutional government in the eighteenth and nineteenth centuries. Institutionally, this evolution meant a gradual passage of the claim of political representation from the more personalised institutions of the monarchy to the more diffuse institutions of modern legislatures. Socially, the transformation reconfigured political space, from the more fragmented and hierarchical structure typical of feudal societies, to the more unitary and undifferentiated relations underlying modern commercial, and eventually industrial societies (Violante 1982). 'Democratic' representation built on this early modern, state-centric conception of representative government. The study of modern political representation has followed these same channels, focusing upon electoral systems and the relationship between elected representatives and their constituencies.

Recently, this 'standard view' has come under increasing pressure (Saward 2010, 2014; Mansbridge 2003, 2009; Disch 2011; Rehfeld 2006, 2009), and it has become increasingly evident that political representation in democracies is a rather more complex process. For these reasons, looking at political representation from a democratic perspective now requires that we step back from the patterns of thinking we have inherited from the standard account, in favour of a more abstract and normative evaluation of the forms representation might take.

Imagining different spaces for democratic representation requires that the idea of democracy be conceived at a general level of abstraction, divorced, at least in the first instance, from any particular institutional arrangement, so that it is possible to identify representative relationships within a variety of possible institutions and practices, and then to judge them in terms of their contributions to democracy.

The abstract, but we hope robust, norm of democracy that we adopt for our analysis judges the effects of collective decisions on individuals rather than being defined by the institutions common in democratic government, even though we also assume that collective goods are relational and irreducible to individual goods. The degree to which a representative relationship is 'democratic' would depend upon the degree to which it enables individuals potentially affected by a collective decision to have opportunities and powers to affect the decision itself, in some way proportionally to his or her stake in the outcome. The corollary action norm is that collective actions should reflect the purposes decided under inclusive processes. In short, the basic norm of democracy is empowered inclusion of the community of those affected in collective decisions and actions (see, for example, Habermas 1996: 107; Dahl 1998: 37–8; Held 1996: 324; Young 2000: 23; Goodin 2007; Warren 2006b; Fung 2013; Castiglione 2015).

In all but directly democratic venues (and even sometimes then), this norm of democratic inclusion is achieved through representation. Thus, we are conceiving of representation as the concept identifying the normatively significant structure of democratic institutions. An account of representation that is sufficiently generic to respond to emerging political practices and institutions, as well as specific enough to identify their democratic elements, will have a number of theoretical features, which we summarise in the form of eight issues.

The first four are concerned with extending the conceptual dimensions of political representation, building on theoretical insights and debates that we believe will continue to be productive. The first concerns the specific sense in which political representation is a relationship. The second relates to the way in which democratic representation involves forms of trusteeship. The third is concerned with the criteria according to which representation, as a political relationship, can be judged either for what it is or for what it achieves. The fourth identifies the modes of agency embedded in political representation as forms of political practice. The last three issues seek to capture the new ecology of political representation, while the fifth issue serves as a conceptual bridge between normative and institutional dimensions of representation.

ISSUE 1. DEMOCRATIC REPRESENTATION IS A RELATIONSHIP OF AUTHORISATION AND ACCOUNTABILITY

A great virtue of Hanna Pitkin's approach to political representation was that she was clear about its ontology: influenced by ordinary language philosophy, she viewed the meanings of representation as enacted within social relationships (Pitkin 1967). As a political theorist, Pitkin was interested in political representation, particularly within representative government. But she recognised that an understanding of political representation (conceptually, normatively and institutionally) involved placing the concept within two interlocking narratives. One narrative showed how the very concept of representation (and more generally the 'represent-family of words') had come to mean what it means in the standard account of political representation. This involved placing the political meaning of 'representation' within a larger group of meanings, as those used in contexts such as artistic, theatrical, mental, religious and legal forms of representation. The purpose of this comparison was not just to trace its historical and etymological character, but also to make the point that meanings first developed in other contexts had left their imprints on our political usage. The second narrative was concerned with the process of institutionalisation of the idea of political representation, which reflected successive historical experiences of power struggles and ideological disputes. This second narrative eventually resulted in the standard account, which took political representation to mean the institutional and formalised relationship between a 'representative' and his or her constituency, seen as the democratic feature of legislative power in a representative form of government (see also Manin 1997).

The point Pitkin was making was that one cannot understand representation without recognising the way in which it could be used from different perspectives, and that these perspectives were the results of linguistic, semantic and institutional processes.[2] Out of these processes, however, Pitkin identified a number of discrete groups of meanings. She first distinguished between 'formalistic' and 'substantive' understandings of political representation. Formalistic understandings and theories focus on the presence of the formal features of authorisation (by the 'principal') and/or accountability (of the 'agent'). In contrast, substantive theories are concerned with the way in which these relationships work. She divided substantive approaches between those that understand representation as 'standing for' someone or something else, and others that conceive it as 'acting for' someone else (or a collectivity). With respect to the former she further distinguished between 'descriptive' and 'symbolic' ways of 'standing for'. The latter she treated as a single group, though she recognised that there are different ways in which one can act for someone else.

However different, each of these formulations assumes that at the core of political representation there is a relational element between the entity that represents and the entity that is represented. Although this observation is obvious, its implications are not always fully appreciated. There are, for instance, important consequences for how we understand the agency of the representative (Plotke 1997: 29–30), to which we shall return in Issue 4. Here we wish to draw attention to two other aspects of the relational quality of political representation: its ambiguity and its social construction. There is an intrinsically dynamic quality to political (and democratic) representation, which the standard account fails to emphasise, a point to which we will return in our discussion of Issue 8.

'Formalistic' theories, as Pitkin notes, may emphasise either authorisation or accountability, almost to the complete exclusion of the other. From a formal perspective, we can therefore characterise the core relationship established by political representation in at least two ways:

1. Political representation involves a representative X being authorised by constituency Y to act with regard to good Z. Authorisation means that there are procedures through which Y selects/directs X with respect to Z, and that while authority for decisions with respect to Z resides with X, ultimate responsibility for actions/decisions of X rest with Y.
2. Political representation involves a representative X being held accountable to constituency Y with regard to good Z. Accountability means that X provides, or could provide, an account of his or her decisions or actions to Y with respect to Z, and that Y has a sanction over X with regard to Z.

Each account can produce different political conceptions. Democratic theories tend to combine authorisation and accountability, but the way in which they combine is neither obvious nor necessarily fixed once and for all. Indeed, democratic societies and institutions often propose different equilibria between these two kinds of relationships. Westminster-style representation, for example, loads heavily onto the initial authorisation of governments, with weak accountability between elections, but strong post-hoc accountability. American-style presidential systems only weakly authorise governments, as elections cannot produce results that align representatives into a single governing body, owing to the separation of constituencies that is at the heart of separated powers. Instead, the system subjects individual elected officials as well as institutions to numerous mechanisms of accountability; in the American case, biannual election of members of the House of Representatives, Congressional oversight of executive agencies and checks on presidential powers, an auditing agency controlled by Congress, and strong judicial review.

A similar ambiguity with respect to the relational quality of representation emerges when we look at it from a more substantive perspective. 'Standing for' and 'acting for' understandings point towards distinct ways in which 'representation' constitutes political relationships. We often conceive of our political or democratic institutions as doing both, thus using one or the other of these understandings as a way of justifying a particular conception of how the institution should either work or be organised. Some of the disputes about the merits of descriptive representation – a clear case of representation as 'standing for' – stem partly from this ambiguity. Moreover, both 'standing for' and 'acting for' can give rise to different ways of representing, to which we may give different political consideration. For instance, think of the way in which opinion polls (a form of descriptive 'standing for' through statistical generalisation) can be used to orient government's action. Or consider the way in which activism and political mobilisation can act as a form of symbolic 'standing for', and occasionally 'acting for'.

'Acting for' can also give rise to different understandings of the relationship involved in representing: as a trustee; as a deputed agent; as a fiduciary (in the sense of a 'free' agent); as an expert. Each of these ways of understanding what 'acting for' involves on the part of the agent refers to a different relationship between principal and agent. Mansbridge's argument that the practice of political representatives cannot be captured by the simple 'promissory' model of the standard account makes this point as well: she builds out the standard model by ideal-typing three other common understandings of what political representation involves, including 'anticipatory' representation that is forward-looking; 'gyroscopic' representation, in which a representative is trusted to make good decisions owing to their strong moral gyroscope; and 'surrogate' representation, in which representatives take on causes not organised into electoral constituencies (Mansbridge 2003). Such arguments point to ambiguities embedded in the standard account and move us towards analysis of representative relationships as they are understood and enacted.

The second relational aspect we wish to note has to do with the socially constructed and contextual nature of political representation. Of course, all relationships are socially constructed and contextual. Formalising their structure may make them easier to define, at least in the normal course of events, but this conceptual technique should not substitute for enacted meanings. As Hans Wolf perceptively maintained in a passage rightly singled out by Pitkin (1967: 9), 'the making present of A by [B] is merely a formula; what is important is how that is to be understood, what it means, under what circumstances and assumptions it is possible, and how it is justified'. Representing is a 'conceptual construct, particularly a construct of group opinion and ideology'. The socially constructed aspect of representation is evident in all discussions about what is represented in the political process: people, interests, values, characteristics, and so on, as we discuss in Issue 6 below.

But there is another aspect of the social construction of political representation as expressed in the standard account that is worth remarking, particularly because it has implications for how we understand political representation within the globalised conditions of modern democracy and politics. This feature of the concept can again be illustrated by reference to Pitkin's work. In the 'Appendix on Etymology' in *The Concept of Representation* she shows how, at least in English seventeenth-century politics, the idea and function of political representation is first attributed to the whole legislature before being assumed by individual members of it as representatives of their own constituencies. But a very similar story, she suggests, applies to the development of the Latin equivalent in the late Middle Ages. In other words, the claim to political representation does not emerge piecemeal as the aggregation of particular representative claims. Rather, it is mediated by the more general claim that political authority of a body derives from its collective representation of the whole of the people, realm, caste or class. Of course, this is a complex intellectual and political story, with implications for the sharp controversy that developed in the late eighteenth century over whether representatives carry 'mandate' from their constituents, or can act independently of constituents' instructions. These observations suggest that there never was a simple and operative relationship between the principal and the agent; indeed, both are constructed by relationships embedded in the larger political communities to which they belong. This construction of principal and agent appears to be unproblematic in the standard account because both the unity and the boundaries of the political (or democratic) community are assumed as being largely territorial and relatively easy to identify – a condition that stabilised only with the rise of the nation-state, and is now being destabilised by the circumstance of politics we discussed above.

ISSUE 2. TRUSTEESHIP IN DEMOCRATIC REPRESENTATION

Representation, argued Edmund Burke, should be 'virtual': representatives should not be delegates, but rather trustees who use their best judgment on behalf of those they represent. The 'delegate' versus 'trustee' dichotomy has been rightly rejected: when representatives serve as pure trustees, no democratic elements remain, and they are little more than paternalistic aristocrats (Pitkin 1967; Mansbridge 2003, 2009; Manin 1997). Yet insofar as the 'delegate' model implies that representatives simply mirror their constituents' preferences, it fails to anticipate the key political functions of representatives as deliberators and bargainers within political institutions, and as agents whose activities define and refine constituencies and their interests. The contemporary popularity of 'accountability' as a feature of democratic representation seems to split the difference, enabling representatives to use their judgment, but in ways responsive to those they represent (Castiglione 2006).

But the 'accountability' approach to trustee representation has limits, even within the terms of democratic representation (see also Issue 8 below). Consider the following:

1. No citizen can participate in all decisions that affect him or her, owing to scarcities of time, knowledge and attentiveness. For the same reasons, it is unthinkable that citizens can actively hold accountable those who represent them. 'Accountability' directly to citizens requires a level of citizen participation in monitoring their representatives that is impossible in large-scale complex democracies.

2. Similarly, accountability is costly: it requires monitoring regimes. Trust is, from this perspective, simply more efficient: it lowers the costs of monitoring. Ideally, because accountability is costly, it should be 'allocated' to the relationships where it is most important.
3. Accountability regimes may cultivate a culture of suspicion that damages cultures of professional responsibility and undermines public trust.

In practice, relatively passive representative relations based on trusteeship are ubiquitous – and it is hard to see how they could not be in today's societies. We therefore need to ask whether it is possible, at least in principle, to understand 'trusteeship' as a feature of democratic representation.

Burke's aristocratic formulation will not do: the judgment to trust is, in large part, a judgment that the interests and/or values of the person or entity trusted are convergent with one's own. Democracy emerged, in part, on the basis of distrust of aristocrats who, for the most part, did not have the people's interests in view, and so provided little basis for trust.

Yet we do have another conception of trust that is consistent with democracy, if not democratic in itself: bureaucrats, judges and many kinds of professionals hold a 'public trust'. They are not elected but rather chosen for their competence and expertise. Theoretically, they serve purposes that have already been settled and generalised by the political process. In government, trustee relations are, for the most part, limited to the domain of administration – that is, arenas in which purposes are agreed and administrators hold a public trust. In contrast, the domain of politics is defined in part by conflicting interests and values, and so relations of trust are not, as a general matter, appropriate (Warren 2016).

But once we understand the notion of trust in terms of its basis – the congruence of interests and/or values between the truster and trustee – we should also notice that many representative relationships exhibit this congruence (Mansbridge 2009). Under these circumstances, might political representative function as trustees?

Circumstances do exist that satisfy these conditions, but on case-by-case bases. We might say that trusteeship is democratic when a citizen makes a decision to trust, based on knowledge of convergent interests or values (Warren 2006a, 2016). Clearly, this kind of representative relationship is common in civil society through voluntary association membership: we trust Greenpeace to represent some of our environmental interests in their political activities, even if we are not active in the organisation. Likewise, we may trust certain of our elected representatives on the basis of what Mansbridge (2003) calls their internal moral 'gyroscope', which holds the representative steady and aligned to our own values and interests; therefore (we think) this will ensure that the choices the representative makes are the ones we would make under the same circumstances. We do not, therefore, delegate decisions we have made, but rather trust the representative to make decisions in our name and on our behalf in ways that we are likely to find acceptable.

In complex democracies, then, even the most active citizens engage in something of a division of labour with respect to representative relationships: they may reserve their participatory resources for monitoring representatives whose values and interests conflict with theirs, or who are subject to cross-cutting pressures in such a way that they are more inclined to represent those who actively voice their interests and values, and who monitor their conduct.

We might, then, develop a democratic conception of representation based on trusteeship along these lines, on the assumption that it is one kind of representative relationship within a broader ecology of representative relationships. The democratic element resides not in citizens' active monitoring of the representative relationships, but rather in their initial judgment that trust is warranted, perhaps checked periodically – say, at the times of membership renewals or elections (Mansbridge 2009; Warren 2016).

ISSUE 3. INPUT VERSUS OUTPUT REPRESENTATION, PROCESS VERSUS PERFORMANCE

Insofar as democratic representation is a relationship that benefits the represented, it must be possible to judge it from both internal and external perspectives – that is, from the perspective of the integrity of the representative relationship from the citizen's perspective, as well as from the perspective of how the relationship functions or what it accomplishes within the political system. There are two reasons for being attentive to both kinds of judgments. First, as already noted, the institutions of political representation have multiple meanings, allowing them to perform more than one relational function at the time. Some institutions or persons may symbolically 'stand for' a group of citizens or the collectivity, while at the same time they may be 'acting for' them. The good that derives from the 'standing for' is more likely to be of an expressive nature and therefore not readily comparable with the more instrumental good that we presume should come from the 'acting for'. The problem in each particular case is to judge how their different functions can be made mutually supportive or, failing that, how they can be balanced within the political ecology of a democratic system of government. Overall, we assume that in a democratic society, where the effects of collective decisions on individuals is what ultimately counts, there must be a presumption in favour of the instrumental over the expressive side, so that the latter must in some way made be congruent with the former.

Second, within democracies, the concept of representation is associated with the norm that citizens have equal standing in collective decision-making processes, typically institutionalised as political rights attached to citizenship status – rights that should be operative both in process representation or input legitimacy, and in output representation, output legitimacy or performance-based legitimacy. Neither process nor output representation, however, has in itself its own criteria of validation, since each refers to the other as its ultimate test of legitimacy. So, the evidence of a good or fair system of representation is that overall it produces outcomes that satisfy the citizens. But in order to judge whether the citizens are really satisfied we need to have in place some fair or good system through which the interests, values and opinions of the citizens can be expressed.

ISSUE 4. REPRESENTATION AS A POLITICAL PRACTICE

Representation, we noted above, is not the opposite of participation (Plotke 1997). But historically, early modern period arguments in favour of representative government were often directed against a classical conception of direct democracy, and as a way of tempering presumed excesses of growing social and political egalitarianism. Indeed, the practice of democratic government has relied on various forms of representation as a way of retaining aristocratic and elitist features of government (Manin 1997). However, it is also true that the emergence of mass democracy has meant that representative institutions, such as large popular parties and class-based organisations, have broadened political and democratic participation. The practice of political representation should therefore be seen as a two-way relationship, which can be used as much to exclude (Rehfeld 2005, ch. 1) as to include (Plotke 1997) people from politics. Such a dualism has conceptual roots. Representation can indeed be seen as much as an 'absence' as a 'presence' (Runciman 2007). Since representation is 'making present something that is literally absent', much depends on where we place our emphasis. Indeed, the tension between presence and absence in representation is indicative of some of the general tensions of modern democracy, as in the conflicts between its populist and elitist tendencies.

These points suggest the more general point that we ought to view representation as political practice in which a central constitutive role is played by the 'claims' made by the representatives (Saward 2010, 2014). When we do so, we can see that there is no necessary (as opposed to contingent) antagonism between democratic representation and participation. Indeed, far from excluding, many forms of representation encourage and channel forms of direct participation, making them both more meaningful and effective. In part, these effects have been the experience of mass democratic organisation. The problem that we now face with the decline of some mass organisations that historically mobilised participation – political parties in particular – is to find new and meaningful ways of reconciling political representation with democratic participation. This problem implies several tasks, such as rethinking grounds (the idea of the 'constituency', of individual and group representation, and so on) on which the represented should have their identities and interests recognised, and then identifying the channels of representation through which the represented can make their voice heard and effective (Rehfeld 2005; Phillips 1995; Williams 1998; Young 2000; Dovi 2007; Fung 2013).

Another aspect of the presence/absence dichotomy embedded in the concept of representation that may be essential to the kinds of judgments citizens bring to representative practices is the reflexivity that these practices can induce. This effect of representation was noted by Madison and Kant, who were concerned by the distorting effects that self-interest tends to have on judgment. Representation can induce reflexivity through the disjunction of the interests between the representative and the represented. Positions and arguments are, as it were, displayed before constituents for their consideration. Representation can in this way underwrite cognitive distancing between persons and arguments, between the 'who' and the 'what', thus creating greater space for public discourse, deliberation, and various forms of accommodation and compromise. Within such a process, representatives can also function as conduits of other reasons and interests to the individuals they represent, thus making these individuals potentially more reflexive in the way they hold their interests, for reasons of now having to view and justify them from a public perspective (Ankersmit 2002; Urbinati 2000, 2006; Dryzek and Niemeyer 2008). All of this, however, implies a reconsideration of the various levels at which public discourse takes place within a democratic society, and the various conversations that go on among the citizens, among their representatives, and between the citizens and their own representatives. In short, we need to understand representation as a relational political activity, rather than simply a Rousseauian dichotomy of active versus passive relations to power and legitimacy – a dichotomy that still has inertia within democratic theory.

ISSUE 5. REPRESENTATION IS CONSTITUTED BY/WITHIN POLITICAL PROCESSES

If we understand representation as a relational (or enacted) political practice, then, of course, we shall need to theorise the features of political contexts that constitute representative relationships (or which structure their enactments). Although representation will always be contextually determined by its constitutive relationships, from a theoretical perspective we can identify the kinds of relationships that would be involved in any adequate understanding. In particular, representation is constituted by:

1. The rules and norms that define representative roles, constituted not simply by the self-understanding of the representative, but also by the expectations of the represented. In many cases, representative roles are formalised, with normative expectations that attach to the role. To be sure, even formal representative roles are typically subject to conflicting expectations, with many possible ways to understand duties and responsibilities (Mansbridge 2003, 2009).
2. The incentives and opportunities produced by institutions. Adversarial processes, for example, provide opportunities for political entrepreneurs to articulate issues and claim representative status, not only within government, but within society and even markets. Differing electoral systems provide different kinds of incentives for parties, groups and representatives to broker, express or stand firm, as does the relationship of each – close or distant – to power and resources.
3. The nature of conflict and cleavage within society, defined by power relations, distributions of resources and culture. These structure the field of issues and arguments that, at any given point

in time, provide opportunities for political representation, some
of which come to bear upon public opinion and culture, others of
which connect more directly with centres of decision-making.
4. The group and associational structure of society, providing capacities, opportunities and patterns of representative relationships.
5. The self-understanding of participants and participation within
   representative relations. Citizens' education and representatives'
   qualifications both determine and are determined by the process
   of representation, so that citizens and representatives continuously contribute to one anothers' formation and transformation.

Owing to these contextual elements, representative relationships are
both intrinsic to political practices and institutions and constitutive of them. Indeed, they are also so ubiquitous that most of the
classical formulations we have inherited, such as the polarisation
between direct and representative democracy, or between trustees
and delegates, are unhelpful. Representative relationships are themselves venues of participation, deliberation and political struggle;
they range from trust to monitoring and suspicion; they increasingly
combine identity and instrumentality, input and output legitimacy,
'standing for' and 'acting for', and so on. These dichotomies are no
longer useful in identifying 'kinds' of representation. They remain
valuable primarily as analytic tools we can use to highlight features
of representative relationships.

ISSUE 6. OBJECTS OF REPRESENTATION: WHAT IS REPRESENTED?

Because our views of democratic representation have too often been
limited to formal, electoral representative models, the question of what
the objects of representation are has been constrained by the assumption that representatives represent constituents, either as individuals
or aggregated into (usually territorial) constituencies. As a normative
proposition, the assumption is warranted: in a democracy, ultimately
the goods of collective actions must be justified as goods for individuals who are co-dependent within a collectivity. Within the standard
model, however, the norm often functions as an ontology, such that
the objects of representation are viewed as individuals, usually understood as their revealed interests, preferences and values.

More recently, the standard model has expanded to include the
descriptive characteristics of persons that bind them to ascriptive
groups. The best recent literature holds that descriptive representation

is justified because it introduces the social perspective and experiences of disadvantaged groups into representative institutions (Mansbridge 1999; Williams 1998; Phillips 1995; Young 2000; Dovi 2002). When representative bodies look like their constituencies, they do a better job of representing the full range of experiences, perspectives and situations in society. But combined with the view that the objects of representation are constituted within representative relationships, these theoretical developments suggest that the question of what is represented should itself become a question (Disch 2011).

At least four considerations should frame this question. First, from the perspective of those who are represented, what is represented are not persons as such, but some of the interests, identities and values that persons have or hold. Representative relationships select for specific aspects of persons, by framing wants, desires, discontents, values and judgments in ways in which they become publicly visible, articulated in language and symbols, and thus politically salient. While individuals hold some interests, identities and values quite consciously, many others are formed in response to representative entrepreneurship, which may function to evoke latent interests, raise consciousness or overcome collective action problems (Urbinati 2006, 2014). Thus, we should not say that 'interests' or 'identities' or even 'values' pre-exist the representative relationship. They become objects of representation through the constituent features of the relationship, even if they owe their existence to situated experiences and individual biographies. Likewise, 'groups' are never objects of representation as such, because we should think of them as complexes of shared experiences, moulded into group form by a shared consciousness of belonging (Young 2000). It is very often the case that political representation outside of formal political venues – representation by social movement leaders or counter-hegemonic symbols and argument – is instrumental in bringing the group as objects of representation into existence, and then stabilising its existence over time.

Second, persons are not just bundles of interests, identities and values; they are also agents. It is distinctive of democratic representation that persons actively participate in asserting, authorising and approving that which is represented on their behalf – through arguing, reflecting, demonstrating, writing and voting. So it is intrinsic to democratic representation that individuals are represented in their capacities as citizen-agents; these capacities are reflexively instantiated in every representative relationship. To put the point another way, democratic representation also represents the political standing

of individuals as citizens who are empowered to authorise representatives and then to hold them accountable.

Third, objects of representation are further 'objectified' by their
functions within democratic processes, where they are, as it were,
detached from persons to become social movements, interest groups,
public goods, social perspectives, narratives, empathies and moral
identities. Representatives often say that they 'stand for' entities
of these kinds – for the common good, for 'the family', for climate
change action, for human rights, for free enterprise, for the marginalised or for the hard-working citizen who plays by the rules. Each
type of entity is contingent, of course – real, but dependent upon the
combinations of experiences, biographies, and social and political
processes through which such entities are created and reproduced,
and objectified in acts of representation.

Finally, it is precisely this detachment of collective entities from
persons that enables representatives to represent positions in public
discourse and argument, in this way serving as both conduit and structure of public spheres. Without this detachment from specific persons
and interests, politics would fail to have a discursive locus, and would
be reduced to the aggregation and bargaining of interests and identities (Urbinati 2006). The issue here is related to, but not quite captured by, the old distinction between the delegate versus trustee roles
of representatives. When representatives – groups, public individuals,
the media – carry interest positions into public decision-making, they
engage in more than 'individual' judgment. They function as key figures in representing and mediating public debates, in this way reflecting interest and identity positions back to their constituents. This
reflexive representation of positions and arguments should, ideally,
enable constituents to follow debates and to reflect upon and defend
their own positions, such that representatives can, ultimately, claim to
represent the 'public will' as reflected in a developed 'public opinion'
(Manin 1997; Urbinati 2000, 2006). That is, a fully developed theory
of democratic representation would capture the discursive functions
of representatives in the public sphere – functions that are served in
different ways, depending upon whether representatives are inside or
outside of formal politics.

ISSUE 7. WHO IS A DEMOCRATIC REPRESENTATIVE?

As politics has become more complex, multi-layered and perva-
sive within society, so too has the question of who can legitimately
claim to be a democratic representative. The standard answer, that

representatives are elected, is increasingly inadequate, owing to the de-territorialisation of political issues, the mismatch between representation based on territories and the scale of issues, the devolution and deconcentration of some kinds of powers and the globalisation of others, and the increasing importance of discursive and symbolic influence. Each of these developments introduces new domains for political representation with the possibility of democratic legitimacy.

We might think of these domains as expanding in two dimensions. On the one hand, politics is increasingly spilling out of formal, electoral politics into non-electoral and informal domains, suggesting that we need to theorise the democratic possibilities of informal forms of representation (Montanaro 2012). On the other hand, modes of influence are expanding – or are at least more visible – from those that are parasitic upon state powers of decision-making and administration to those that work through public influence and economic power. Combining these distinctions suggests the domains of representation shown in Table 2.1.

The significance of these distinctions is that the growth of representative activities is most rapid in the domains outside of elected representation and familiar forms of corporatist and interest group representation. Many of the new forms of representation have ad hoc qualities which democratic theorists have been poorly equipped to judge. Thus, in the domain of direct action, some three decades ago groups of college students claimed to represent the interests of sweatshop workers. They were not elected, and few had direct contact with those they claimed to represent – but their actions produced regimes that monitor work conditions in the clothing industry

Table 2.1 Domains of representation

Mode of power	Sphere	
	Electoral politics	Non-electoral politics
State-based power	Elected representation	Corporatist, interest group and CSO representation
Public Influence	Electorally oriented political organisations and advocacy groups	Voice representation (media, social movements, advocacy groups, citizen panels)
Economic power	Public-private partnerships	Stakeholder representation, direct action representation, NGOs

in many countries. In voice representation, individuals and groups claim to be the representatives of women, gays, ethnic groups, religious groups, the poor, the persecuted, the unborn, animals and even the Earth. In cases of public-private partnerships, real-estate developers assume public purposes and come to 'represent' them in exchange for opportunities to profit. The European Union, the United Nations and the World Trade Organization are all seeking to include 'civil society organisations' in their decision-making processes but are faced with the question of which organisations have legitimate claims to speak for, say, women or peasant farmers.

In short, the emerging political landscape provides more and more opportunities for individuals and groups to propose themselves as representatives, and to function in representative capacities. But once representation no longer has an electoral basis, who counts as a democratic representative is difficult to assess (Alcoff 1995). Democratic theorists should not rule out any such claims *a priori*, but we do need ways of judging the democratic credentials of representative claims (Saward 2009; Montanaro 2012).

Issue 8. Authorisation and accountability in informal representation

Granting Pitkin's point about the excessive formality of the authorisation/accountability distinction, it nonetheless suggests one approach to non-electoral or 'informal' forms of representation. We might ask in such cases about the functional equivalents to the relationship between authorisation and accountability at work in election cycles. Through elections, representatives are authorised to represent interests, identities and values, and to bargain, deliberate and decide. Once they have done so, they can be held accountable for the results through the potential sanction of being voted out of office. Elections should function to motivate discursive accountability: representatives should, and often do, give retrospective accounts of their representations, actions and decisions (Dryzek and Niemeyer 2008). While account-giving is discursive in form and can be ongoing throughout a term of office, representatives often act prospectively, looking towards the next election in which voters have the opportunity to judge the adequacy of the account (Mansbridge 2003; Thompson 2004; Young 2000: 128–33; Fung 2006).

Non-electoral representation lacks the clear temporal sequencing of authorisation and accountability that is produced by regular elections. Appointed positions in government such as judges and administrators usually have authorisation procedures that are relatively clear-cut, at least from a conceptual perspective. In other non-electoral areas, however, the dimension of authorisation is wide open: where there are no regularised means such as an election, authorisation can grow from the ability of groups to attract followers (memberships, petitions, and so on), mission statements that converge (or claim to converge) with a constituency, descriptive characteristics such as gender or race presented to potential constituencies as declaratives ('as a woman, I believe . . .'), experiences or simply public visibility as measured in book sales and media appearances.

It is also possible that where elections are lacking, accountability may reflexively and retrospectively provide authorisation. Does a mission statement converge with a group's subsequent activities? Do an association's members agree that the association represents their purposes? This is why, we think, representation is increasingly identified with 'accountability' in non-electoral politics. We need general accounts of political landscapes that are increasingly populated with entrepreneurial representative claims that connect to possibilities for authorisation and accountability by some constituency (Castiglione 2006; Saward 2009, 2010; Montanaro 2012). So, for example, we might start mapping the landscape of representative entrepreneurs by noting some differences among the many kinds of groups that populate civil society. With respect to authorisation and accountability, for example, we might distinguish among voluntary membership groups, ascriptive groups and well-resourced civil society groups or NGOs organised around a cause or a mission. We can then ask more specific questions about potential mechanisms of authorisation and accountability. Table 2.2 summarises some of these possibilities:

In the case of voluntary associations, for example, the possibility of joining and exiting provides strong indicators of both authorisation and accountability within the association (Goodin 2003a). Likewise, the existence of internal democratic mechanisms, including elections and transparency, can underwrite claims made on behalf of constituent-members. We might also notice that, in contrast to elections, the temporal sequencing of authorisation and accountability in voluntary associations might not be very important. For individuals, the ability to enter and exit an association is likely to be based on a judgment of whether the informal representative has common interests. If individuals make this judgment, then the representative serves more as a trustee, that is, simply trusted rather than being called to account (see Issue 2 above).

Table 2.2 Authorisation and accountability of informal representatives

	Group Characteristics		
	Voluntary associations	Involuntary-ascriptive group memberships	Resourced groups: foundations, NGOs, media organisations
Authorisation	Membership entrance	Descriptive characteristics of spokespersons Website readership, book sales, public appearances, and so on	Convergent missions
Accountability	Public justification Membership democracy Membership exit 'Horizontal policing' by groups, media	Public justification Membership democracy 'Horizontal policing' by groups, media	Public justification Resource base (boards, contracts, market forces) Transparency Performance indicators 'Horizontal policing' by groups, media

In contrast, in formalised venues specialised for collective decision-making, conflicts of interest are the rule rather than the exception. Political interactions among representatives will usually include bargaining and brokering, meaning that the interests, identities and values of the represented will often be compromised. Accountability is especially important in these domains, since the bases for trust will usually be uncertain.

The democratic legitimacy of representation claims on behalf of involuntary or ascriptive groups, however, is likely to be less clear, since there are no organisational features through which group members may either authorise representatives or require accountability. This is why descriptive representation in formal bodies is inherently problematic, even if ultimately justifiable (Alcoff 1995; Mansbridge 1999). In such cases, democratic legitimacy may depend upon proactive attempts by self-appointed representatives to develop accountability to the variety of experiences and perspectives within a group (Young 2000; Dovi 2002, 2007). But it may sometimes be that representation of ascriptive groups in informal domains is less problematic, owing to the need for representatives to attract a following, which might be evident in, say, book sales or media attention. In still other cases, voluntary advocacy groups form on the basis of ascriptive characteristics (such as the National Organization for Women), bringing with them the authorisation and accountability mechanisms of voluntary associations.

Finally, a third category includes organisations with resources such as foundations, NGOs and media organisations that often simply propose themselves as representatives (of the poor, the community, drug users, and so on). The only initial authorisation in such cases resides in missions that converge with the constituencies identified by the organisation, while often the only accountability mechanisms are those inherent in the resource base of the organisation (the board, government contracts, market forces, and so on), combined with whatever public justifications the organisations offer (Saward 2006). The weakness of the authorisation-accountability cycles in such cases is driving the increasingly widespread focus on accountability of INGOs, NGOs and the media (Ebrahim 2003; Held and Koenig-Archibugi 2005). It is also clear that this is an area that requires imagination: are there informal but effective 'horizontal' forms of accountability – peers answering to peers, for example – that might function in democratic ways? Can accountability be the result of networks of voluntary organisations that police one another (Grant and Keohane 2005; Goodin 2003a)? Can accountability be strengthened by introducing mechanisms of organisational performance and organisational learning typical of the private sector and of the new managerialism in the public sector? Again, we should not rule out accountability mechanisms that may seem suspect from a democratic perspective, such as transparent performance indicators initially forced on public institutions by management styles that originated in the private sector; or organisations, even corporations, that find profits in presenting themselves as accountable to a constituency, as in the 'corporate social responsibility' movement. Such mechanisms may sometimes function in democratic ways. Or they may sometimes evolve in response to public debate provoked by representative claims about organisational constituencies.

Conclusion: challenges of the new ecology of representation

If, as we argued at the start of this chapter, a normative conception of democracy entails the *empowered inclusion of the community of those affected in collective decisions and actions*, then simply conceptualising new, non-electoral forms of representation will not be sufficient. We will also need to step back and assess their functioning within the broader ecology of governments, markets and society. This task presents a broader and tougher set of problems. In conclusion, we suggest three of them. First, the growth of informal representation, though inevitable, may erode the simple equality made possible by electoral representation. The norm of democracy does not require simple equality, but it does require inclusion of those affected by collective decisions – a norm that will result in a complex conception of equality attuned to multiple and overlapping forms of representation (Warren 2002; Fung 2013). Yet it is far from clear that the new ecology of representation will realise a more complex equality. On the one hand, there are more opportunities for representation than ever before: individuals can increase their representative presence by joining advocacy groups, organising expertise or using the internet to enable direct action. On the other hand, the proliferation of representative opportunities outside of the electoral system may disproportionately advantage those who are educated and socially well connected. As points of access and opportunities for participation multiply, so do the resource requirements for participation – education, money, time and social capital. It is likely that those interests, identities and values attached to those with organisational capacities will be better represented than those populations without. In some ways, of course, this problem is simply an expansion of an older and more familiar problem, the undue influence of special interest groups and corporatist arrangements. Still, group representatives may often fill this void, especially when those with some political sophistication (say, college students or the Ford Foundation) take on the job of representing the unorganised (say, sweatshop labourers or inner-city youth). And it may be that increasingly diverse kinds of informal representation will tend to counterbalance the traditional access, influence and sometimes outright corruption of moneyed interests. For these reasons, citizen panels comprised through random selection may provide a promising way of countering systematic biases in informal representation (Brown 2006; Warren 2008).

Second, democratic legitimacy has to do not only with the relative equalities of representation, but also with the universality of inclusions (Rehfeld 2005). Electoral representation can claim universality within territorial constituencies, and an elected representative is charged with representing those within the constituency, whether in fact he or she does so or not. Informal representatives cannot claim this kind of universality, but they may claim other kinds – for example, representing those who are affected by collective decisions of a territory, but not represented, as, for example, residents of Ontario who are affected by air pollution from coal-fired power plants in the Ohio Valley. Informal representatives can help to fill this void. But while we can find many instances in which informal representatives supplement electoral representation, we do not have a functional equivalent of the equal right to vote to judge their democratic legitimacy (Montanaro 2012).

Finally, the growth of informal representation may also result in the diffusion of loci of accountability for broad public goods, even if accountability to specific constituencies increases (Mansbridge 2004). If institutions become open to more representation without being designed to unify responsibility for decisions, accountability may become so diffuse that representation will fail to connect citizens and decision-makers. Multiple forms of accountability may demand so much of citizens that they become overloaded or disaffected. Or it may be that multiple forms of representation so gridlock political processes that no single entity can take responsibility for public goods. These possibilities are, however, hypothetical. And even if they could in principle be empirically investigated, we still lack the theoretical frameworks for doing so. We democratic theorists will need to get busy.

Postscript

The working paper that formed the basis of this chapter, written in 2007, concluded with the observation that democratic theorists had work to do. Surveying the theoretical panorama more than a decade later, we observe that democratic theorists have indeed been busy. Much interesting work has been done, and new ideas and insights developed, many of which we have tried to reference in this new version. But the final invocation of the original paper still holds: we still need more work to understand and evaluate the new landscape of political representation.

The eight issues we originally identified still, we think, provide an agenda. Much of the interesting work written recently can be located in relation to the issues we raised, and, as a whole, the eight issues provide a comprehensive view of the problems faced by the theory and practice of representation in the changing conditions of modern politics. Of the eight themes, three are concerned with ways in which we understand the representative relationship, particularly from a democratic perspective. Issues 1–3 highlight substantive aspects of the relationship that the 'standard account' tended to conceal: the dynamic and socially constructed nature of the relationship itself; the micro-processes of trusteeship involved in democratic leadership; the necessary circularity between input and output, which characterises the way in which democratic communities define, through the representative process, the idea of the public interest. Each of them emphasises a particular way in which representation can be (or fail to be) a democratic practice. Issues 6 and 7 question the standard account from a different perspective. They suggest that rethinking democratic representation involves rethinking both the objects and the subjects of political representation. Much of the standard account was scripted by the electoral selection of legislative assemblies; perhaps the key problem of democracy as nation-states expanded the franchise. Electoral representation is, and will remain, central to democratic government. But the standard account is also distracting from problems of representation in rapidly changing political landscapes. The remaining three issues we surveyed – representation as a political practice (issue 4); the contextualisation of representation within the political process (issue 5); and the formal-informal distinction (issue 8) – offer more analytic ways of examining the political context within which the act of representing acquires meaning.

Some recalibration and qualification of our analysis may, however, be needed. Here we can only mention a few points, without discussing them in full. In our analysis, as in recent discussion, much has been made of the limits of the 'standard account'. But it is often unclear what is meant by the latter. Overall, we think of the standard account as the consolidated view of a model of political representation institutionalised in the course of the twentieth century across a number of constitutional democracies, and not as the particular theoretical construct of a single author or even a group of authors. The work of Hanna Pitkin, for instance, is a theoretically sophisticated reflection about such a dominant view, but cannot be described as the 'standard account' itself, nor can some of the limits of the standard account be attributed to her own theorisation, which in a number of cases offers elements for a critique.

One other important qualification is that rethinking representation has become part of a more general reassessment of democratic theory. Democratic theorists are questioning the simple opposition between different models of democracy, suggesting, for example, that participation, deliberation and representation may need combining for democracy to work effectively as a legitimate form of government. Democratic innovations such as increasing uses of deliberative mini-publics in policy development and as precursors to ballot measures make use of a variety of modes of democratic action rather than instantiating a single model of democracy. This point is also linked to the realisation that the democratic nature of representation does not consist in simple responsiveness to the people's will (however this is conceived), but in the more systemic way in which the institutions and practices of representation enable the inclusiveness of decision-making. The systemic nature of the 'standard account' of representation was largely dependent on the constitutional structure of the democratic state within national boundaries, which is no longer adequate to the scope of either the problems or possibilities. As we argued in the conclusion, a challenge to recent theories comes from the question of how it is possible to overlay the new ecology of representation on the older constitutional order, while providing, at the same time, political systems that effectively guarantee proportionate standing for those affected or potentially affected by political decision-making processes.

Finally, from a more analytic perspective, recent theories of representation have challenged the traditional dual structure encapsulated in the relation between principal and agent, or in the symmetric processes of authorisation and accountability. They have done so introducing a third element, such as the audience, or more informal processes, such as claim-making or audience recognition. These are important insights into the way in which representation, as a social construct, works. It remains to be seen whether the democratic imagination can give concrete institutional expression to these more fluid aspects of the representative relationship, so that they contribute to democratic empowerments rather than masking elite manipulations of representative systems.

Notes

1. As we explain in our postscript, we originally wrote this paper in 2007, as the agenda for a workshop of the same name. The decade and more that has passed since then has seen the growing of an enormously productive new scholarship on the theory and practice of democratic representation – so much so that we could not write the same paper today. But we also believe our agenda-setting paper remains valuable for its relative simplicity, and generally valid in the issues we identify. We have therefore opted to publish with only minor revisions to the original.

2. Pitkin's conceptual analysis was meant to show that representation theory needed to recognise the plurality of meanings of the idea of representation (what she metaphorically called the different snapshots of a three-dimensional object), but she went on to suggest that by knowing the different ways in which the 'word is used' one would know 'what the thing is' (Pitkin 1967: 11). It should, however, be noted that she

was probably aware of the excess of reification that the passage from 'words' to 'things' may imply. In a footnote to the passage where she suggests the photography metaphor, she writes: 'I now believe, on the basis of reading Wittgenstein, that the metaphor is in some respects profoundly misleading about concepts and language' (Pitkin 1967: 255, note 20). In a previous note, she states: 'this book is primarily Austinian and not Wittgensteinian in its orientation; if I were to write it over again now, it would be a different book' (Pitkin 1967: 254, note 14). Compare also Castiglione 2012.

3

Machiavelli against the Venice myth: a sixteenth-century dialogue on the nature of political representation

Jan Bíba

Introduction

The established reading of the political history of the Italian Renaissance suggests that Florentine political theory and praxis were among the key sources of modern democracy. Proponents of this reading believe that Florentines acknowledged certain key political values constitutive of modern democracy, such as freedom of speech, equality before the law, free access to public offices, active citizenship, and so on (see, for example, Baron 1993). Some scholars – above all, members of the so-called Cambridge School – even recommend classical republicanism as a panacea to the ills of Western democracies. Under severe criticism in recent works of many commentators, this optimistic view has been revised. Many scholars no longer understand republican Florence as a democratic regime built on citizens' equality, participation and representation. Instead of celebrating the birth of democracy, they show a wholly different picture of the republican regime – a triumph of oligarchy and elitist republicanism that has nothing, or almost nothing, in common with democracy (see, for example, Hankins 2004; Najemy 2008).

Even though these two theories seem contradictory, they are not mutually exclusive. Students of the history of representative government should not be surprised by this disagreement. It has been acknowledged many times that the relation between representation and democracy is at least an 'uneasy alliance' (Pitkin 2004). And Bernard Manin depicted representative government as – at best – a mixed regime that combines oligarchic and democratic elements, and even suggested that Francesco Guicciardini's conceptualisation of Florentine political praxis was the main source of modern theory of representative government (Manin 1997: 53–62). However, this is only one part of the story, and, as I will explain, Renaissance Florence was also witness to a theoretical countermovement that attempted to think of representation in a more democratic way. I believe theorists of democracy can learn a lot from this historical debate.

In this chapter, I seek to reconstruct the discussion between ideological opponents in early-sixteenth-century Florence – between elitist republicanism defending a narrow government (*governo stretto*), whose main proponent was Francesco Guicciardini, and Machiavelli's republicanism defending a more inclusive government (*governo largo*). In my analysis, I concentrate especially on Guicciardini's and Machiavelli's respective proposals for a constitutional reform for Florence. I offer a re-reading of Machiavelli's *Discourse on Remodelling the Government of Florence* that allows me to claim that at stake within this debate was the role and nature of representative institutions and their relation to conflict.

While Machiavelli looked up to the tumultuous ancient Rome and its institutions, Guicciardini and the elitists modelled their desired institutional arrangement on oligarchic Venice. It seems to me that one of the sources of deficiency of contemporary democracies is the persistent 'Venice myth'. By this myth I mean a strong conviction of many Renaissance – and, of course, later – writers that sixteenth-century Venice represents an ideal mixed regime and should provide a kind of a blueprint for all future republics.[1] According to this narrative, Venetians have succeeded in putting together two opposing values: liberty and stability. In other words, they are praised for forming a republic devoid of strife among its citizens, as if conflict were anathema to republican government. The dark side of this myth dwells in a strange limitation of democratic life in that political power is consigned into the hands of a few elite citizens and ordinary people are restricted in their ability to influence political decisions.[2] And, as we will see, it was the setting of representative institutions that was supposed to do the trick.

I suggest that Machiavelli, against this background, emphasised the positive role of Roman tumults, of strife between the nobles and the plebs, as a necessary precondition of liberty and a republican regime. And, as I claim, he intended to incorporate this view into his constitutional proposal and into his proto-democratic understanding of representation. In sum, I propose that Machiavelli provides an antidote to the Venice myth. A crucial aspect of his argument is a rearticulation of the relationship between conflict and representation and their constitutive dimension.

To prove this thesis, I will first pay attention to Guicciardini's constitutional proposal, his understanding of representation, and I will also point to a similarity between Guicciardini and the Schumpeterian version of democratic elitism. Then I will propose a re-reading of Machiavelli's *Discourse* that, drawing on Claude Lefort's insights, enables me to highlight the link between representation and a foundational humoral conflict. In the concluding section, I will summarise the historical argument and suggest its relevance to contemporary debate.

Guicciardini, the Venice myth and democratic elitism

In the year 1494 the Medici regime in Florence collapsed and a popular republic based on an unprecedentedly inclusive Great Council was established. The Great Council became a place of strife between the city's elites (*ottimati*) and the *popolo* until the Medicis returned to power in 1512. The leitmotiv of Guicciardini's writings is severe criticism of the post-1494 order in an attempt to change the popular republic to an oligarchic one. However, due to the presence of the notions of active citizenship and equality in Florentine political discourse, he could not start by denying them in the name of a government of a few. Instead, Guicciardini elaborated a complex set of ideas that reinterpreted the nature of popular government in order to argue that popular government must be narrow (*stretto*).

According to Guicciardini, the principle of political equality present in Florentine political discourse, mainly introduced by the inclusive Great Council, gives rise to social conflict and thereby threatens the stability of political order.[3] To save the republic, it was necessary, in his view, to contaminate the original demand of equality by inequality. This move enabled Guicciardini to refuse as illegitimate not only any demand for economic and social equality, but also demands for effective political participation and representation. As a result, Guicciardini provides us with a fiction of a popular republic that actually masks the rule of oligarchy.

This strategy can be demonstrated by the first of two speeches that form Guicciardini's treatise *Del Modo di Eleggere gli Uffici nel Consiglio Grande*. The first speaker is a proponent of aristocratic or elitist republicanism. He starts his speech by acknowledging basic republican principles. The speaker claims that those who order free republics should have two goals in mind. The first goal is equality before the law and in this regard there should be 'no distinction made between rich and poor'. The second concerns citizens' participation in government, where the speaker declares that public offices should be 'distributed in such a way that each citizen can participate as much as possible', because all citizens 'are children of the same mother'.

This strong claim of equality (children of the same mother) is devalued immediately. While the first goal must be realised 'without reserve', realisation of the second goal is eventually pernicious for the republic because it brings 'disorder and ruin'. For this reason it is important that all citizens do not have equal access to magistrates and that not everyone can participate (Guicciardini 1932: 176).

The same logic of democratic devaluation applies also to Guicciardini's proposals for a constitutional reform of Florence that draw on alleged similarity between Florentine popular and Venetian oligarchic government (Guicciardini 1994: 103). The main aspect of the reform is introduction of the Senate.[4] Guicciardini proposes to move the Senate to the centre of Florence's political life as a necessary measure for the survival of the popular republic. The Senate is supposed to provide balance and protection against excessive power of the Gonfaloniere, on the one hand, and arbitrary power of the Great Council on the other. Importantly, the Senate should supplant the Great Council by taking from it the authority to decide the most important matters in the city. The Great Council should remain a universal legislative body in which all eligible citizens would participate, but the effects of their participation would be rather limited, as they could not propose or amend laws. In Guicciardini's model, the Great Council is allowed to do only two things – first to elect magistrates and members of the Senate (who, due to the effect of electoral aristocracy (Manin 1997), will always (or nearly always) be from the rank of *ottimati*), and second to approve laws that were drafted by the Senate. It is important not to overlook the distinction between deliberation and approval – as Guicciardini says, 'the making of new laws or correction of old ones must be deliberated by more restricted Councils and shouldn't be presented to the people for consultation or discussion' (Guicciardini and Brown 1994: 99).

It cannot be denied, and has been emphasised many times, that this separation of the making of new laws and their approbation has some positive effect in depersonalising the decision-making and consequently achieving a greater degree of universality of laws (for example, Pocock 1975). However, it also has a dark side: in the name of freedom and equality, Guicciardini proposes a regime that provides for some form of participation – a sizable part of population is allowed to vote and approve laws through the Great Council – that is ineffective because the voting public can only approve laws, not change them. In other words, a certain group of (almost always wealthy) citizens controls the supply of political solutions, submitting them only for approval. Freedom, according to Guicciardini, requires that political and economic elites control the political supply and therefore even the political demand. People can demand (approve) only such political solutions and policies that are offered to them.

Many have noted that this arrangement is strikingly similar to the theory of democratic elitism and minimalist democracy (see, for example, McCormick 2003; Manin 1997; Przeworski 1999; Schumpeter 1976). Both Guicciardini and the proponents of democratic elitism condition the preservation of a free regime by the rule of elites and by the exclusion of ordinary people. As we have seen, this task has been accomplished by understanding representation restrictively, as a mechanism of elections and collective authorisation. Both democratic elitists and Guicciardini reduce participation to voting in elections, and all other forms of participation or representation are forbidden or at least regarded with suspicion.

This shared conviction about the necessity to exclude ordinary people has its origin in another important similarity that can be found between Guicciardini and Schumpeter, who is understood to be the godfather of democratic elitism. This is their critical attitude to existing proto-democratic or democratic theories, respectively: Guicciardini's rejection of the political vocabulary of civic humanism and Schumpeter's rejection of the so-called 'classical doctrine' of democracy. Both these attitudes have their origin in a strong belief in the congeniality of politics and entrepreneurship. For both authors, the political knowledge that distances common people from elites has its origin in entrepreneurship.

These similarities are not a coincidence – they testify to a peculiar transformation of both theoreticians' political language. The essence of this transformation rests in gradual infiltration by strategies of argumentation that have more to do with economics than with politics and with the replacement of arguments that appeal to equality, participation, common good and civic virtues by ones related to calculation, effectiveness and efficiency (Viroli 2005).

It is possible, drawing on this brief overview of Guicciardini's proposal, to briefly summarise the nature of the Venice myth. Its core belief is that freedom and stability are threatened by excessive participation of ordinary people. This participation is a threat for two main reasons. First, common people lack necessary political knowledge, which has a certain economic and social status as its prerequisite.[5] Second, large-scale participation of common people would bring confusion and conflict that are seen as detrimental for well-ordered republics. Thus, the institutional arrangement of a republic must be ordained in such a way to eliminate or drain conflict. This task is achieved mainly by reducing participation to voting. Due to the principle of distinction (Manin 1997), elections form a representative body compound of elite citizens, who are supposed to possess qualities necessary for effective governance. After this brief overview of the Venice myth and of the role it assigns to representation, I will turn to Machiavelli's political theory that challenges some key aspects of Guicciardini's view.

Machiavelli's perfect republic

It has been suggested many times that Machiavelli in his writings – especially in the *Discourses on Livy* – defends a popular (or as some would say populist) republic modelled on the ancient Roman republic (see, for example, McCormick 2011; Levy 2014; Coby 1999). A different picture emerges if one focuses on Machiavelli's half-forgotten piece, the *Discourse on Remodelling the Government of Florence*. The *Discourse* is unique among Machiavelli's writings as it provides a concrete proposal for a constitutional reform of Florence in Machiavelli's age. In this republican blueprint, Machiavelli also challenges some of the basic presuppositions of the Venice myth.

There are two broad streams of interpretation of Machiavelli's *Discourse*. While the first stream emphasises the continuity of its teaching with populist republicanism presented in the *Discourses on Livy*, the other stream, on the contrary, sees the *Discourse* as a kind of a watershed in Machiavelli's writings between the more populist *Discourses on Livy* and his allegedly elitist later writings such as the *Florentine Histories*. The populist interpreters suggest that Machiavelli in his *Discourse* proposes a constitutional reform that brings together a set of pro-popular and anti-elite institutions – an inclusive Great Council, a mixture of sortition and elections, quick rotation of offices, Provosts (*Proposti*) resembling Roman tribunes of the plebs and a Court of Appeal – and that in this respect he draws on Athenian democracy (see, for example, McCormick 2006; Dowlen 2008: 119). The elitist interpretations, on the other hand, suggest that Machiavelli in his *Discourse* refused key aspects of the populist model of the *Discourses on Livy* – especially the notions of expediency of internal conflicts or tumults, of civic virtue and of the eminent role of exceptional persons (founders and innovators) – and adopted the Venetian constitutional model that gives priority to interlocking and balancing institutions (see, for example, Najemy 1982; Jurdjevic 2007; Silvano 1990). Proposed by historians of ideas, this second view seems to be embraced by some political theoreticians' broader interpretations of Florentine political life and some of Machiavelli's proposed instruments, which highlight the need for 'impartial resolution of conflicts between different factions' or concord (see, for example, Sintomer 2010: 476 and 2009: 70; Urbinati 2013: 149).

As I have already suggested, my interpretation departs from both of these streams. In my reading of the *Discourse*, Machiavelli proposes a republic that is more democratic and inclusive than the Venetian constitutional model, but is also far from being a populist republic. In fact, I claim that Machiavelli sees both the elitist and the populist republic as degenerate regimes. Instead of situating the *Discourse* in either the populist or the elitist tradition, I emphasise its proto-democratic[6] character that is based on a strong link that he establishes between representation, conflict and inclusion.

Machiavelli composed the *Discourse on Remodelling the Government of Florence* in the year 1520, after the death of Lorenzo di Piero de' Medici whose premature demise called into question the continuation of the Medicis' governance in Florence. Not only did no one among the family members seemed suitable for this task but, even worse, the heads of the Medici family were also important church dignitaries without the possibility of having legitimate descendants to become new Florentine rulers. In this situation, Giovanni de' Medici (Pope Leo X) asked several Florentines to design proposals for a prospective constitutional settlement for Florence without the reign of the Medici family (Najemy 2008: 426–34). Surprisingly, given his previous relation to the Medici family (see, for example, Butters 2010), Machiavelli was among those asked and his answer comprises the body of the *Discourse on Remodelling the Government of Florence* (Machiavelli 1999).

Interpreters who read the *Discourse* with an eye to placing Machiavelli in either the populist or elitist tradition miss the fact that Machiavelli actually proposes two republics in one: first, an oligarchic republic for the Medicis and their friends, and, second, a more popular republic which is supposed to emerge from the first one after the inevitable death of the Medici Pope Leo X. While the first republic is a very strict and narrow (*stretto*) form of government able to sat-isfy the Medicis, and Machiavelli does not hesitate to admit that it is actually a monarchy,[7] the inevitable death of the Medici ruler starts a process that will significantly alter the republic.

Machiavelli opens by explaining to Giovanni de' Medici (Pope Leo X) that given the historical development and societal conditions of Florence, a republic is the only possible stable regime that could be established (Machiavelli 1999: 101–7). Yet, much like Guicciardini, he proceeds to propose, under cover of this term, an oligarchy of the most restrictive kind. Machiavelli contends that in each city there are three diverse social groups or classes – the wealthiest, those in the middle and the lowest – and he also suggests that in a remodelled Florence each of these classes should occupy a different institution and have a different task (Machiavelli 1999: 107). The wealthiest are supposed to create the so-called Council of Sixty-five, which will be the seat of the executive and legislative powers – the 'chief head and chief arm of the government', according to Machiavelli (1999: 109). From these sixty-five wealthiest citizens will be selected the Gonfal-oniere of Justice, with the remaining sixty-four members divided into two groups of thirty-two members each. The two groups will take it in turns every year to form the Signoria together with the Gonfaloni-ere. The distribution of positions in the Signoria should be regulated by strict rules of rotation. It is noteworthy that Machiavelli assigns this prerogative to the wealthiest not because of their superior practi-cal knowledge but due to their pernicious desire to dominate, as they 'have ambitious spirits and think they deserve to outrank the others' (Machiavelli 1999: 107–8). Machiavelli also warns Giovanni that the republic would be ruined should this desire remain unsatisfied.

The middle class is supposed to create the Council of the Selected, with 200 members, and its main task is to approve legislative pro-posals coming from the Council of Sixty-five. And finally, the lowest class is supposed to create a new Great Council consisting of 1,000 (or at least 600) citizens. The only task of this council is to allot some less significant offices and magistrates in the city.

These institutions form the first republic, but, as Machiavelli acknowledges, this body politic is actually a monarchy as the Pope and his friends firmly hold all the power in the city – it is the Pope who is supposed to decide who is going to be appointed into the coun-cils and who can even control the results of sortitions in the Great Council through the institute of couplers who make sure that only candidates that were preselected by the Medicis are put into pouches (Machiavelli 1999: 110). It is revealing that Machiavelli uses the term 'monarchy' in this context, a word he otherwise uses reluctantly.[8] In the parlance of *The Prince*, a 'monarchy' is a 'hereditary principality', a form of rule that differs from a new principality not in its legitimacy but only in the fact that the founding violence of the regime has sedimented – it has been forgotten (Machiavelli 2005: 7–8).

I believe that Machiavelli uses the word monarchy not only to please Giovanni but also to show that the Pope's legitimate claim to government rests on his sacrosanct power.[9] However, the inevitable death of the Pope starts a process that brings into question the relation between legitimacy, power and representation. Using Claude Lefort's vocabulary, we may describe this process as disincorporation: due to the disappearance of the Pope's body and of his indisputable transcendental claim to government, the locus of power 'appears as an empty place and those who exercise it as mere mortals who occupy it only temporarily' (Lefort 1988: 17). As we will see, this process of disincorporation ultimately reveals a fundamental conflict in the city, and introduction of new institutions into the republic's constitutional arrangements is required to cope with the conflict.

The death of the Pope starts a process that changes the first republic-monarchy into a second republic that is, as Machiavelli claims, a perfect republic (*repubblica perfetta*). Launched by a disconnection between the person and the body of the Pope on the one hand, and political power and its representation on the other, this process involves three steps. The first consists in creating the institution of the Provosts, an institution that radicalised the first republic by providing for popular surveillance over the Council of Sixty-five and the council of the Selected. Reminding us of Roman tribunes of the plebs, the Provosts are to be elected by the Great Council. They cannot be selected from members of the Council of Sixty-five and their time in office is limited by strict rules of rotation, both to prevent corruption and to distribute the office widely through the city. A Provost oversees deliberations and decision-making in the Council of Sixty-five and in the Council of the Selected. He is empowered to veto any decision taken by these two councils and move that decision to the other council for co-decision.

A Court of Appeal is formed in the second step. This institution reminds us of the so-called public accusations in ancient Rome. Public accusations are different from calumnies and they enable each citizen to initiate a public hearing on political offences or concrete policies (Machiavelli 1995: 23–8). The third step consists in transferring the right to appoint the Council of Sixty-five and the Council of the Selected from the monarch to the Great Council.

How are we supposed to understand these institutional changes? What is their real meaning? As I have already suggested, there are two main interpretations of the *Discourse*: one sees it as an artful exemplar of populist republicanism, as Machiavelli's attempt to trick the naïve Medici into establishing a populist republic, while the other sees the *Discourse* as an expression of elitist republicanism. To me, they both seem to be wrong. In my opinion it would be difficult to interpret Machiavelli's proposal in a populist manner as the body of citizens involved in the Great Council is still very limited (1,000 or at least 600) and the most important offices in the city (the Council of Sixty-five) are still reserved for the *ottimati*. It seems to me that it is also impossible to interpret this proposal in a strictly elitist or Venetian manner because the institutions of the Provosts, extensive use of sortition and the Court of Appeal add a popular flavour, allowing – in certain circumstances – the lowest class not only to approve or disapprove proposals but also to influence, deliberate on or even change a decision made by the Council of Sixty-five or the Council of the Selected.

I have already suggested that the key to interpreting the *Discourse* might be found in the concept of disembodiment, which insists – contrary to Guicciardini – that conflict is pivotal and not antithetical to a stable polity. Machiavelli makes conflict central to his vision of politics and republicanism and this is how we have to understand conflict's nature and origin. In a famous passage in *The Prince*, Machiavelli claims:

> [T]hese two different humours are found in every body politic. They arise from the fact that the people do not wish to be commanded or oppressed by the nobles, while the nobles do desire to command and to oppress the people. From these two opposed appetites, there arises in cities one of three effects: a principality, liberty, or licence. (Machiavelli 2005: 35)

According to Machiavelli, in every city there are two conflicting humours or dispositions – one to dominate and the other to avoid domination – and the specific character of a city and its political regime (principality, republic or anarchy) stems from the way it copes with this conflict. Similar formulations can also be found in other Machiavelli writings (see, for example, Machiavelli 1995: 18; 1990: 105) and the author of the *Discourse* ensures Giovanni that contemporary 'vexations' to the Medici government come from a conflict between two humours, between those citizens 'who in asking are arrogant and unbearable', demanding domination, and those who 'suspect they are not secure in their present way of life' (Machiavelli 1990: 114) and want to avoid being dominated.

Machiavelli uses the analogy of humour to suggest that, in the polity as in the body, there should be conflictual relations among contending elements. The concept of humour comes from ancient Greek medicine where it designates distinct bodily fluids (blood, yellow bile, black bile and phlegm) that form a human body and also shape the temperament of a person. These four bodily humours were believed to correspond to four basic elements (air, fire, earth and water) and basic qualities (warm, dry, cold and moist). Ancient medicine believed that a condition of health could be described as a form of equilibrium between the different humours that are present in the body. However, as these humours are composed of opposing elements and qualities, there is an agonistic dimension to that equilibrium (Hankinson 2008). Health thus requires both balance and instability, both unity and division, and these in turn require specific relations of equality between the different humours that are present in a physical body – not in a quantitative but in a qualitative sense. In other words, a health condition requires *isonomic* relations between the four bodily fluids in a sense that no humour prevails over others (Magni 2012: 80). In contrast, a state of dominance of one humour over the other humours was described as disease by ancient medicine. It should also be emphasised that each temperament requires a specific form of equilibrium and instability between the humours, and so to be healthy means to live in conformity with the idiosyncratic nature of a particular conflict.[10]

Machiavelli applies this medical metaphor to the body politic to explain why conflict between humours is constitutive of the political and social space. However, to ascribe such a role to humoral conflict has at least three consequences. Firstly, the body politic can only remain united or healthy if it simultaneously maintains its constitutive division. The conflict itself becomes a necessary condition of a society. Secondly, this foundational conflict also constitutes its opposing parties. In other words, the fact of the dialectical nature of political humours (to dominate and to avoid domination) suggests that these humours and the social and political forces they represent should be understood rather as arising from the conflict than as its prerequisite.[11] As Machiavelli makes clear, the demand to avoid domination can be born only as a result of experiencing domination or its threat (see, for example, Machiavelli 1995: 17). And last but not least, Machiavelli claims that opposing humours as a political force do not exist before their representation. In other words, representation has a constitutive dimension: it is only after being represented that humours become political subjects capable of articulating and pursuing their political demands. As Machiavelli states, 'A multitude without a head is useless' (Machiavelli 1995: 92). Such representation can be provided either by a charismatic leader, when humours or parties act in an extra-institutional context – as in the case of *secessio plebis* or in that of Michele di Lando during the Ciompi revolt – or by orders and institutions of a well-ordered republic (see, for example, Machiavelli 1995: 92; 1990: 127).

Several conclusions could be drawn from this brief overview of Machiavelli's appropriation of the theory of humoral conflict. Above all, a serene republic devoid of conflict is an oxymoron; wherever there is a body politic there is conflict between humours. Moreover, an oligarchic republic dominated by elites would be as unhealthy as a populist republic dominated by the *popolo*.[12] Ongoing conflicts presuppose some form of equality or *isonomic* relations (Magni 2012: 80) between humours (no humour can prevail over others) and this equality is achieved via conflictual interlocking of representative institutions that also bring humours or classes as political forces into being. In other words, it is because of conflictual representative institutions that power is not appropriated by any social group or humour, that its locus is kept empty and at stake. And, finally, the task of a reformer, then, should not consist in effacing the constitutive conflict. On the contrary, a reformer should seek both to embody and to express this conflict in institutional arrangements.[13]

Such analogies between the theory of four humours and Machiavelli's republicanism are central to the constitution he proposed. The representative institutions must perform two tasks at the same time: become an expression of the foundational humoral conflict and prevent the conflict from destroying the body politic. Representative institutions must re-present the conflict and thus also its opposing parties, providing the conflict with a non-violent and non-factional outlet. The conflict is possible only when power is permanently kept at stake, when there is no person or social group that is able to make itself consubstantial with the locus of power, when the contingency of its occupation is made visible. The constitutional reform proposed by Machiavelli is designed to fulfil this task in that the class-specific councils should re-present the competing interests of different strata of the Florentine society and embody the conflict of humours. Extensive use of sortition coupled with quick rotation of offices prevents individuals and groups from permanent seizure of power through magistrates. It also makes visible the contingency and temporality of occupying a position and thus undermines any claim to special legitimacy, for example one based on a religious belief, particular political or economic knowledge, or praxis. The Court of Appeal and the Provosts can use their veto powers to challenge any attempt (both by private individuals and by council members) to seize power in the city.

Now we find ourselves in a position that enables us to understand the nature of Machiavelli's attack against the Venice myth. At the heart of this myth lies an idea that the existence of a free, or democratic, regime presupposes both limits on popular participation and elimination of conflict. To achieve this task, Guicciardini and his more recent followers rely on an impoverished notion of representation, one reduced to collective authorisation. The crucial innovation introduced in Machiavelli's constitutional proposal for a perfect republic consists in a reworking of the relation between conflict, representation, and inclusion. While Guicciardini sees conflict as detrimental to the existence of the republic, Machiavelli paradoxically understands conflict between humours as a source of vitality of the body politic – when embodied in representative institutions, conflict creates an idiosyncratic agonistic equilibrium and provides stability. Representative institutions play a key role in the relation between conflict and stability for both theoreticians: whereas Guicciardini uses electoral representation and the distinction between the Senate and the Great Council as an ideological instrument to cover and efface conflicts, Machiavelli creates a strong bond between conflict and representation. Inevitable humoral conflicts do not have to be detrimental when embodied in representative institutions; they have to be re-presented.

These different views on the relation between conflict and representation advocated by Machiavelli and Guicciardini have important consequences also for the relation between representation and inclusion: Guicciardini sees participation of common people as a source of conflict and confusion and thus he limits participation to elections to the Senate and approval or disapproval of legislative proposals coming from the Senate. The permanent threat of conflict justifies exclusion, and representation is an instrument of this exclusion. In contrast, Machiavelli emphasises the urgent need to keep the locus of power in check, to preserve conflict, and thus provides a legitimation for inclusion. The very existence of conflict requires inclusion of diverse segments of society but this inclusion can only be achieved on the basis of representation: representation brings social groups or humours into being as political actors and, through its institutions, it creates an agonistic space of equality. To summarise the crucial difference between Guicciardini's and Machiavelli's approach, we might say that while Guicciardini uses representation to foster a rule of oligarchic elites and in fact to tame democracy, Machiavelli opens an inchoate trajectory that establishes strong connections between democracy and representation. In other words, for the author of the *Discourse* there is no *vivere libero* (republic or democracy) outside and beyond representation.

In lieu of a conclusion: representation and conflict

Many have noted that representation has undemocratic origin and that representative institutions were designed to limit rather than to encourage democracy. Scholars of democratic theory usually situate the origin of democratisation of representation (articulation between representation and democracy) in the eighteenth century. However, this chapter has looked at a debate about representation and its possible connection with democracy that took place in sixteenth-century Florence between Guicciardini, as a proponent of the oligarchic Venetian model, and Machiavelli, who defended the more popular Roman model. Comparison of Guicciardini's and Machiavelli's constitutional proposals has revealed two different articulations of the relation between representation, inclusion and conflict.

Guicciardini, following the myth of Venice, believes that social conflict and wide participation are incompatible with a free way of life (*vivere libero*) and that representation reduced to the electoral mechanism and collective authorisation is an appropriate way of providing an illusion of participation and thus avoiding the risk of emergence of social conflict. In his view, representation fulfils the ideological function of concealing conflict in the city and maintaining the pretence of social harmony. In contrast to Guicciardini's view, I proposed a proto-democratic reading of Machiavelli's *Discourse on Remodelling the Government of Florence*. However, my reading of the *Discourse* differs from common interpretations of this piece. While the *Discourse* is usually read either as a defence of a populist republic or as a proof of Machiavelli's late inclination to the elitist model of Venice, my reading instead emphasises the role of temporality, contingency, conflict and representation. Machiavelli, in the reading proposed, is far away from Guicciardini's approach as, in an attempt to provide wider and effective participation, he connects conflict and representation. Machiavelli uses representative institutions to make the fundamental humoral conflict visible and, instead of serenity, proposes an unstable agonistic equilibrium that ensures both representation of that conflict and its non-violent solution. This seems to be the most important disagreement between Machiavelli and proponents of the myth of Venice and, I believe, also an important lesson for democratic theory: a free regime – be it republic or democracy – requires a robust social conflict that finds its non-destructive outlet in and through representative institutions. Representation of conflict is inevitable, because it is its continuing existence that makes the regime free by keeping political power at stake.

Notes

1. For Machiavelli's and Guicciardini's intellectual background, see, for example, Pocock (1975); Skinner (2004).
2. In certain aspects, this depiction of the desired goal of elitist republicans strikingly resembles the workings of contemporary liberal democracies. See, for example, Gilens and Page (2014).
3. Guicciardini stated his criticism of Machiavelli's view of Roman tumults in his *Considerations*: 'praising discord is like praising a sick man's illness, because the remedy that has been used on him is the right one' (Guicciardini 2007: 393).
4. During his life, Guicciardini elaborated several proposals for a constitutional reform of Florence. Among them, the most important are *Dialogue on the Government of Florence* and *On Bringing Order to Popular Republic* (also known as *Discorso di Logrogno*, Guicciardini 1998). Interesting insights can also be obtained from less significant writings such as *Del Modo di Eleggere gli Uffici nel Consiglio Grande* and from some of the speeches presented in his *The History of Italy*. Even though these proposals are different in details they all shared the same basic intention. I draw mainly on the most developed and sophisticated proposal that was presented in the *Dialogue on the Government of Florence* (1521-6).
5. However, it is necessary to emphasise that both Guicciardini and Schumpeter are also proponents of meritocracy, holding that it is not enough to be born into the rank of *ottimati* or a particular 'social stratum' (Schumpeter 1976: 291).
6. While I claim that Machiavelli's view contains an important insight for democratic theory and representative democracy, it is still important not

to confuse his proposals with modern democracy. As I will explain, what is supposed to be represented or included are not individual citizens but social groups like classes or humours, and nor does Machiavelli's proposal involve the modern notion of equality or provide equal access to magistrates or equal standing under the constitution.

7. 'I believe, considering all this organisation as a republic, and without your authority, that it lacks nothing necessary to a free government according to what is above debated and presented at length. But if it is considered while Your Holiness and the Most Reverend Monsignor are still living, it is a monarchy, because you have authority over the armed forces, you have authority over the criminal judges, you keep the laws in your bosom' (Machiavelli 1999: 113).

8. The instances of the word monarchy (*monarchia*) are scarce in Machiavelli's writings. The word is used only once in each of Machiavelli's main works (*The Prince*, *Discourses on Livy* and *The Art of War*).

9. Machiavelli also seems to highlight this moment by using a simile from medieval canon law: 'you keep the laws in your bosom' (1999: 113). See Kantorowicz (1997: 152–4). However, it does not mean that Machiavelli himself believes in a sacrosanct origin of Giovanni's power. See, for example, Machiavelli's discussion of a religious fraud committed by legendary founders or reformers (like Moses or Numa Pompilius) who were also religious leaders.

10. Just as there is a difference between healthy equilibria of fluids in the bodies of a melancholic and a phlegmatic, there is a difference between the healthy forms of equilibrium in a republic and a monarchy.

11. This reading of Machiavelli's theory of political conflict differs from two broad streams of interpretation that see conflict as arising from a pre-political nature of political actors. For example, while Quentin Skinner sees political conflict primarily as a consequence of a corrupt human nature (Skinner 2000: 63–6), John P. McCormick emphasises a class conflict (not in a Marxian sense) between rich and poor (McCormick 2011). It seems to me that McCormick, in contrast to Skinner, rightly recognises the difference between individual and collective identity (*uomini* vs *popolo*) in Machiavelli's writings, but he fails to fully acknowledge its constitutive dimension. It should not be overlooked that in some historical examples discussed by Machiavelli, *popolo* or *plebe* can also demand domination and elimination of an equilibrium between opposing humours. In other words, their identity is not given irrespective of such conflict and may change in its course (see, for example, Machiavelli 1990: 105, 122–4, 128–30; see also Leibovici 2002).

12. For this reason, I find it misleading to interpret the role of the Provosts in a populist manner, as an expression of popular sovereignty over elites. Both the Provosts and the relatively inclusive Great Council (relatively in comparison to Venice) should be read rather as

an expression of Florence's more popular idiosyncratic equilibrium (see, for example, Sintomer 2009: 58–81).

13. This can take many different forms, depending on the nature of a given regime. For example, whereas a republican reformer has to embody conflict in the city's institutions, a new prince in a new principality has to side with a stronger humour against a weaker one (see, for example, Machiavelli 1995: 34–7; see also Parel 1992: 107).

4

Power without representation is blind, representations without power are empty

Bernard Flynn

Introduction

In this chapter I will argue that, in the modern period, power can be exercised only insofar as it is represented. I will begin by evoking in the broadest outline what I take to be the essence of Claude Lefort's interpretation of the *œuvre* of Machiavelli, that is, his description of the metamorphosis by which natural force is transformed into political power, being no longer located in the body (or bodies) of the prince but rather in a symbolic register, a register that is not reducible to real social processes.

In his important study *Adventures of the Symbolic*, and in his contribution to this volume, Warren Breckman characterises recent political philosophy in France as having effected a 'symbolic turn' (analogous with the 'linguistic turn'). Notably absent from this work, and for good reason, is Michel Foucault. Foucault has refused this 'symbolic turn' and attached himself to an older tradition according to which there is an equation between de-symbolisation and secularisation.

Foucault famously laments that in political theory we have not yet 'cut off the head of the king', by which he means we have not responded to the progressive irrelevance of the juridical and sovereign exercise of power. Foucault will pursue his analysis in accord with a tradition of 'realism', a realism that would unmask the representations of power, both juridical and symbolic, as occulting the true operation of power on the level of the real. His analysis maps grids of power and the resistances that they engender. He views power as being exercised directly on the body, without need of representation. His radical antinomianism has led him to very questionable judgments in concrete historical situations.

In this chapter, I will argue that Foucault's de-symbolisation has, as is the case with Marx, issued in a denegation of the political as such, which, in the mind of the author, one would be ill advised to follow. My critique of Foucault can be captured in two closely related and complementary claims: power without representation is blind, and representations without power are empty. Taken together, these claims can help one to understand the role of representation in the constitution of power, the inevitability of the symbolic in the exercise of power and the potential risks that its de-symbolisation entails.

Power without representation is blind

At issue is power and its visibility. In an article entitled 'Merleau-Ponty and Thinking From Within', Françoise Dastur reflects critically on a 1966 article by Michel Foucault: 'Maurice Blanchot: the Thought from Outside'. Foucault's article contrasts 'thinking from the outside', which he identifies with Blanchot, with a 'thinking from interiority' that epitomises Western notions of conscience and subjectivity (Foucault 1987: 7–60). Dastur argues that Merleau-Ponty's thinking from within refuses the binary between these two to 'renounce the idea of an absolute exterior' and that of subjectivity as interiority in favour of a 'relationship of belongingness' that implicates 'the seer in the visible' (Dastur 1993: 25–36). In the Preface to *The Phenomenology of Perception*, we recall what Merleau-Ponty says of Augustine's inner man, 'There is no inner man'. Rather, 'thinking from within' is a thinking within the density of the flesh of the world. According to him, the vision of the visible is formed within the visible itself. Our inherence within the visible is not an obstacle to our perception of it; on the contrary, it is the very condition of that perception. I shall follow Dastur's line of thinking, but I will extend it into the domain of the political philosophy elaborated by Claude Lefort; then I will contrast it with the political philosophy of Michel Foucault.

Lefort responds to classical political philosophy's question 'What are the natures of different regimes?' He considers different regimes as forms of society 'in order to identify a principle of internalisation that can account for a specific mode of differentiation and articulation between classes, groups and social ranks and at the same time a specific mode of discrimination between markers, be they economic, juridical, aesthetic, religious, which order an experience of coexistence' (Lefort 1988: 218). A putting into form (*mise-en-forme*) by which a society is instituted involves an engendering of sense (*mise-en-sens*) as a system of intertwining meanings. There is also a *mise-en-scène* of social relationships, by which Lefort means that society gives itself a 'quasi-representation of itself' (Lefort 1988: 219). By 'quasi-representation' he does not mean an actual picture. He is inspired by *The Phenomenology of Perception*, where Merleau-Ponty speaks of a 'corporal schema', which is not an image or a picture of the body; nonetheless, it tends towards visibility (Merleau-Ponty 1962).

Merleau-Ponty further elaborates this notion, reflecting on the experience of a touching/touched, where he sees a 'sort of reflection that the body effects on itself' (Merleau-Ponty 1968). This reflection is never completed. It is always short-circuited at the last moment, and thus the body's identity with itself is suspended across a gap, an *écart*. Immanence is never achieved; the phenomenological reduction cannot be completed. Nevertheless, the body does not experience itself as 'parts outside of parts' but as a body, by way of the corporal schema.

The *mise-en-scène* by which a society constitutes its own identity is, likewise, a quasi-representation consisting of a synthesis or intertwining of the visible and the invisible. The identity of the body politic is also suspended across a gap, an abyss, but it is not annulled. Lefort criticises political science for its failure to think society's tenuous identity; in like manner, one could criticise Foucault for his inability to think the unity of a society.

To warrant this claim and demonstrate what is at stake in making it, I will now turn to the thought of both Lefort and Foucault on Machiavelli's *The Prince*. It might be objected that the comparison is unfair, since Lefort has written a 700-page book on Machiavelli, while there are only scattered references to him in Foucault's Collège de France lectures. Obviously, I am not concerned with which one 'got it right' (an idea incompatible with Lefort's conception of interpretation). I will view their readings of Machiavelli as symptomatic, that is, as they bear on the place of power and its visibility. The two readers differ on the importance they accord to Machiavelli in the history of political thought. For Lefort, Machiavelli is central; for Foucault, he is 'overrated' as compared to Bacon.

According to Lefort, it is the lack of a theological or natural foundation that marks the novelty of the Florentine, who remains silent on the question of the divine or natural foundations of political authority. Lefort remarks that 'his silence is deafening'. Machiavelli introduced a void in the space where thought formerly found reassurance in the presence of a divine or a natural order.

The articulation of ruler and ruled in pre-modern society is founded on religious principles. For Machiavelli, modern political society is generated by a symbolic exchange. In Chapter 9 of *The Prince* he tells us that two classes exist in every city. They are in conflict, and the conflict is between two desires. The common people want neither to be governed nor oppressed by the grandees, the big shots, and the grandees want to govern and oppress the common people. The regime is instituted by an exchange between the prince and the people. Note that pre-political society, according to Machiavelli, is already structured by class conflict. There are the big shots and the people. However, it is not, as Hobbes would have it, a war of each against all.

Why must the prince not ally himself with the grandees? The prince is motivated by a desire for power, as are the grandees. If the prince allies himself with them, he will just be one of them, useful in their pursuit of class interests. However, his alliance with the people, who want not to be oppressed by the grandees, puts him in a position to command both the grandees and the people. Assuredly, the prince will oppress the people in his turn, but the violence of his power is of a different nature from that of the grandees. In the grandees, the people 'encounter their natural adversary, the Other, who constitutes them as the immediate object of its desire' (Lefort 2012: 141). The prince frees them from this relation by the very fact of not being a part of it. By his presence, the prince disabuses the grandees of their claim to natural domination. Prior to the institution of the political by the symbolic exchange between the people and the prince, there are two poles: the grandees and the people. Their relationship is immediate and natural: big fish eat little fish. However, when the prince forms an alliance with the people, he institutes a third position, above the conflict of class. There is no ontological or theological foundation for this position of the third; the position of the third is the institution of the political.

This institution of the political accomplishes a metamorphosis of force into political power. Violence and coercion remain, but they are no longer immediate and natural; rather, they are instituted and mediated through the position of the third, and thus visible. Nevertheless, the institution of the political involves a 'deception'. The people support the prince to be protected against the grandees. But Lefort writes:

> In lending him their support, they do not know what they are doing. While they struggle not to be oppressed, they are about to take on an oppression of a new kind. While they expect the good, they receive the lesser evil. (2012: 142)

Here we see the anti-utopianism of both Machiavelli and Lefort. The 'third' institutes the unity of society, 'but such an image cannot hold up against the discovery that an irreducible conflict rends society'. The prince can modify this conflict and create conditions for some form of coexistence, but cannot resolve it. If the people do not get what they wanted (the dissolution of power) they get the next best thing (its political institution).

The symbolic exchange which engenders the position of the third has what Levi-Strauss called 'symbolic efficacy'. It does something. It confers on a society a fragile unity, in default of which it would devolve into the immediate and natural conflict between the grandees and the people. The political is suspended over a void: it covers a gap between natural relations of force on the one hand, and the political image that a society constructs of itself on the other. In other words, it renders an identity to a society that does not have one – and thus serves to constitute it as a society. This position of the third is the *mise-en-scène* through which a society constitutes its fragile unity. In a detail we cannot pursue here, Lefort insists that the prince, in the thought of Machiavelli, must deflect onto his image the affect, even love, that the people wish to project onto him. In a particularly 'scandalous' part of *The Prince*, the Florentine lists the virtues that the prince must appear to have, but not actually have. If he must appear to have virtues, to whom must he appear? Obviously, it is to the people. The being of a prince is a being recognised. The place of power must appear. Political power is essentially visible. The prince, far from occupying a position of exteriority *vis-à-vis* the society, is constituted by the 'sort of reflection' the society affects on itself. It is for this reason that political power without representation is blind: power has to be represented in order for society to be able to see itself. At the same time, the representation of power stages society to itself as a particular kind of unity.

In contrast to Lefort, for whom Machiavelli is the first thinker of modern symbolic power, Foucault holds him up as the last theorist of sovereignty. Foucault does not present an interpretation of *The Prince* in his own name. He presents an image of Machiavelli culled from pro- and anti-Machiavellian debates which he does not claim as the 'true' meaning of *The Prince*. Nonetheless, when he is situating Machiavelli in the history of political thought as the last thought of sovereignty, and not as a precursor to the art of governmentality, he seems to affirm precisely this reading of *The Prince*. To Foucault, 'The *Prince* is characterised by a single principle: For Machiavelli, the Prince exists in a relationship of singularity and externality, of transcendence, to his principality [. . .] he is not a part of it, but external to it' (Foucault 2009: 91). As a consequence of his exteriority, his hold on power is fragile. Thus his sole interest is the maintenance of his power, which is under constant threat. The prince must be constantly on the alert for conspiracies and plots arising from the grandees.

Now I wish to highlight certain aspects of this reading of Machiavelli, which if not underwritten by Foucault himself are at least employed by him. Then I will contrast them with Lefort's reading and explore their consequences for the political thought of Foucault. The contrast between Lefort's and Foucault's readings of Machiavelli emerges through the examination of three philosophemes: singularity, externality and transcendence. I begin with transcendence. According to Lefort, the new object that Machiavelli wishes to bring centre stage is the becoming anonymous of political power. In a monarchy, the king, in his person, is transformed by the sacrament of coronation. Through the grace of God his body is doubled and becomes a body of nature and body of grace. He is not deified, but he has a special relationship to God not shared by other men. According to Lefort's reading of *The Prince*, there is no such transformation of the person of the prince. Power is not invested in his body, but rather in the place he occupies by virtue of his symbolic exchange with the people. If he cannot be loved, he must be feared, but, most of all, he must avoid the hatred of the people. In this reading, he must avoid both love and hatred, because they focus on the singular person of the prince.

According to Foucault, the transcendence of the prince is a consequence of his exteriority. Since there is no natural relationship between the prince and his people or territory, he is not a part of them; there is no blood-and-soil relation. As we have seen above, for Lefort, the transcendence of the prince exists in virtue of the constitution of the position of the third. His power is based on the projection, or the phantasm, of a position above the conflict of class, and, in a sense, external to each of the conflicting desires. However, it is the position of the third that inscribes the conflict as taking place in one social space. It effects the fragile identity of the society with itself, delivering it from the immediate and natural conflict of pre-political society.

Foucault characterises the prince's exteriority from his people. He writes, 'Machiavelli's Prince receives his principality either through inheritance, or by acquisition, or by conquest; in any case, he is not a part of it, but external to it' (Foucault 2009: 91). According to

Lefort, far from being external to the society, the prince, who is a being of appearance, has his being in being recognised. This is not the case with the medieval monarch, who, anointed by the grace of God, remains a king even if deposed and imprisoned. The modern prince is constituted by a symbolic exchange, thus his being is a being of appearance.

If it be objected that I am making too much of Foucault's brief remarks on Machiavelli, my point is to bring centre stage, by contrast with Lefort, the lack of any conception of the symbolic in Foucault's thinking. Warren Breckman, in his monumental study *The Adventures of the Symbolic*, speaks of a symbolic turn in French political philosophy, analogous to the linguistic turn in Anglo-American philosophy (Breckman 2013). Lefort features centrally in his profoundly informative account of those philosophers who have taken the symbolic turn. Notably absent from his study, and for good reason, is Michel Foucault. If Foucault were to be considered within the categorical system elaborated by Beckman, it would be in a tradition that considers secularisation as radical desymbolisation. In this tradition, there is an equation of secularisation and desymbolisation. It is a tradition that extends through the Enlightenment, the left Hegelians, to Marx. When Foucault claims that political philosophy has not yet cut off the head of the king, he means that the concern with the question of sovereignty and the juridical approach to law, where power is framed as law, are not fully secularised.

Foucault makes his rejection of a symbolic dimension of the political clear in the beginning of *Discipline and Punish*, where there is a juxtaposition between the tortured body of the prisoner and the magnificent body of the king. Here Foucault evokes Kantorowicz's (1977) analysis in *The King's Two Bodies*; however, he misinterprets it. I bring this up not out of pedantry, but because his misreading reveals his denegation of the symbolic. In *Discipline and Punish*, he writes, 'The surplus power of the king gives rise to the duplication of his body' (Foucault 1977: 29). For Kantorowicz as well as for Lefort, it is not the king's power that gives rise to the duplication of his body; it is, on the contrary, the symbolic duplication of his body which gives rise to his legitimate power. In detail that I cannot pursue here, there is a secularisation of the Christian notion of the dual nature of Christ, as both God and man. The Mystical Body of Christ as the head of the Church defines the king not as a god, but as a representative of God on Earth. The doubling of his body is the basis of his sovereignty. It is precisely the problematic of sovereignty that Foucault wishes to reject. In *Power/Knowledge* he writes, 'What we need, however, is a political philosophy that is not erected around the problem of sovereignty, and therefore around the problem of law and prohibition' (Foucault 1972: 121). This is to say that we need to 'cut off the head of the king'. For Foucault, the representation of the king's body is not the source of his power, rather its mask. The figure of the sovereign and the law occult the true operations of power.

Representations without power are empty

As we have seen in Lefort's reflection on Machiavelli, the representation of power is the *mise-en-scène* through which a society gives itself its fragile unity. For Foucault, this representation is not productive as it is for Lefort but, rather, deceptive; it occults the true operations of power. In *Power/Knowledge*, Foucault writes, 'The state is superstructural in relation to a whole series of power networks that invest the body, sexuality, the family, kingship, and knowledge, technology and so forth' (Foucault 1972: 122). It is striking that Foucault employs a Marxist vocabulary to express his conception of the relationship of the state and power. For Marx, at his worst, the superstructure is epiphenomenal in relation to the base, which is, for him, the forces and relations of production. Of course, for Foucault, a base is not the forces and relations of production, but the operations of power, of micropolitics. He writes, 'The state consists in the codification of a whole number of power relations which render its functioning possible' (Foucault 1972: 122). Notwithstanding the differing content between Foucault and Marx, the structure of the arguments is the same: power subtends appearance. Foucault says as much himself. In response to a question concerning his work prior to *Discipline and Punishment* he writes, 'When I think back now, I ask myself, what else is it that I was talking about in *Madness and Civilization* and *The Birth of a Clinic* but power?' (Foucault 1972: 115).

In *Discipline and Punishment* Foucault writes, 'Corporal disciplines constitute the foundation of formal juridical liberties' (Foucault 1977: 222). He contends that we have paid too much attention to the Roman forum and not enough to the military camps. The reduction of the political and juridical spheres to products of real operations of power has profound effects on Foucault's political judgment. The murder of a young woman in a northern town, which was linked circumstantially to a prominent local bourgeois, and a mining disaster in the city of Lenz, put the subject of popular justice centre stage. Foucault and *gauche* proletarian leader Pierre Victor (aka Benny Levy) debated the merits of popular justice in Sartre's

Les Temps modernes. Victor wanted to set up 'people's courts' to carry out popular justice. He proposed as examples the popular justice of people's courts set up by the Red Army in China. The people who 'love the army' delegate a part of their power to the army, which establishes people's courts (Foucault 1972: 10). Foucault is adamantly opposed to this, because he claims that a 'people's court' would too much resemble normal juridical institutions. It would not express people's justice, but rather subject it to the juridical ideology of the bourgeois. At base, what Foucault objects to is the idea of a third. This is the idea that there can be people who are neutral in relation to the two parties, that they can make judgments about them on the basis of ideas of justice which have absolute validity, and that their decisions must be acted upon. This notion of the third is far removed from and quite foreign to the very idea of popular justice. 'In the case of popular justice, you do not have the three elements. You have the masses and their enemies' (Foucault 1972: 8). Foucault contends that when the people identify an enemy, they do not rely on an 'authoritative judgment' which has the power to enforce their decision. They carry it out, pure and simple. Foucault, at this point, seems to be advocating lynching.

This is not merely an extreme position taken 'in the heat of the hunt'. It follows from his conception of power and representation. Towards the end of this discussion on popular justice, Foucault writes, 'Now, when a kind of power is exercised, the manner in which it is exercised –which must be visible, solemn and symbolic – must only refer us to that kind of power which is exercised in reality at this particular time' (Foucault 1972: 34). The debate ends by Foucault expressing his position in a more general way:

> for my part, the idea which I wanted to introduce into the discussion is that the bourgeois juridical state apparatus, of which the visible, symbolic form is the court, has the basic function of introducing and augmenting contradictions among the masses, principally between the proletariat and the non-proletarianised people, and that it follows from this that the forms of this juridical system, and the ideology associated with them, must become the target of our present struggle. (Foucault 1972: 35–6)

This idea that the juridical system, its checks on power and its claim to impartiality, are mere ideology that must be the 'target' of struggle condones, not to say celebrates, the exercise of raw power outside of any lawful restraint.

This is not the only instance where Foucault condones the
exercise of power unconstrained by law. In his debate with Noam
Chomsky he declares, 'When the proletariat takes power, it may be
quite possible that the proletariat will exert toward the classes over
which it has triumphed a violent, dictatorial, even bloody power.
I can't see what objection could possibly be made to this' (Lilla
2006: 150). A few years after this debate, Solzhenitsyn's *The Gulag
Archipelago* was published in France. In *The Reckless Mind* Mark
Lilla writes, 'Foucault used to provoke nervous titters by joking
about cruelty and pain, but no one was laughing anymore' (Lilla
2006: 153).

One could contend that Foucault changed his position in his later
writings. This is true in many respects but not so in his denegation of
the law and the symbolic dimension of society. In his 1978 *History
of Sexuality* he poses the question of 'why power masks itself as law'.
His reply that seems self-evident (to himself) is that 'power is tolerable
only on condition that it masks a substantial part of itself' (Foucault
1978: 86). The history of the monarchy 'went hand in hand with the
covering up of the facts and procedures of power by juridico-political
discourse' (Foucault 1978: 88).

Turning to his lectures given at Leuven in 1981, the tone could
not be more different from the discussion with the half-mad Mao-
ist referred to above. Yet the content of the argument remains
unchanged. The first lecture takes the form of an excruciatingly
detailed exposition of lines 257–650 of Book 23 of Homer's *Iliad*.
At issue is a conflict over who should be awarded second prize in a
chariot race initiated by Achilles. Foucault's point is that the conflict
is settled within the *Agon* itself. The conflicting parties do not refer
to a third to adjudicate this conflict. Foucault claims that there is no
judge in this story.

While it is true that there is no judge, it is, in my reading of
the text, not clear that there is no reference to a third. Antilochus
claims to deserve the second prize; however, he won it by cheating; he recklessly 'cut off' Menelaus at a turn in the race course.
As the incident was taking place his rival called out, 'Antilochus
– no one alive is more treacherous than you, Away with you, mad-
man – damn you. How wrong we were when we said you had
good sense. You'll never take the prize unless you take the oath'
(Homer 1991: 573). The oath referred to is a ritual in which the
rider stands before his horse with the handle of the whip touch-
ing the horse's face and swears that what he is about to say is
true. Which in this case would be that he did not cheat. With this

reference to the oath, 'Antilochus came to his senses and backed off quickly' (Homer 1991: 577). He blamed his rashness on his youth and refused to take the oath, thereby abdicating his claim to second prize. Were he to swear, he admits that he would 'swear a false oath in the eyes of every god'. In the translation used by Foucault, Antilochus claims he would 'be guilty in the eyes of the gods' (Foucault 2014: 34).

Foucault does not quote these lines in his detailed exposition of the text. This is not surprising. For what is the fear of swearing a false oath in the 'eyes of every god' but a reference to a third? In pre-modern society the transcendent position of the third is occupied by the gods and the law is based on the fear of offending them. Book 23 of the *Iliad* does not justify or illustrate Foucault's anti-juridico-political discourses. On the contrary, it suggests that a third position has always been required, even though it was located in various places throughout history.

For a final example of this refusal of the third, one that brings its political significance into even sharper focus, I will turn briefly to Foucault's reflections on the Iranian Revolution. That Foucault thoroughly misunderstood what he witnessed in Tehran goes without saying. But what is interesting is how he misunderstood it. According to Janet Afary and Kevin Anderson, what Foucault actually saw in Tehran was a religiously inspired insurrection against an authoritarian modernising regime, which had been framed consciously by Khomeini as the re-enactment of a battle between Hassan, the grandson of the prophet, and the evil Yazid, his rival. This battle happened in the seventh century and it ended with the massacre of Hassan and the martyrdom of his supporters. What Foucault thought he saw was the birth of the concept of 'political spirituality', lost to the West since 'the good old days' of Savonarola and Oliver Cromwell. In the willingness to die, Foucault saw the expression of a 'perfectly unified collective will'. He claimed that 'Khomeini is the focal point of a collective will'. And, in addition, he insisted that 'Khomeini is not a politician' (Afary and Anderson 2005: 222). He, Khomeini, is the incarnation of the collective will of the Iranian people. He is the incarnation of the people as one.

The notion of 'the people as one' is familiar to those who have knowledge of Lefort's conception of the totalitarian phantasm. While I am not claiming that Foucault is a totalitarian thinker, I am claiming that his rejection of the symbolic and of the political opens the door to a form of thought well expressed by one sympathetic to him, Johanna Oksala, who writes:

Similar to Benjamin, Foucault's idea of political spirituality is an exploration and recognition of the ontological structure of the messianic inherent in politics. Political spirituality is an attempt to contribute to a completely different understanding of the political. The possible interruption of all previous history opens up an unrealised future, a 'world yet to come'. Politics is the realm of the messianic, in the sense that it is the realm of necessary contingency, a realm in which anything is possible, a realm of hope and the promise of a different world. (Oksala 2012: 153)

The messianic voice would seem unlikely for Foucault. By dissolving the state into a network of operations of power, Foucault understood himself to engender a changed role for the intellectual. In the past, the intellectual represented the voice of the universal. However, with the demise of the grand narrative and the centrality of sovereignty, the intellectual becomes a 'specific intellectual', who studies micropolitics and bio-power in institutions such as asylums and prisons. In his thoughts on Iran, the specific intellectual has become something of a prophet. It is my hope that the profoundly creepy concept of political spirituality does not come to be rooted in the political culture of the Left.

5

Two regimes of the symbolic: radical democracy between Romanticism and structuralism

Warren Breckman

The leading post-Marxist theories of radical democracy share various common features, but perhaps none of these aspects is more fundamental than their reliance upon the idea of the symbolic. Indeed, the claim that society is a constructed symbolic order was the key move allowing radical democratic theorists to stake out a new territory beyond the Marxist orientation that dominated radical thought throughout most of the twentieth century. The turn to the symbolic inverts Marxism's structure/superstructure, or, more precisely, the symbolic bypasses the dualism by arguing for the constructed quality of all social phenomena, including economic activity. The symbolic turn also opens up a space of contingency, frequently identified with the 'political' as such, insofar as the symbolic accentuates the *sui generis* status of the social world, a world without grounding in an anterior natural or metaphysical order. This association of the symbolic with contingency created new imperatives for political philosophy as well as new possibilities for conceptualising political action. At the same time, however, the symbolic turn has had paradoxical effects because the loss of foundations makes it seem impossible to find a position 'outside' the 'gargantuan matrix', as Slavoj Žižek once called the symbolic order (1999a: 34). The tension between the possibility to escape from determinism and open the social space to creative political action, and the symbolic order as a ubiquitous ideological grid that always already inhabits our subjectivity, will be familiar to anyone who is conversant with recent radical democratic theory.

When we think of contemporary radical democratic treatments of the symbolic order, we readily think of France and of a genealogy that unfolded in the discourse of what Americans like to call

'French Theory'. This genealogy is complicated and reaches back to poststructuralists like Derrida, Kristeva and Baudrillard, then further back to structuralists like Barthes, Althusser, Lacan and Lévi-Strauss, and further still to interwar figures like Bataille, and even to earlier thinkers like Mauss, Durkheim and Saussure. It is a commonplace that Claude Lévi-Strauss was above all the key figure steering French thought towards a preoccupation with the symbolic, insofar as he built structural anthropology on the linguistic model pioneered by Saussure, Jakobson, Greimas and others. Repeating Saussure's exclusion of the historical, diachronic dimension of language in order to establish a synchronic science of language as a system, Lévi-Strauss defined the symbolic as a closed order of social representations that form a system, the function of which is to render the perception of the world coherent by superimposing on the continuum of reality a grid of taxonomic oppositions and syntagmatic associations. Likewise, Lévi-Strauss's new symbolic approach to cultural systems emphasised not the meaning of individual symbolic images or themes as such, but the system of their differences or reciprocal relations (Hénaff 1998: 6). Of course, this structuralist approach underwent critical revision in subsequent French thought, with Jacques Derrida criticising the structuralist concept of centred or, if you will, homeostatically stable systems, and Jacques Lacan theorising an unsurpassable conflict between the symbolic and the real. In different ways, both Derrida and the later Lacan deconstruct the structuralist idea of the symbolic as a self-sufficient, closed order and instead describe a flawed symbolic, shot through with that which it is not and cannot be. This move has been crucial to the radical democratic theory of Ernesto Laclau, Chantal Mouffe, Derrida and the early Slavoj Žižek, each of whom builds upon the paradox that society's ceaseless attempt to create an adequate symbolisation of itself is propelled by the inherent impossibility of ever achieving such a symbolisation.

Despite the fact that this approach clearly differs from structuralism, when the term 'symbolic' appears in radical democratic theory, commentators' first impulse is to think of the structuralist definition of a system in which values emerge through differential relations among elements within the system. The structuralist definition of the symbolic thus continues to dominate our understanding of radical democratic theory, even if that definition persists mainly *ex negativo* as that which such theory overcomes.

This familiar genealogy may be challenged if we set contemporary democratic debate into dialogue with a deeper history of thinking about symbolic representation. This history takes us back to the

Romantic era, when thinkers developed a more polyvalent idea of symbolism than that associated with the classic structuralist idea of the symbolic order. In what follows, a foray – even if necessarily brief – into this Romantic mental landscape will allow us to return with sharpened gaze to a contemporary scene, namely the rancorous debate between Slavoj Žižek and Ernesto Laclau. My gambit is that the recovery of a historically nuanced understanding of the symbolic illuminates the situation of present radical democratic theory.

Numerous critics of the structuralist idea of the symbolic have emphasised the polyvalence of the concept. For example, already in the early 1950s, Claude Lefort pitted Lévi-Strauss's impulse to mathematise the symbolic order against the use of symbols within the unmasterable complexity of lived social experience (1951: 1400–17). More recently, Vincent Descombes has underscored the irreducible duplicity of the concept of the symbol, which encompasses both the strictly conventional sign and the motivated sign that evokes the unsayable. Or, in terms that evoke a tension between Lévi-Strauss and Durkheim, Descombes emphasises that on one hand the symbolic is the 'algebraic' and on the other hand it is the 'sacred'. In a similar vein, Jean-Joseph Goux insists that the concept of the symbol oscillates between what he calls 'abstract operational symbolisation' and 'cryptophoric symbolisation': 'There is no true symbolism,' writes Goux, 'that is not cryptophoric: the symbol is a visible substitute that replaces something hidden, something that is not presentable' (1990: 130, 124). Echoing these French observations, the German historian Rudolf Schlögl has conceded recently that there is no unified theory of the symbolic; but the French commentator Daniel Fabre correctly insists that far from being crippling, this lack of unity has created a 'fecund uncertainty', a fertile zone of indeterminacy that has enabled a considerable range of theoretical projects (Schlögl 2004: 13; Fabre 1989: 61; 1996: 250).

The same fecund uncertainty applies to Romantic thinking about the symbolic. It is necessary to say this because in twentieth-century critical discourse, Romantic symbolism was subjected to a reductionist process. Walter Benjamin set the terms for a negative assessment of Romantic symbol theory that has dominated much discussion ever since. As is well known, Benjamin valued Baroque allegory because its reliance on arbitrary conventions seemed to accentuate the gap between meaning and being; Romantic symbolism, by contrast, rested on a dream of fusion and identity, whereby the gap between signifier and signified is ostensibly transcended by what Benjamin calls 'the idea of the unlimited immanence of the moral world in the

world of beauty' (cited in Cowan 1981: 109–22). The literary theorist
Paul de Man contributed to this critique when he contrasted Romantic symbolism to the deconstructive ideal of a literary writing that
resists closure and the illusion of presence (De Man 1984). Indeed,
modernity, or more precisely postmodernity, has sometimes been
seen as intrinsically *allegorical*, in that it claims to foreclose forever
on the fantasy of immediacy, presence, identity and transcendence
(Day 1999: 103–18). Insofar as such twentieth-century approaches
distinguish strongly between allegory and Romantic symbolism, they
are not without some grounding in Romanticism itself. Hence, for
example, the young Friedrich Schelling insisted that the symbol over-
came the division between Kantian schematism, which signifies the
particular through the general, and allegory, which signifies the general through the particular, by fusing the general and the particular
in an absolute identity: Schelling could thus assert that Mary Magdalen 'does not only *signify* repentance, but is living repentance itself'
(Schelling 1856: 555).

If Schelling's definition of the symbol seems to confirm Benjamin's
and de Man's worries about fantasies of totality and closure, we
immediately encounter polyvalence and indeterminacy if we look to
yet another canonical formulation of the new Romantic theory of the
symbol. 'True symbolism,' wrote Goethe in 1797, 'is where the particular represents the more general, not as a dream or a shadow, but
as a living momentary revelation of the Inscrutable' (Goethe 1994:
471). Unlike an allegory, which equates a concept with an image
in such a way that the concept is contained in the image, the symbolic, claimed Goethe, 'changes the phenomenon into an idea, the
idea into an image, such that the idea remains always infinitely active
and unapproachable in the image, and will remain inexpressible even
if expressed in all languages' (Goethe 1994: 470–1). Goethe's definition vacillates between an ideal of the symbol as a form of presence or, better, presentification (*Vergegenwärtigung*), and as a figure
that initiates a disruptive, open and above all *inexhaustible* dialectic.
At times this vacillation could prompt descriptions that evoke an
insurmountable circularity in this play of difference and identity: the
symbol, wrote Goethe, 'is the thing, without being the thing, but
nonetheless the thing' (Goethe 1898: 142).

The Romantics took over the core of Goethe's idea of the symbolic,
but they radicalised it in various ways that cannot be detailed here. It
suffices to emphasise that whereas Goethe believed that the greatest
work of art could achieve a demonstrably perfect mode of aesthetic
symbolism, the Romantics were simultaneously less restrained in their

fantasy of a symbol that could unify everything and more sober in their sense that human efforts to create such a symbol will inevitably fail. That formulation underscores yet again that we must not elevate one dimension of Romantic symbol theory over the polyvalence that lies at its core: the symbol is simultaneously a figure that concentrates and disperses meaning; it is a powerful figure, not just one sign among all others, but one that has the paradoxical power both to present or body forth and to accentuate the gap between sign and signified. It is, in sum, a special kind of representation, a representational form that oscillates between creating a certain kind of presence and remaining permanently flawed, shot through with that which it is not and cannot be. With good reason Umberto Eco once asked whether the Romantic symbol is an instance of 'an immanence or of a transcendence', and then left the question unanswered (Eco 1984: 143). The polyvalence is further accentuated when we consider that the same Romantics who distinguished between symbol and allegory often used the terms interchangeably and collapsed the two into a general idea that the modern age is itself allegorical. That is, modernity is a state of longing for an impossible unity, a unity lost in the past or waiting in the unforeseeable future. In the Romantic meta-historical imagination, the idea of the symbol becomes itself a symbol, namely a symbol of that impossibility. Thus, in the late 1790s, during the full flush of the radical years of the *Frühromantik*, Friedrich Schlegel could assert, 'All beauty is allegory. One can only express the highest allegorically, precisely because it is inexpressible' (Schlegel 1967: 324). The Romantics did not doubt that there is a highest, a totality towards which the self should strive; that it remains mysterious and elusive did not undermine the dream of reaching it. Indeed, precisely this dynamic interchange between possibility and impossibility seems to underpin the Romantics' sense of the moral grandeur of their striving spirit, what Friedrich Schlegel called the 'unformed colossalness of the moderns' (Schlegel 1957: 46).

No necessary political direction attached to this symbolic sensibility. Without question, it could lend itself to conservative political thought. Characteristically, this took the form of a search for a means to stabilise the limitless mobility of symbols. Hence, Friedrich Schlegel's conversion to Catholicism in 1809; hence, the frequent Romantic turn towards Catholicism, medievalism, monarchy and originary myth. But the symbolic sensibility could produce more nuanced conservative strategies as well. For example, Samuel Taylor Coleridge defended the 'ancient Constitution' of England not simply by reasserting the power of tradition, as had Edmund Burke, nor by defending its obscurity against Tom Paine's calls for transparency, but by emphasising that the idea behind the Constitution remains inexhaustible in relation to the form it might take at any historical moment. As David Aram Kaiser writes, 'Coleridge's account of the inexhaustibility of the English Constitution is an expression in romantic political theory of a hermeneutical model well known in romantic aesthetic theory, that of the symbol' (Kaiser 1993: 47).

Conservative strategies such as these must be countered by examples of progressive, and even radical Romantic uses of the symbolic. Take, for example, Friedrich Schlegel's 1795 essay on Republicanism that challenges Kant's argument that a republic cannot be democratic because a democratic republic lacks a clear separation of executive and legislative powers. Insisting that a republic, if the name has any real meaning, must be democratic, Schlegel nonetheless recognised the danger of coercion. His solution mobilised a symbolic logic that uses Kantian categories against Kant:

> '. . . how is republicanism possible?' asked Schlegel. 'The general will is its necessary condition; but the absolute general (and therefore absolute enduring) will does not occur in the realm of experience and exists only in the world of pure thought. The individual and universal are therefore separated from one another by an infinite gulf, over which one can jump only by a *salto mortale*. There is no solution here other than, by means of a *fiction*, to regard an empirical will as the *surrogate* of the a priori absolute general will. Since a pure resolution of the political problem is impossible, we have to content ourselves with the *approximation* to this practical X'. (1996: 101)

In a quite different context some thirty years later, the French Romantic socialist Pierre Leroux transferred the poetic description of what he called the 'style symbolique' to political thought in his effort to create a third-way politics between what Leroux calls the '*socialisme absolu*' of the Saint-Simonians and the '*individualité absolue*' of liberalism. The Romantic notion that the symbol is a visible representation of the invisible connected Leroux's aesthetics and his politics, for the symbolic mode suggested a way to think of social relations without reifying them; the gap between representation and objects such as 'individual', 'society', 'humanity' and 'God' seemed to open for Leroux a space for artistic and political creativity (Breckman 2005: 61–86).

Even if the Romantic symbolic sensibility has often been denounced for its alleged affinity for conservative politics, examples such as Leroux and the young Schlegel suggest a much more indeterminate relationship to political choice. Nonetheless, one still has to answer to yet another longstanding criticism of the Romantics, a criticism also closely associated with Walter Benjamin, namely the critique of aestheticised politics. Within that critical context, the German Romantics have been harshly criticised for their willingness to transfer their yearning for a harmonious fusion of form and content from the work of art to the realm of politics. Yet the image of Romanticism I am presenting supports a different kind of aesthetic political philosophy suggested in an unjustly neglected book by Frank Ankersmit titled *Aesthetic Politics: Political Philosophy Beyond Fact and Value*. Ankersmit bases his aesthetic politics not on the organic unity of the work of art, but on 'the insurmountable *barrier* between the represented and its representation'. Ankersmit calls this an aesthetic of 'brokenness'. From this position, he proceeds to describe a politics that is aware of the irreducible non-identity of the representation (the state) and the represented (the democratic electorate). 'Political reality,' writes Ankersmit, 'is not something we come across as if it has always existed; it is not found or discovered, but made, in and by the procedures of political representation' (Ankersmit 1996: 48). In a pivotal chapter titled 'Romanticism, Postmodernism, and Democracy', Ankersmit locates the emergence of this awareness of the complex work of political representation in the Romantic era.

In our historical memory, the legacy of Romantic ideas about the symbolic has tended to be repressed. It may well be that these ideas have been victim of a general tendency whereby engagement with the history of the symbolic typically involves some form of exit narrative. As Sven Lütticken recently wrote, 'In the end, all genealogies of the symbol seem to end in practices of radical de-symbolisation' (Ankersmit 2008: 113). Indeed, one could see this as a basic premise of Enlightenment: myth yields to science, a world thick with opaque symbols evolves into a world of rationally transparent relations, belief in the real power of symbols gives way to a recognition of their status as fictions, the power of symbols to present fades before the function of signs to represent. We see this dialectic of de-symbolisation at work in the history of the Marxist Left, beginning with Karl Marx himself. In truth, no one accorded more power to symbols than Marx – after all, the capitalist world, as Marx understood it, was governed by two symbols, money and commodities. Yet Marx's critical task was to dissolve what he called these 'social hieroglyphics' by tracking them to their root. Marx took this impulse directly from the Left Hegelian effort to demystify the sacred symbols of Christianity, and it is no accident that Marx readily drew analogies between his critique of social symbols and the

radical Hegelian critique of religion. Nor is it surprising that, like
the Left Hegelians, Marx attacked the Romantic concept of symbolic form. Just as the Romantic ideal of the symbol was anchored
in the impossible desire to present the unpresentable, so too was
the Left Hegelians' rejection of the symbolic deeply implicated in
their campaign against religion. Marx followed the Left Hegelians
in associating human emancipation with the task of overcoming the
otherness, heteronomy and unmasterability implied by symbolic
representation.

In the period of Marxism's collapse, the intellectual Left's suspicion of symbolic form eased. And with it, the dialectic of de-
symbolisation in certain ways went into reverse. If we now turn,
finally, to Ernesto Laclau and Slavoj Žižek, it is clear that neither of
them accepts the Romantic belief that the symbol corresponds somehow to an ineffable outside, what Novalis once called the 'numinous'.
For both Laclau and Žižek, symbols belong strictly to the human
domain; they do not reveal ontological correspondences between sign
and world, but rather specific human acts of conferring meaning. At
the same time as the Post-Marxists thus share a disenchanted terrain
with Marx, nonetheless the symbolic performs work for them that
requires us to recapture the polyvalent possibilities in the theory of the
symbolic. It is important to be clear on the claim being made here. This
is not a claim for some sort of direct influence of Romanticism upon
thinkers like Laclau or Žižek, but rather a suggestion that in the present context, the polyvalence that seems to be intrinsic to all notions
of the symbolic, and which was first given its modern formulation by
Romanticism, has re-emerged from prohibition and has come to play
a productive role in radical democratic theory.

Let us consider just one illustration, namely the treatment of universality in Laclau and Žižek. Universality is a particularly good
example because of the productive relationship between the impossibility of representation and the necessity of symbolisation. To
begin with Laclau, since the early 1990s, he argued vigorously that
the Left will be reinvigorated only if it can move beyond postmod-
ern identity politics and recapture the category of the universal. Of
course, the question is vexed because Laclau recognised that there
is no such thing as a pure universal, one untainted by particularity
and awaiting discovery in a metaphysical beyond. Keeping with this
rejection of foundationalist universalism, Laclau theorised a conception of 'relative universalism' 'pragmatically constructed through
the "equivalential" effects of struggles carried out by actors that are
always limited' (Laclau 1985: 219, 229). This formulation built on

the initial theory of hegemony offered in *Hegemony and Socialist Strategy*, namely that in the absence of any sort of determining base or foundational logic, political positions emerge through practices of articulation that build equivalential links between elements within the discursive field of politics. Yet, in his new search for a viable notion of the universal, Laclau shifted his attention from elements within a field or system, to the field itself. Where his earlier notion of hegemony stressed the operation of metonymic links within a system of differences, Laclau's more recent approach emphasised that a differential system operates according to a complex play not only of differences, but also of equivalence, insofar as all the elements stand on this side of an exclusionary limit. Yet, if the system's limit is to be a real limit, it cannot be just another element within the system. So, the constitutive ground of the system is exterior to the system. And that means the ground cannot be represented as such, because to do so would simply place it back among the elements within the system.

Transferring this basic deconstructive logic to the social domain, Laclau concluded that the universal is the fullness of society itself; but that fullness itself cannot be represented. The topos of an 'empty place' emerges in Laclau's thought in the form of the empty place of the universal, of the social totality. The logic of equivalence now orients itself to the system itself, or more precisely to the empty place of the system. Social relations are fuelled by a dynamic interchange between the desire to fill the empty place of the universal with positive content and the subsequent inevitable failure of every such attempt at symbolisation. If universality as such cannot be represented, then a particular signifier will have to assume the function of representing the universal, of becoming the 'symbol of a missing fullness'. Laclau insisted that this is a contingent process, with no rational or ontological ground granting priority to certain signifiers. Rather, the elevation of a particular into the position of universality is always the result of hegemonic struggle within an antagonistic political field, and hegemony always involves a synecdoche in which a particular lays claim to a constitutively absent social fullness.

Laclau and Žižek shared many common grounds, yet after the late 1990s they grew increasingly distant, culminating in an acrimonious fight in the pages of *Critical Inquiry* in 2006. I have dealt at considerable length elsewhere with the wider range of issues that divided them, and these cannot concern us here (Breckman 2013: ch. 6). In the final section of this chapter, I would like to consider their dispute strictly in the light of my foray into Romanticism. One of Žižek's recent books bears the title *In Defense of Lost Causes*. The cover of the American edition presents an image of the guillotine blade, symptomatically expressing Žižek's turn away from post-Marxist radical democratic thought and his embrace of the rhetoric of revolution and the canon of revolutionaries, from Robespierre, through Marx to Lenin and Mao. Žižek's title immediately invites the word 'romantic'. After all, what could be more romantic than lost causes? What is more romantic than desperate acts, driven by passions that burst through all constraints with such power that the world itself might be changed? To call Žižek such a romantic is to play with a readily available signifier that circulates freely in our culture, is usually negative, and is almost always devoid of actual reference to the historical phenomenon of Romanticism.

What if we move beyond cliché and consider Žižek from the more informed standpoint developed in this chapter? Here, it seems evident that Žižek's revived enthusiasm for the idea of revolution and total transformation has led him to seize upon only one aspect of the polyvalent Romantic idea of the symbol, namely the power to presentify, to make present. We see this emphasis in an approach to universality that differs profoundly from Laclau. As Žižek's opposition to democracy and capitalism intensified throughout the 1990s, he came to advocate what he calls 'partisan universality'. This, he tells us many times, is a universal worth fighting for. As with Laclau, Žižek had from his earliest writings insisted that the universal always carries the stain of the particular, but his approach could hardly be more different from Laclau's. Where Laclau imagined a relative universalism constructed through a series of equivalences bound together by a desire to symbolise the absent fullness of society itself, Žižek insists that

> [t]he key component of the 'leftist' position is the equation of the assertion of *Universalism* with a militant, *divisive* position of one engaged in a struggle: true universalists are not those who preach global tolerance of differences and all-encompassing unity, but those who engage in a passionate fight for the assertion of the Truth that enthuses them. (Žižek 1999b: 226).

Whereas Laclau insisted on the impossibility of a symbol occupying the place of the universal and hence the inevitable failure of every such attempt, Žižek's politics hinges on the claim that a figure can and must embody or present the universal. This insistence upon the power of a figure or embodiment also explains the paradoxical fact that this self-proclaimed 'fighting atheist' is also a profoundly

Christocentric thinker, who recognises in Christ the power to short-circuit the endlessly deferred longing for real presence. As in the early history of Christianity, so too in the history of revolutionary politics, Žižek believes that the concrete, positive presence of a redeeming figure creates the conditions for a genuine rupture, a 'Conversion' that can reorder reality and create a new symbolic order in which even our past can be retroactively re-symbolised. Knotting together this Christocentric idea with his conception of revolution, Žižek writes that the true test of the revolutionary is 'the heroic readiness to endure the conversion of the subversive undermining of the existing System into the principle of a new positive Order which gives body to this negativity' (Žižek 1999: 238). The 'authentic Master' in the revolutionary situation is thus he who is willing to occupy the 'untenable' place of power and assume the 'impossible position of ultimate responsibility' (Žižek 1999: 237). The dynamic structure of impossibility that links Romanticism to post-Marxist radical democracy is here pushed aside, at least rhetorically: Žižek's latest word is not *demand the impossible*, but rather, 'THE IMPOSSIBLE DOES HAPPEN' (Žižek 2001: 84; 2000b: 326).

Žižek thus departs from the polyvalence of Romanticism and lays a one-sided stress on the power of a figure to incarnate, present and embody. He thus re-enacts the short-circuit enacted by the young Friedrich Schelling, whereby the symbol overleaps the gap between particular and universal, such that a figure like Mary Magdalen 'does not only *signify* repentance, but is living repentance itself' (Schelling 1856: vol. 5, 555). By contrast to Žižek, it is Laclau who is the heir of the subterranean legacy of the polyvalent Romantic symbol.

We can conclude with a very revealing moment in Žižek and Laclau's debate in the book *Contingency, Hegemony, Universality*, published in 2000. Žižek there poses a series of rhetorical questions to Laclau: What if the

> political itself (the radically contingent struggle for hegemony) [. . .] *can be operative only in so far as it 'represses' its radically contingent nature, in so far as it undergoes a minimum of 'naturalization'?* What if the essentialist lure is irreducible . . .? (2000a: 100)

That is, Žižek asks, what if it is necessary for political struggle that political actors forget or repress the contingency of their own representations of social reality? In his response, Laclau acknowledges that Žižek does not really believe that any positive entity can truly fill the lack in the social; but he proceeds to make a very telling point:

> ... in the endless play of substitutions that Žižek is describing, one pos-
> sibility is omitted: that, instead of the impossibility leading to a series
> of substitutions which attempt to supersede it, it leads to a symboliza-
> tion of impossibility *as such* as a positive value. This point is important:
> although positivization is unavoidable, nothing prevents this positiviza-
> tion from symbolizing impossibility as such, rather than concealing it
> through the illusion of taking us beyond it. (Laclau 2000: 199)

The possibility of creating such a symbolic understanding, writes
Laclau, 'is important for democratic politics, which involves the
institutionalization of its own openness and, in that sense, the injunc-
tion to identify with its ultimate impossibility' (Laclau 2011: 199). In
his 2006 exchange with Žižek, Laclau insists that the very definition
of politics is the creation of symbols, and the highest of all symbols
is impossibility as such, recognition of which is itself a basic imperative of post-Marxist radical democracy. This is a need that moves
outside the ubiquitous and orthodox twentieth-century definition of
the symbolic as a differential system of signs. Laclau's symbol is not
merely a sign; rather, it mobilises the polyvalence that we saw in
the Romantic symbol. That is, the radical democratic symbol must
simultaneously on the one hand body forth and present and on the
other hand expose the impossibility of ever establishing identity with
the social totality. Or, to recall the words of Friedrich Schlegel, 'One
can only express the highest allegorically, precisely because it is inexpressible' (1967: 89–90).

6

Political representation: the view from France

Raf Geenens

Contemporary Anglophone literature on political representation has recently undergone a so-called 'constructivist' turn. As Lisa Disch explains elsewhere in this volume, authors partaking in the constructivist turn seek to dismantle a somewhat simple, yet very widely accepted account of political representation, according to which political representation is little more than a process of 'mirroring'. In this simple view, the term 're-presentation' is understood, almost literally, as 'making present again'. The people's opinions and preferences are purportedly present within the people's own minds; political representatives have the straightforward task of detecting these opinions and preferences and making them 'present again' on the political stage.

According to 'constructivist' authors, representation plays a more complex role in our democracies. Rather than functioning as a mere conduit for their constituents, political representatives are actively involved in the construction of the opinions and preferences they are supposed to express. Citizens' opinions and preferences are not the pre-given substrate of representative procedures but are partly constructed by the very process in which they are presumably expressed. Political discourses are now seen as co-constitutive of the ideas and interests which, on a more naïve understanding of representation, should be present before they can be re-presented. Thus, the political stage is not a mere reflection of a society's political makeup, but is itself *constitutive* for the political feelings and attitudes that can be found within a given society. This does not necessarily reduce the masses to passive recipients of elite-constructed representations, but it does mean that the roles of the 'representatives' and the 'represented' are interwoven in a more complex manner than is often assumed.

Although I am broadly sympathetic towards this 'constitutive' or 'constructivist' account of representation, I argue that it remains myopic in an important sense because it focuses on what could be called 'micro-aspects' of representation. Most constructivist authors are interested in the interplay between claims made by politicians – 'representative claims', as Michael Saward calls them (2010) – and the political views of individual citizens. They argue that this interplay is more bi-directional than is assumed in a 'naïve' understanding of representation, and they investigate how such representative claims – when they are no longer understood as reflections of an already existent substrate – can be democratically legitimate. Are leaders genuinely expressing the interests and opinions of their constituents, or are they rather manipulating them? Where should we draw the normative line and claim that the representative mechanism is no longer democratic? To be sure, these are important issues. But the narrow focus on the representation of interests and opinions leaves many other aspects of democratic representation out of view. Missing in such an approach is attention to the broader, 'systemic' effects of representative processes. Obviously, uttering representative claims is an important part of these processes. But it might be the case that the representative system seen in its entirety (including political institutions but also other areas of social life) has normatively valuable effects that are not directly related to the mechanism of interest and opinion formation.

In this chapter, I will demonstrate that zooming out of this interplay between representative claims and voters' opinions can bring more encompassing and more fundamental societal mechanisms into view. Political representation, and the way it is organised in democratic societies, does not only have important effects on the political opinions of individual citizens. It might also, more generally, influence the way society understands itself (to begin with, as a democratic society), the way individuals within that society see themselves (to begin with, as individuals) and how individuals within society interact with each other, even when they are involved in activities that have no apparent link with politics. Thus, I will be defending the following idea: the way in which a democratic society represents itself on its political stage is constitutive for the self-understanding of that society and its members as a whole.

In order to elucidate this holistic account of political representation, I will build on the work of the late French philosopher Claude Lefort. According to Lefort, a society's political regime, rather than just a mechanism for making collectively binding decisions, is intimately interwoven with the nature of all social relations to be found within that society. As I will explain in the first section below, political power is primarily understood here as a 'hermeneutic' tool, a tool used by society to construct an interpretation of itself. As a result, power cannot be disconnected from collective processes of self-representation.

Note that it is not just Lefort who defends this view. Similar ideas can be found in some of the younger political philosophers who dominate much of the debate in France today (and who are strongly influenced by Lefort), such as Marcel Gauchet, Pierre Manent and Pierre Rosanvallon. Looking backwards, one can discover antecedents to Lefort's ideas in the work of classical French liberal thinkers, such as Alexis de Tocqueville or even Montesquieu. It seems therefore justified to speak of a typically 'French' view on politics and representation. The core intuition of this view is that political institutions play a key role in the 'self-representation' or the 'self-understanding' of society, and are thus deeply intertwined with the 'moeurs' (to use Tocqueville's term) or the 'spirit' (in Montesquieu's words) of society as a whole. There are of course important differences between the views of these various authors, who are divided by centuries (see Geenens and Rosenblatt 2012), but I will not delve deeper into these differences here. Instead, this chapter will mostly focus on the way Claude Lefort describes the role of politics in a democratic society's self-understanding.

I will demonstrate that, for Lefort, this role is threefold. First, political representation is necessary for sheer reasons of *identification*: it is through political discourses that we come to see ourselves as members of one and the same society, and as members of this specific society. Second, Lefort observes that the representation of societal opinions and conflicts on the stage of politics is always a translation of these opinions and conflicts into the normative language of principles and rights. Such a translation is important because it *transforms* the way we, as citizens, understand our own attitudes and interactions. Third, the democratic self-representation of society matters because it allows us to understand ourselves as collectively autonomous or *sovereign*, that is, as members of an entity that is not governed by the laws of history or by economic necessity but that is – at least in principle – self-steering. In the concluding section of this chapter, I will offer some brief reflections as to why it is important today – maybe more so than ever – to take stock and to become conscious of these broader effects of democratic representation.

Lefort and the 'hermeneutic' role of political power

Claude Lefort's central thesis can be summarised as follows: the process of democratic representation, taken as a whole, has a number of normatively valuable effects that have relatively little to do with the actual decision-making, and that can only be grasped by taking into account the 'symbolic' role of politics in the life of a society. Before looking into these various normative merits of democratic representation, I will say something more about what is meant by this symbolic understanding of politics.

Lefort's interest in the symbolic aspects of politics is by and large the result of his extensive readings of Machiavelli. In his 1972 book on Machiavelli (Lefort 1972),[1] Lefort starts by inquiring into the practice of reading itself. Whoever reads and interprets a book, Lefort claims, can only do so by pretending that the text has a clear and coherent meaning. But a lucid (or honest) interpretation does more than this. It also acknowledges that there is – and remains – a 'lack of certainty' about what the proper interpretation would be. This uncertainty is an effect not just of the distance between writer and reader, but also of the fact that the writer him- or herself was engaged in an enterprise – setting up a meaningful construction – that is never completely consistent or self-transparent. The reader, trying to get a grip on this construction, inevitably exercises power over it; he or she coerces the text's meaning into a stable form, but the material itself remains unstable. Careful readers will proceed with their interpretation nonetheless, all while being aware of the precarious nature of their task.

This 'reading ethics' will guide Lefort when making his way through Machiavelli's *œuvre*. Yet, somewhat surprisingly, this reading ethics also epitomises the conception of politics he claims to find in Machiavelli's *The Prince*. Political power, in this conception, is a *hermeneutic* tool, used by society to read and interpret itself. Society never has a direct or automatic access to itself, so its self-understanding will have to pass through a detour; that is, it requires *mediation*. When speaking about who we are, about the nature of our mutual interactions, or about the society in which we find ourselves, we invariably look at society (and at our own positions in it) as if from an imaginary point floating above society. For Lefort, whoever speaks or thinks about society necessarily presumes it is possible to adopt such a perspective, that is, to occupy a panoramic point that reveals all social relations and thus 'transcends' these relations that really exist.

According to Lefort, this is the task Machiavelli ascribes to the prince. Through the things a prince says and does, society acquires a concrete, stable image of itself. The prince's power thereby serves as a focal point, revealing society to itself as *this* society and as *one* society. At the same time, the prince's office also divides society, as there is now a distinction between the citizens and the prince. Thus, all while creating unity, the appearance of power also divides society and prevents it from fully coinciding with itself. Society, Lefort claims, is always saddled with an 'original division' (Lefort 1992: 313). If Machiavelli announces the beginning of political modernity, it is, according to Lefort, for this specific reason: he was the first to sense that there is an original 'fracture' in our collective self-understanding.

This fracture can also be understood as the gap between the 'real' and the 'symbolic'. Establishing what society *really* is can only be done through *symbolic* representations. Someone has to take up the (never-ending) task of interpreting social reality and instituting collective representations of it. These representations are *original* in the sense that they do not cover up social reality, but rather make it visible to us. Lefort also notes that this 'symbolic layer' has a certain inertia. In consequence, the images, ideas and norms in which we express our current self-understanding inevitably connect us to a specific history. Alas, this also implies that society cannot change this symbolic layer at will.

Lefort's emphasis on the 'symbolic order' clearly betrays the era in which his thinking originated. Lefort rarely refers to Blanchot, Derrida, Lacan or Laplanche, but it is these (and related) authors who determined the philosophical universe in which Lefort wrote his study on Machiavelli. Within this context, Lefort's originality lies in the fact that he did not approach the symbolic in metaphysical, linguistic, or psychoanalytic terms, but rather in *political* terms. For Lefort, the primacy of the symbolic means, first and foremost, that the meaning of our social interactions does not precede its political expression, but is inevitably shaped by the political order in which we find ourselves (an idea that Lefort's thesis supervisor, Raymond Aron, had earlier defended under the label 'the primacy of the political').

It is clear, then, that for Lefort political institutions do not play a merely functional role in social life. Instead, they are intimately interwoven with the very meaning of social life. This raises the theoretical stakes. The process of political representation should now not just be understood in light of its democratic mission (channelling citizens' opinions into policy decisions), but also in light of its broader societal role. If political representations are crucial in making society into what it is, one should investigate the manifold connections between democratic modes of representation and various other features of a democratic society. This is precisely what Lefort will do from the late 1970s onwards in his extensive writings on democracy: he will tease out the links between the mode of 'being' in democratic societies, and the political institutions of such societies. According to Lefort, this is not a novel type of exercise; it is rather a return to the original task of political philosophy, namely to investigate the complete *form* of a society in light of the way power is exercised (Lefort 1988: 11).

Lefort's investigation rarely follows a strictly methodical path, but for the sake of clarity I will argue that Lefort sees three types of 'connections' between democratic procedures on the one hand and the broader 'mode of living' in a democratic society on the other: democratic representation plays a role in the self-identification of citizens within a society, it shapes the way we interact with each other, and it reminds us of our collective freedom.

Collective self-identification

A first and rather important normative merit of democratic representation lies in that it provides citizens with a locus of self-identification: the political stage is the mirror in which citizens come to see and identify themselves as members of *this* society, of *one* society. This was already the key message of Lefort's Machiavelli book. The first and primary task of politicians, rather than expressing the interests and opinions of citizens, is to provide society with an image of itself. Political representatives are there to 'read' or 'interpret' society (Lefort 1972: 306–9).

Pierre Rosanvallon, in his book on the history of political representation in France, captures particularly well the difficult nature of this task in a democratic society (Rosanvallon 1998). While pre-revolutionary France had an organic order that could easily be read off from the myriad institutions and rituals in which it was embodied, the democratic France that emerged in the nineteenth century had no clear or obvious image of itself. The people had been appointed as the subject of sovereignty, but 'people' was a term so vague and abstract that even its most ardent supporters hardly knew how to depict it. As the nineteenth century unfolds, various strategies are deployed, from strengthening the historical imagination so that one can recognise the people as a real, biographical person (Michelet) to the political representation of different professional groups so as to lay bare society's economic structure. For a long time, proportional representation emerged as the winning formula. Accepting that society contains no 'natural' bodies or corporations, proportional representation reveals society to be composed of individuals who vote *as* individuals. At the same time, the party system – representing the plurality of opinions – caters to the perennial need for identification. Yet it does so in a highly modern manner: the entity of identification (the party) is an abstract artifice, and its voters are seen as individually voting citizens.

Rosanvallon's historical narrative confirms Lefort's conception of politics as the place where society comes to recognise itself as *this* and as *one* society. It also shows that this unity does not necessarily require a thick, homogeneous sense of identity. Different political actors can tell different stories about society. Even if these stories contain multiple or conflicting plotlines, citizens do acquire an image of their society as the entity that sits at the heart of these different stories. What matters is that there are stories and that they are heard by citizens, so that these citizens come to understand themselves as citizens of one and the same society.

It is easy to forget this and to overlook why this matters. Another Lefort disciple, Pierre Manent, warns us – amid pessimist musings about the rise of individualism – that the loss of this perspective might have disastrous consequences. According to Manent, it is especially the abstract institution of the state that allows citizens to see themselves *as* citizens. The state, as brought to life by the words and deeds of visible political actors, has a 'spiritual or symbolic function', he writes; it is 'indispensable to me becoming conscious of being a citizen' (Manent 2006: 29). He goes on to say that 'in the scheme of representation, the state constitutes the neutral place, abstract and raised above society, to which I can turn as a citizen so that it can represent *me*' (Manent 2006: 29). On Manent's republican anthropology, human beings can only thrive if they can sacrifice something of themselves to a common project, that is, if they live in a community where something is held in common: the 'body politic' or the 'res publica'.

No matter whether one emphasises the stable role of the state or the more fluid ecosystem of political parties, it is always through such institutions that individuals adopt a perspective from where they see themselves not only as individuals, but as political agents with a responsibility for the fate of a specific collectivity. And this, in turn, is what supports all further bounds of civic and economic solidarity.

This, then, is clearly an important normative merit of political representation: democratic institutions are 'representative' because they construct and uphold the point of view from where citizens can see and understand themselves as members of this specific society.

Freedom and equality

Lefort also points to a second normative merit of representative institutions. Accepting that political representations – the things said and done on the political stage – have a formative influence on society's self-understanding, it is obvious that the concepts and the terms of these representations can make a significant difference. Democratic politicians compete against each other on a stage that is visible to all, and, as they do so, they mobilise certain images of the citizens, of these citizens' interests and of their opinions. But to the extent that these politicians are indeed *democratic* politicians, they will normally do so in a specific vocabulary. They will refer to principles such as *freedom* or *equality*, they will describe the members of society as individual *citizens*, they will claim that these *individuals* have certain *rights*, and so on.

Thus, to the extent that social interests, conflicts and ideas are 'represented' in democratic institutions, these interests, conflicts and ideas are also translated into a distinct idiom, namely that of justice, equality and individual liberties. This is why Lefort says that politics is not just a *staging* (*mise-en-scène*) of society, but also a *giving meaning* (*mise-en-sens*) and *giving form* (*mise-en-forme*) to it (Lefort 1988: 11). Politics puts all social things into a specific form. That form is not necessarily a democratic form; in totalitarian societies, for instance, it is most certainly not. But for a society to be democratic, these forms have to be specific ones, that is, principles such as equality or individual freedom.

Even if these terms are sometimes used as mere code for naked self-interest, the fact that interests have to be veiled and coded in order to be presentable on the public stage matters a great deal. Hypocrisy does have a civilising effect, and nowhere more so than in the theatre of politics. For the principles and values that circulate in the political realm inevitably end up fashioning citizens' self-image, as well as the way citizens interact. It is the public language of rights and principles, of fairness and equality that activates and upholds our self-understanding as individual citizens endowed with rights, and that teaches us to treat other individuals as respectable citizens endowed with these same rights. It is only because it is first enacted on the stage of politics, Lefort says, that we can adopt such an image of ourselves and of our interactions.

This is not just an effect of the *language* used by politicians. The complex procedures typical of representative democracies are similarly important. Not unlike rituals, these public procedures are strong embodiments of certain principles we hold dear, from the inviolability of individuals and the legitimacy of dissent to the presumption of innocence. And as we are constantly exposed to them, these procedures cannot but shape how we interact with each other, even in areas of life that are far removed from the public eye. Thus, when political representatives compete with each other yet at the same time, constrained by a variety of procedures, recognise each other as equals worthy of respect, they are – whether they are aware of it or not – influencing the 'style' of social relations throughout society.

In pointing to this connection between political interactions and non-political interactions, Lefort takes more than a page out of Tocqueville's classical *Democracy in America*. Indeed, if the two volumes of Tocqueville's *Democracy* occupy such an important place in the history of political thought, it is precisely because Tocqueville was unusually sensitive to the connection between political principles – the principles that structure political procedures and shape the discourses of political actors – and the way individuals speak and interact in other, non-political realms of society. It is this sensitivity that allowed Tocqueville to describe the change from an aristocratic to a democratic society, not so much as a material change, but as a change in our collective imagination: that is, a change in the *image* through which individuals perceive themselves and their role in society.

Tocqueville explores several elements that are crucial in this regard. Most famous is of course the rise of equality. Tocqueville describes the transition towards democracy as the displacement of an 'image of hierarchy' by an 'imaginary equality' (Tocqueville 1992: 692, 695). I am referring here to a passage in the second *Democracy*, where Tocqueville discusses the changing relation between masters and servants. In a democratic society, master and servant are no longer tied to each other by a 'permanent hierarchy' (Tocqueville 1992: 694). Instead, they come to see each other in light of an 'imaginary equality', despite the 'real inequality of their conditions' (Tocqueville 1992: 695).

Similarly, the idea of popular sovereignty is, according to Tocqueville, not an isolated notion but rather the 'last ring' in a chain of ideas that 'envelops' the entire Anglo-American world (Tocqueville

1992: 462). Tocqueville emphasises that the principle of popular sovereignty is much more than just a proposition about the legitimacy of collective decisions. According to Tocqueville it is intimately interwoven with the way individuals perceive themselves in all areas of their life. Americans are confident that Providence has given each of them a sufficient amount of reason to guide his or her own behaviour. As such, this principle is not just a formal principle for legitimate decision-making, but, in Tocqueville's terminology, a 'generative principle' of American society as a whole (Tocqueville 1992: 462).

The connection Tocqueville draws between political principles and the nature of human interactions in other, non-political realms of society is exactly what his contemporary followers are after. Whether it is Lefort, Rosanvallon or Manent, they all believe that the principles democratic representatives enact on the political stage matter, not so much because these principles warrant democratically legitimate decisions, because they ensure 'responsiveness', or because they result in high-quality policy outputs, but rather because they generate a specific type of society, a specific type of human beings and a specific style of social relations.

George Kateb, in his essay entitled 'The moral distinctiveness of representative democracy', makes a very similar point (Kateb 1981). According to Kateb, representative democracy's most important merit does not lie in its 'responsiveness' to citizens' preferences, in the formal legitimacy of its procedures, or in the quality of the resulting policy outcomes. The real virtue of representative procedures is rather to be found in their side-effects. Within the political sphere, political representatives bring certain values to life which unintentionally produces a specific way of 'being' elsewhere, outside of the political realm:

> In its distinctive way of forming political authority, representative democracy cultivates distinctive ways of acting in nonpolitical life [. . .] [It] helps to foster certain traits of character and hence certain ways of being in the world that no other form of government does. (Kateb 1981: 363)

Kateb extensively enumerates the many moral qualities which he believes to be nurtured by representative democracy. He mentions, for instance, the fact that representative democracy 'politicizes' all non-political relations of life because it constantly inspires and incites individuals to claim the status of citizens and to assume the role of a political actor, even in non-political settings (Kateb 1981: 360).

Furthermore, because the practice of representative government constantly displays, on a very large stage, that all authority can be questioned (there is a constant 'chastening' of authority), it breeds independence of spirit (Kateb 1981: 359–60, 368). Kateb also claims that the public practice of representative democracy creates a widespread sense of moral indeterminacy. This is not the same as scepticism or relativism. It is rather an awareness that even when a moral or political answer is accepted as correct, it is never certain that this is indeed the *ultimate* correct answer, that it is the *only* correct answer or that it will always *remain* the correct answer. Finally, and most subtly, Kateb claims that the practice of representative democracy infuses social relations with a certain delicacy and an attitude of fairness, self-doubt and self-correction. He summarises this attitude under the heading 'serious playfulness'. This is the attitude of those who know that the game is bound by constitutional rules and checks and balances, yet vigorously play to win, but are also willing to admit defeat. This attitude is generated by the procedural and staged nature of representative democracy, but it eventually pervades *all* social relations, both formal and informal. Thus, for Kateb, the truly remarkable effect of political representation is what he calls 'the nonpublic manifestation of the "spirit" of the public sphere' (Kateb 1981: 368) – a phrase that involuntarily (or so I assume) echoes Montesquieu.

Political autonomy

A third and final merit of representative procedures has to do with *conflict*. According to Lefort, the pivotal difference that distinguishes democratic regimes from non-democratic regimes is the democratic regime's explicit acceptance of conflict. All human communities are shot through with tensions and divisions that have the potential to erupt into full-blown social conflicts. Yet most societies are ill equipped to deal with visible conflicts. Instead, they deploy a variety of strategies to maintain at least the appearance of social unanimity and prevent the development of deep conflicts. Democracy is unique for Lefort in that it does not try to muffle or deny the existence of societal oppositions. Instead, democratic societies openly acknowledge the presence of conflicts; they even welcome them and make space for them at the heart of their most important institutions. This is exactly what happens in representative institutions: they give room for parties and politicians to engage in an endless tug of war over the power to rule. Moreover, the legitimacy of this never-ending game is formally recognised: the presence of disagreeing parties is applauded, and cyclical elections demonstrate that those in power do not coincide with their position but are only occupying it temporarily and might be removed come the next elections. Through this process, the opposing forces present in society can become visible, and their tensions and conflicts are openly played out. In this way, representative procedures emphatically provide us with an image of society as intrinsically *conflictual*.

The rewards of that strategy can hardly be overestimated. Within society, these divisions could lead to real and potentially very chaotic struggles. By evacuating the conflict to a place outside of society the conflict does not disappear, but it is *domesticated*. Political actors dramatise the conflict on a stage that is visible to all, which allows us to identify with it (in the way we identify with actors in a theatre play) without having to engage in it ourselves. Paradoxically, the conflict can now even become a source of unity, as we are all turned into spectators of this same public stage.

This visible staging of societal conflicts matters for several reasons. For starters, this ongoing conflict makes it very clear that society has no fixed purpose or identity. With politicians engaged in a never-ending conflict over the interpretation of society, citizens learn that society will never fully coincide with any determinate self-image. Instead, the meaning of society, its purpose and the way it is organised are always up for grabs. As Bernard Flynn explains in this volume, the political institution of society requires a symbolic 'third position'. Lefort famously claims that in a democratic society, this third position is to remain 'empty': no one has a natural (or supranatural) title to rule. In consequence, *all* hierarchies and power structures can be put into question. This is the message citizens receive, on a daily basis, in a society that represents itself through a proceduralised conflict. Of course, the different claims to rule are all rooted in a fixed reference point, 'the people'. But as there are so many different voices claiming to speak for the people, their only lasting message is that 'the will' of 'the people' is not quite a uniform whole.

According to Lefort, the 'emptiness' of the place of power affects social relations far beyond the realm of politics. When political conflict becomes legitimate, social conflict in all its forms becomes legitimate as well. The symbolic mutation brought about by democracy opens up a history, and I am paraphrasing Lefort here, in which citizens have the experience of a final indeterminacy, not only with regard to the foundations of power, law and knowledge, but also with regard to the relation of the one to the other, in all domains of social life (Lefort 1988: 19). In other words, by representing political power relations as changeable, democratic procedures in one and the same move sanction the dynamic nature of human relations throughout society.

Furthermore, the never-ending conflict confronts us with the openness of our collective future.[2] Every party embodies a specific ideological position and also translates this position into concrete policy proposals that have the potential to push our society in a specific direction. Thus, different parties offer competing interpretations of the present and of the future, thereby reminding us of the fact that our current situation is ambiguous and contains more than one possible future. As such, the conflict between political parties not only teaches us to adopt an attitude of tolerance towards other ideological positions. It also shows us, most fundamentally, that our society can move in different directions and thus that we are collectively free. By putting forward different policy proposals and different visions of the future, the multiplicity of representatives confronts us with the undecidedness of our future – keeping at bay the idea that we are on a predetermined path. This latter idea is of course very popular, and Lefort detects various versions of it (such as the belief that we are governed by material laws of history, or by economic necessity) which he sees as direct threats to democracy. The best protection against such threats is precisely *conflict*. The staged conflict between representatives constantly reminds us of our collective autonomy, that is, it activates and maintains an image of ourselves as *sovereign*.[3]

Conclusion

Taking together these three points, the thrust of Lefort's ideas on political representation should be clear. In comparison to much of the contemporary literature, he presents us with a much richer vision of representation. While authors in the constructivist turn have been showing a keen awareness of the 'aesthetic' effects that are part and parcel of political representation, I believe they could, and *should*, extend the scope of their inquiry. For these 'aesthetic' or 'constitutive' mechanisms do not just affect the political process (narrowly understood as the procedures and interactions that lead to a collectively binding decision) but might have *constitutive* effects far outside and beyond the realm of politics. This is exactly the message of Lefort and other likeminded French thinkers: democratic representative procedures matter because they give rise to a specific type of individual beings, to a specific style of social interactions and, ultimately, to a specific type of society.

The relevance of that message is not limited to discussions about representation. It can be noted today that an increasing number of scholars (as well as actors in the real world) see no need to maintain the old-fashioned institutions of representative democracy, for instance because they believe that, in a postnational world, these institutions cannot be saved or reconstructed. But many scholars also seem to genuinely believe that the core normative criteria of democratic decison-making (such as formal equality, rational justification, and so on) can just as well be satisfied in various sorts of novel institutional arrangements, such as deliberative supranationalism, comitology, networked governance, direct-deliberative polyarchy (cf. Cohen and Sabel 1997; Joerges and Neyer 1997; Neyer 2000). These proposals are particularly prevalent in discussions about supranational political institutions (such as the European Union), but not only there.

What is wrong with such theories? The authors of these theories are misled by what one could call a 'positivist' illusion. They believe that the role of political institutions coincides with their visible, empirically observable function (to find solutions for collective problems) and that the normative criteria guiding this function can be adequately captured in a clean list of bullet points (such as responsiveness, inclusiveness, and so on). In consequence, they claim that this function can be fulfilled and that these normative requirements can be realised not only in classical representative institutions, but also in very different types of collective decision procedures, such as 'direct-deliberative polyarchy'. They might even claim that such novel decision procedures can fulfil some or all of these requirements better than classical democratic institutions.

This optimism towards novel political decision procedures is not without risks. Yet to explain why, one needs a substantial account of the normative merits of classical representation, an account that goes beyond thin formal criteria such as responsiveness or inclusion. The French account seems more equipped for this task than those theories of representations that pay no attention to the 'symbolic' effects of representation. In this regard, these French thinkers seem to have understood, better than anyone else, what exactly is at stake when the role and the credibility of our existent representative institutions continues to be eroded – or, alternatively, when we do not succeed in constructing equivalent institutions outside and beyond the nation-state.

Notes

1. The book was translated into English in 2012 (Lefort 2012).
2. This is also of importance for Ernesto Laclau's constructivist account of political representation (see Warren Breckman's and Oliver Marchart's chapters in this volume).
3. This idea is further developed in my article 'Sovereignty as Autonomy' (Geenens 2017).

7

Democracy and representation

Claude Lefort (translated by Greg Conti)[1]

'Démocratie et représentation', in Claude Lefort, *Le temps présent* (Paris: Éditions Belin, 2007), 611–24. Originally presented at the Colloquium on Latin America, EHESS, organised by Daniel Pécault, 28–9 April, 1989.

Neither democracy nor representation is a creation of the Moderns, at least if we understand 'modern' in the sense which this word took on at the beginning of the nineteenth century. *Democracy* was born (inasmuch as we can tell by the current state of our historical knowledge) in Ancient Greece. Although historians wonder, with good reason, if democracy has ever realised itself fully given how greatly aristocratic values inherited from the former ruling strata have remained active in it, the democratic regime has nonetheless been immediately identifiable by a specific trait: namely, that the people are supposed to possess supreme authority, and that the majority of the citizens are supposed to decide those actions that bear on their shared destiny (*le sort commun*). As for *representation*, understood in the precise sense of a set of institutions whose members are authorised to deliberate on or even to decide public affairs in the name of those to whom the right of appointing them has been granted, it began to take shape in Europe during the period of monarchical states, and by the end of the seventeenth century it had stamped itself on the English tradition to such an extent that it constituted a model for all enlightened minds. In contrast, *representative democracy* constitutes a completely new form of political society insofar as it unites the principle of the sovereignty of the people with (1) the guarantee of the fundamental liberties of citizens; (2) the abolition of the distinction of orders; and (3) the formation of one or several organs to which public authority is delegated by means of either direct or indirect suffrage, or a combination of the two.

We should briefly remind ourselves that representative democracy was not established in a day. The Americans rallied suddenly to the republic in 1777, but they spent years debating (at the cost of sometimes violent conflicts) the nature and powers of *representation* in the states before settling on a blend of federalism, the representative system and universal suffrage. Thus the authority of the people wound up being rigorously circumscribed to the exercise of the suffrage, although all power – executive, legislative and judicial – was henceforth to proceed from the delegation of this authority. France arrived at representative democracy only at the end of a much longer journey, and without ever accepting the same extension of the idea of *representation*. Recall again that the greatest theorist of representative government in the first half of the nineteenth century, François Guizot, head of the liberal opposition under the Restoration and then leader of the government under the July Monarchy, struggled ardently to combat democracy (Guizot 1988). In general the French took a long time to recognise these two truths: first, that the renunciation of the idea of absolute legitimacy signified that the exercise of supreme authority could not simply be transferred from monarch to people (the contradictions in which the revolutionary assemblies found themselves entangled were a sign of their ignorance of this principle); second, that once the distinction of orders had been abolished it became impossible to find a criterion for the limitation of the suffrage (the failure of the repeated attempts to define political rights in accordance with 'capacities' is instructive here).

The essential point, in my eyes, is that representative democracy – in whatever form it takes – truly establishes itself only after all the consequences have been drawn from what I have thought fit to call, on several occasions, the *disembodiment (désincorporation)* of power. Once the monarch has ceased to incarnate the nation in his person (or the nation is no longer incarnated in the monarchical institution to which parliament has been assimilated, as in the case of England), power no longer has absolute legitimacy; in other words, he no longer bears the imprint of the law nor of the final knowledge of the principles of social order. For the same reason, in the absence of an authority that is generative of the substantial unity of society, society is no longer one with itself or embodied by itself (*ne fait plus corps avec elle-même*). Since power from this time forward is subject to an incessant quest to legitimate itself, the political community can discover and maintain its identity only by confronting the oppositions internal to it, the diversity of interests, opinions, beliefs which beat in its breast; it becomes consecrated to the resolution of its conflicts through the establishment of a political stage (*une scène politique*) onto which division is transposed and made visible. On the one hand, the exercise of power remains dependent on the competition of parties and on the other this competition, strictly defined, confers a sort of legitimacy to the conflicts which play out in society and provides for them a symbolic framework which prevents them from degenerating into civil war.

This is all to say that the efficacy of *representation* is tightly linked to the recognition of political and civil liberties, and that these liberties themselves make manifest the diversity of the social. It is to say, furthermore, that the sovereignty of the people constitutes the fundamental reference of all political action only on the condition of remaining latent – with the exception of those moments in which it brings itself to recognition by the operation of the suffrage. Under this latter operation, incidentally, popular sovereignty takes a paradoxical shape, because voting requires a dissolution of social ties and thereby signifies the sovereignty of the people solely through the enumeration of individual choices.

I have just spoken of the creation of a political stage. In so doing we indicate that even in democracy the concept of *representation* must retain something of the signification that it has in common language. Representative democracy is not merely the system in which the *representatives* hold political authority in the place of citizens who have designated them; it is also the system that gives society a visibility. Without doubt this visibility is not perfect. A sometimes considerable distortion enters into the way that the productions on the political stage reflect the social state. Forces can develop and conflicts can ignite which find no symbolic expression in politics but which are capable of toppling the political order nonetheless. And yet it remains true that, where democracy is firmly established and its principles internalised by the groups that confront one another, every particular social action is led, by the very fact of *representation*, to find its inscription in the generality of the political.

There is perhaps no polity or nation in which power does not express (*ne donne figure*) a unity that transcends the social differentiation of statuses, positions and roles. In this sense, power, whether it be that of the prince or that of magistrates, already institutes a dimension of representation in the city. It does this by holding itself up as a representation. The precisely regulated modes of appearance of the sovereign – the accompanying ostentation and ceremony and the imagery which testifies to the sovereign's grandeur – had the effect of nourishing belief in a common subjection to a natural or divine law. Vestiges of these practices persist, incidentally, in the democratic republic. A particular symbolic order is always required in order to guarantee the idea of the unity of the nation and of its permanence over time. But there are important differences. The possessors of monarchical or aristocratic power reveal themselves only in order to uphold the mystery of power as such, to achieve recognition for the secret of which they are the guardians and which confers on them the supreme right of decision. But the establishment of democratic *representation* has for its end – at least in principle – to exhibit, before everyone, the sources and results of public deliberation, to render legible the confrontation of the issues engendered by the diversity of interests and opinions within society. Finally, we would be neglecting a fundamental aspect of democratic representation if we did not mention that, in detaching itself from the voters, representation marks out a space in which debate is supposed to have no goal other than to bring out the general interest from the array of particular interests, while these latter interests, those which belong to such or such social category, are made the subject of controversy.

We have observed one way in which representation cannot be reduced solely to some citizens standing in the place of others who appoint them: namely, that representation achieves the work of political visibility. For a second reason, representatives should not be thought of as merely standing for the electors: namely, that their being placed in the new setting of a meeting requires for them a freedom of judgment which, in principle, gives them the standing to oppose the opinions of the electors – indeed, it even enjoins them in principle to exercise, if necessary, a pedagogical role. (We can recall in passing the bitter discussions that the formula of the imperative mandate provoked in America and the role that these discussions played in the final clarification of the nature of representation.)

The reality, as we all know well, far from corresponds to the schema which I have just traced. As soon as we take this into consideration, doubts assail us from all sides. For instance, the parties whose competition we have judged to be essential to the life of representative bodies – we do have to admit that they are more often guided by concern for their own conservation or for the expansion of their own power than by concern for the general interest. Hence it has long been noted that they tend to turn into machines which leave hardly any place for selection based on talent. One does not, moreover, need to be a scholar to realise that the demagogy of the representatives of the people tends to destroy the function of political pedagogy that they ought to perform. Nor are the parties alone culpable. The problems of the bureaucracy of the unions are another well-known phenomenon. We must admit, in addition, that the extension of the public space – the space in which information is supposed to circulate freely and the confrontation of opinions to occur – goes hand in hand with the growth of organs which have formidable means for reaching the many, capturing their imagination and moulding their judgment.

If we now turn our gaze to individual citizens, supposed equal *de jure* and free in their political choices, we have to admit that their inequality *de facto*, their inscription in an economic system which maintains power[2] and wealth at one end of the spectrum and mediocrity and destitution at the other, results in the weakening of the belief in political community. We may also note that the more efforts to satisfy the supposed needs of the mass increase, the more, by a kind of rebound movement, new forms of idolatry emerge – especially in the form of identification with the 'leader', the political leader borrowing the traits of the 'champion' or the 'star'.[3]

These criticisms could be multiplied if our purpose was to scrutinise the course that the perversion of democracy has taken in the countries where it has been established longest. For now, what has to be noted is that the perception of this perversion depends on our capacity to identify, as I have attempted only too rapidly to do, the principles which assure the formation of a political society different from all preceding societies; in particular, these are principles the originality of which is to reject concord and the image of an order that is good in itself. In the absence of such principles the anti-democratic polemic, whether from moralists or philosophers or specialists in critical sociology, lacks any real substance. For instance, it becomes inexplicable how a system which we condemn with the terms 'democratic fiction' or 'latent totalitarianism' could shine so brightly in the eyes of those who have known the experience of dictatorship (as in Latin America) or even of actual totalitarian power (as in the USSR, Eastern Europe or China). People in these places consider political and individual liberties to be the most precious asset; they pin their hopes on a regime where a parliament is returned by universal suffrage, where elections are no longer under the control of the government, where the plurality of parties and associations is admitted, where justice is recognised as something independent of mere power, etc.

Perhaps we can better interrogate the hallmarks of representative democracy if we pay attention to the obstacles that it encounters in those countries where it is only just beginning to take shape, as at the end of a dictatorship. The misadventures of what we call 'democratic transition' in Brazil, for example, challenge us to revisit the picture which I just sketched. I therefore propose to (1) re-examine the relationship of political representation with the social state (a term which appears to me preferable to 'civil society' when we are referring to a country in which a large part of the population does not in fact enjoy fundamental liberties); (2) consider the connection between political power and state power; (3) highlight the limits of democracy in a world largely subjected to the necessities imposed by the capitalist system and the development of technique.

Representation acquires its full meaning only if it is supported by a network of associations in which collective projects can manifest themselves. Political *representation*, as indispensable as it may be, is only one of the means by which social groups manage to give public expression to their interests or their aspirations and to gauge their strength and their opportunities within the social whole (*l'ensemble social*). I have remarked that representative institutions play a decisive role in providing society with the visibility that it needs in order to preserve a measure of coherence and to assure a measure of integration for its members. But this should not make us forget that there are often – either due to the absence or the failures of a representative assembly, or arising in competition with it – unions and various other associations, minorities organised within particular communities, and even those things we call 'social movements', all of which exercise a representative function, whether this function is legally recognised or not. I will add that we are also familiar with modes of representation that play an important role for a brief period. For example, I am thinking here of those strike committees that are launched where the union cannot or will not take up the claims of the workers. I am thinking also of the numerous movements recently witnessed in France which led to the formation of organisations ('*coordinations*')[4] dedicated either to defending the interests of a specific category of person or to opposing changes deemed harmful. These movements occurred in settings as varied as the university, the hospital and the post office – with the mobilisation of nurses, a social category which had hardly distinguished itself in the past for its dynamism, constituting the most remarkable of these phenomena.

We must accordingly insist both that institutionalised representation is situated within an ensemble of potentially very rich representative forms and that in the absence of the latter the former risks being rendered ineffective. This is my main remark. What I want to underscore is the idea that representation cannot be fruitful unless it takes root in a certain soil, inscribing itself in a vibrant social space in which information circulates, in which multiple opinions can be expressed, in which, finally, different groups and individuals can acquire a sensitivity to interests and aspirations which are not their own. In brief, representation requires the establishment of a public space in which a mutual modification of points of view can be carried out and the legitimacy of new rights can gain recognition from public opinion.

This brings me to re-examine the concept of participation of which we have been making so much use.[5] It seems to me to be important to grasp the character of participation at its most basic. By this I do not mean participation in elections, for example, and still less do I mean the sort of participation that we associate with 'direct democracy'. Participation at its most basic appears to me to involve the sentiment of citizens that they are a part of the political game (*le jeu politique*) – not the sentiment of having to wait passively for measures favourable to their fate, but the sentiment of being taken into account in the political debate. What *participation* means is above all this: having the sentiment of being involved in it and, more precisely, the sentiment of 'having the right to have rights', to take up an expression of Hannah Arendt. This all supposes in the first place that the majority have the ability to conceive of the motives and the motivations for the conduct of political actors.

In a remarkable book on Greek democracy, translated into French under the title *L'Invention de la politique*, Moses Finley (1985) shows what an extraordinary event it was for the peasants, small artisans and small traders who had never enjoyed freedom of speech (*droit à la parole*) to enter the political space. Contrary to what many historians teach, he explains very well that this phenomenon did not necessarily presuppose the active participation of the whole people, that we give in to utopianism when we claim to discover in Athens a model of direct democracy. What rendered the event so remarkable was that the members of the lower classes (*le petit peuple*) now felt themselves capable of projecting themselves into the world of politics, while the main actors remained for the most part, if not in every case, members of the elite. What was new was the fact was that the lower classes had gained the capacity to evaluate the meaning of the acts of the leaders, to judge their strategy, to comprehend how intrigues were being hatched.

Right here, in this capacity to understand the political game, we encounter part of what characterises the democratic experience. It goes without saying that this is impossible in the Europe of the *ancien régime* and, more generally, in every society where political action unfolds in secret and consists in the private decision of the prince and his council or of an oligarchic power. In this case there is a lack of capacity to appreciate the play of the actors and, hence, by the exercise of imagination, to be oneself a virtual actor. And yet this is exactly what seems to me to emerge time and again in the history of most Latin American countries: the great majority of the people have never been in a position to gain an understanding of political action. In other words, the divide has been so deep between, on the one hand, the many – the peasants, the workers and, more generally, the poor – and, on the other, the elites, that there has been no possibility for the former to grasp what the intrigue of politics really means. I employ this term 'intrigue' in a sense which is not pejorative; what I mean is that current affairs, the language of politicians, the stakes of their conflicts remained opaque. And, in this sense, it seems to me that there was no true representation even if, as we know, it was sometimes established in principle, even to the point that multi-partyism was recognised. The example of Paraguay, where a constitution very liberal in appearance was drafted, is from this angle very striking. There cannot be true representation, even where the competition of parties is admitted, if the political game is circumscribed to an elite and escapes the understanding and the capacity for intervention of those who merely wait for their fate to be decided.

In formulating these reflections, I want to bring out a point that was left partially in the dark at the beginning of this talk: the relationship between the political and the social. Indeed we would stumble into the world of fiction if we let our desire to rehabilitate the analysis of the political, which has for such a long time been ignored and dismissed in favour of economic or class-based analysis, carry us so far as to cut the political off from the social. For the two are inseparable, even if they remain distinct. I will return to this point, but for now I insist on this: we must re-interrogate the reasons for the divide between the elites and the masses that is so manifest in the countries of Latin America. I doubt that such a divide has ever been so great or so deep in Europe, at least since the inception of that process summed up as 'modernity'.

Rereading *L'Ancien régime et la révolution* not long ago, I pondered Tocqueville's extraordinary picture of the French peasantry on the eve of the Revolution. This was a peasantry which had largely become landowners and which suffered, at the end of the day, fewer feudal constraints than the peasantry in most other countries. Tocqueville shows, nonetheless, that the French peasantry remained an excluded mass even though the equality of conditions was becoming ever more widespread and the nobles and the bourgeoisie were taking part in the same Enlightenment and often possessed the same assets, drawn from the same source, namely landed property. And yet, in spite of this portrait of the distress of the peasantry, so striking at the end of the eighteenth century, the author cannot help but observe that these peasants, apparently 'closed off and practically impenetrable',[6] were to the utmost degree sensitive to the movement of ideas and to the discourses about equality which were spreading.

Speaking generally, I don't think that such a large divide between the elites and the masses as exists now in Latin America was experienced in the nineteenth century, even in the early period of the industrial revolution when we know that the urban and working populations were being ravaged. This is true if only because in the masses themselves (as shown by numerous accounts which have now been published) there reigned an incessant effervescence. There were pockets of working men who succeeded in giving themselves an education – a general education and especially a political education – and they felt encouraged in this education by the public debates which were agitating the bourgeoisie. There was also a small fraction of elites who concerned themselves with the fate of the masses, called for their emancipation, published books and investigations from which the workers could gain the inspiration to analyse their own condition. The workers had the sense of belonging to a society in flux, of witnessing an industrial expansion, from which their struggles could benefit. They witnessed the sight of a class which enjoyed rights that it had conquered by force, which had asserted itself through a revolution and which, unbeknownst to itself, was spreading principles that were bound to turn against it. In brief, if the 'social question' could be fully posed, it was because there was a political life which burst through the framework of the state.

It is thus not a question of diminishing the function of political representation in favour of the multiple modes of representation arising out of the interior of society. You cannot have one without the other. On the one hand, it is only because there is a co-penetration of the social and the political that the representative system proves effective. On the other hand, all that is fruitful in associations, in community actions, in the sometimes savage movements which revive the urgency of an active participation in public life – all of this acquires a general and lasting impact only if it is connected with political representation. If the latter is deficient, that is, if it concerns only the few, then the reformation of parties and of parliament can have but little effect in reality. Therefore we must reconcile the idea of the fragmentation of claims and of multiple and sometimes spontaneous forms of representation with the idea of the formation of a true political stage.

My second remark stems from the same preoccupation, although it concerns the relationship between political power and state power. I will tackle the question by evoking the character of the populist ideology which tends to conflate the two.

It is due to democratic representation that the state does not close in on itself, that it cannot figure as a centre of omnipotence and appear as if endowed with a compact force and organisation. In a democracy, the state is subject to the most diverse social demands and, ultimately, it is stripped of political decision. This power of decision, as I have said, is assigned to a government which is fundamentally temporary and which always remains dependent on the support of the people. What it boils down to, it seems to me, is a phenomenon too often ignored: democracy gives rise to two images of power. For one, there is the power of the state, and the state appears as a vast machine; it is in accordance with its administration that the fate of each person comes in many cases to be decided. But this great machine coexists with something which is not a machine at all; it coexists with a mutable system which supposes the periodic reformation of the public organs of deliberation and decision – that is, a system which prevents the people from being crushed by a single power capable of deciding everything and incarnating the nation. In contrast, the temptation of populism is for the government and the state to appear and to become almost the same thing. It is often said that populism rejects in practice the dissociation of civil society and the state, but must we not also observe that it simultaneously rejects the dissociation of political power and the power of the state? It is in this way that all the forms of social representation find themselves perverted once they are integrated into a single, unified system of power.

From the same perspective, there is another theme to which I would like to draw attention, that of the defence of individual rights. Regarding these rights, we must understand that they are not merely attached to each individual but that they make possible a true 'socialisation of society' by placing people from across the whole extent of the social space in a relationship with one another and facilitating the exchange of opinions and the diffusion of information. In Western democracies, new rights have been formulated over the course of the nineteenth and twentieth centuries. Many doubt whether these social and cultural rights are faithful to the inspiration of fundamental rights, that is to say those rights which were announced at the epoch of the French Revolution. Yet the truth is that we will never have definitive criteria which will permit us to distinguish what belongs essentially to the realm of rights from what, under their cover, are nothing but expressions of the interests of a particular social category. Are these repeated demands to have the legitimacy of claims recognised by public opinion not, however, a sign of the democratic vitality of a society? Reflection on new rights tends too often to circumscribe the phenomenon to the relations between groups and the state. What appears to me remarkable in the examination of the struggles which for decades have mobilised minorities for the affirmation of their rights is that public opinion is called upon to grant legitimacy to their claim before the state comes to formulate its measure and modify legislation. In Brazil, individuals and groups remain impotent when it comes to spreading their claims in a real public space and getting them recognised as legitimate. This impotence is a disturbing sign of the persistence of anti-democratic regimes.

My final reflection touches on a much broader problem at which I can only hint. Even if it is certain that democracy is not encompassed wholly by the representative system, it must still be admitted that democracy is inadequate to give a response to all the questions which a modern society poses. I remain convinced that democracy is much more than a system of strictly political institutions, that it constitutes a 'form of society' in the sense that the classics spoke of 'politeia' or Enlightenment philosophers spoke of 'régime'. This form of society, whatever its variants may be, has precisely enough traits to distinguish it without difficulty from totalitarian formations or from the various types of dictatorship. Nonetheless, we cannot forget that social life is shaped by capitalism.

Furthermore, we cannot forget that the expansion of technique ceaselessly transforms the relationship of each person with nature and with other people. Now, we must understand that there is an element of necessity in the working of society. The limits of this necessity can never be grasped exactly because it is not a necessity by nature, but rather a necessity that emerged.

Without going so far as to say that capitalism proceeds from a system of arbitrary values, we must recognise that it is not the necessary product of a process which has been unfolding since the dawn of humanity through the passage from one mode of production to another. It would be absurd, then, to want to hypostasise the capitalist system. Still, the fact remains that within the limits of our own history we are living through the trials of capitalist necessity and of the necessity of technique. And yet democracy does not provide an answer to all the problems posed by the market and the international concentration of capital.

This is an obvious truth that it is important to acknowledge and to spread, above all in those countries where democratic transition gives birth to hopes that are, in the beginning at least, exaggerated. We must have the courage to explain that democracy cannot resolve the problems born of the disorders of the global market. On the other hand, nothing would be more dangerous than to retreat to a narrowly political definition of democracy. In fact, democracy is linked to capitalism at the same time as it distinguishes itself from it. They are linked historically; who would contest this? It is a fact that the relative autonomy of civil society and the expansion of individual liberties were in close complicity with the new economic organisation. But it is one thing to recognise this affinity and another to understand that democracy, in virtue of its own principles, of the connection that it establishes between political and social rights, is faced with the demand to correct the effects of capitalism and to prevent the public interest from being dissolved into the play of private interests.

It is not true that a democratic management (*gestion démocratique*) of society is identical to an oligarchical or a bureaucratic management, nor is it true that democracy simply boils down to the ideology of liberalism. One has only to look at how a savage capitalism reigns in the great ultra-modern country that is Brazil – a capitalism without social compensation, indifferent to the fate of the workers and their rights – to appreciate the immense distance which separates it from a Western democracy. Of course France knows inequalities, but some of these inequalities are judged unbearable as much by the forces of the right as by the forces of the left. Of course poverty and unemployment create new problems here, but there is no doubt that this situation is felt to be intolerable. The polls testify to this. A consciousness of community, however diffuse it may be, makes it difficult, not to say impossible, to accept the fact of the exclusion of a fraction of the population.

This is to say that the 'democratic transition' cannot ignore the demands of a social transformation, that it must prompt the formulation of a clear programme for the limitation of the effects of poverty and be accompanied by a real combat against the phenomenon of exclusion. Liberal ideology does not respond to these demands; it continues to nurture a contempt for mass democracy. But there can be no democracy in our time which does not accept the needs and aspirations of the many as its charge. We can be aware of the perverse effects resulting from the conversion of a limited democracy to a mass democracy; we can be attentive to the dangers of an endlessly increasing levelling and conformism. But nothing can lead us to shy away from facing the challenge of mass democracy.

In this sense, it is important to seek a new political language: a language which is not afraid to lay claim to a democratic ethic, which makes clear precisely how democracy is distinct from liberalism and populism and which is, simultaneously, a 'realist' language which points out the problems which democracy is not able to resolve. On the one hand, democracy *qua* political form of society, *qua* symbolic form, cannot translate its principles into empirical reality and determine the mode of functioning of the economy or the ends of technique. On the other hand, if it is true that democracy has the capacity to welcome conflict, divergence of interests, the very heterogeneity of the social, this signifies that it has a unique capacity to give access to the real. In spite of what liberalism teaches, the real is not merely the effects of the so-called laws of the economy: realism presupposes that what we used to call in the old days the 'social question' be constantly reconsidered.

Notes

1. The translator would like to thank his fellow panelists at an APSA 2016 session on French democratic theory for the occasion to present a draft and discussion of this translation, as well as Xavier Jaravel for his insight regarding a couple of thorny passages in the original.
2. The term here is *puissance*, not *pouvoir*. The latter is the word that Lefort uses in the other cases translated by 'power' in this essay.

3. Lefort uses the English words that have been set in quotations here in the original.
4. The quotation marks are present in the original.
5. It is unclear whom Lefort had in mind as the subject of this clause, whether his fellow speakers at the conference, or academics, or the public more generally.
6. Lefort is quoting Tocqueville here.

Part II

The constructivist turn: normative challenges

8

Representation as proposition: democratic representation after the constructivist turn

Samuel Hayat

Political representation, both as a concept and as a central feature of liberal democracies, is currently undergoing a major redefinition (Urbinati and Warren 2008; Brito Vieira and Runciman 2008; see also Castiglione and Warren in this volume). The power of elected representatives diminishes as they now face competition from other authorities, including unelected spokespersons (Saward 2009; Montanaro 2012). With the development of global governance, power and legitimacy become more and more dispersed (Dryzek and Niemeyer 2008; Rosanvallon 2011). This does not extinguish the political relevance of representation, but it pluralises its form and renders the concept harder to grasp with the traditional conceptual tools of political theory (Sintomer 2013). Among the different theoretical proposals, the constructivist framework of *representative claims* set by Michael Saward appears heuristic from a descriptive point of view, but it does not provide us with normative criteria to evaluate whether a given representative claim is democratic (Saward 2006, 2010). The aim of this chapter is to discuss some of the normative implications of the constructivist turn (Severs 2012; Mulieri 2013; Disch 2015). First, I will argue that the standard account of representation by Hanna Pitkin, but also by many of her critics, is based on a conception of representation as *composition*, which provides a strong democratic criterion to evaluate representation. Then I will distinguish between two ideal-typical conceptions of representation compatible with constructivism: representation as *imposition*, developed most notably by Pierre Bourdieu, in which the represented get their social identities from their representative; and representation as *proposition*, in which the represented acquire in the process of representation both their identity and some agency to judge it – a view of representation that is at the core of pragmatic sociology. Finally, I will discuss possible criteria for representation as proposition and propose inclusiveness as a democratic criterion that can form the basis of an alternate ideal of representation, inclusive representation.[1]

Why a constructivist turn?

The idea of a constructivist turn in the theory of political representation is appealing. But what position are we turning from, and what are the reasons that make this turn desirable, both from a descriptive and from a normative point of view? The question is especially vivid if we consider that the theory of representation experienced not one, but two turns in the past decades: a representative turn in the theory of democracy and a constructivist turn in the theory of democratic representation. How are these two turns articulated and what are the potential contradictions between them?

REPRESENTATION AS COMPOSITION

The representative turn in democratic theory, based on the idea that there was no contradiction between representation and democracy (Plotke 1997), could be said to occur in the wake of Hanna Pitkin's *The Concept of Representation* – in a way, it was her triumph. The same does not hold true for the constructivist turn, which is a departure from Pitkin's famous core definition of representation as 'a making present again [. . .] the making present *in some sense* of something which is nevertheless *not* present literally or in fact' (Pitkin 1967: 8–9). This definition rests upon the idea that *something* (the people, a social group or an institution) exists before its representation and that the act of representation is a certain way of making this something present *again*. When applied to democratic government, it is based on the vastly shared principle that the origin of any legitimate government should in a way be found in the people themselves – and thus that there is something called the people, a body of citizens, that should lie behind the acts of the government and the decisions of legislatures.[2] If one believes in national or in popular sovereignty, then any legitimate government or legislature should be a *composition* of elements that exist in the people or the nation, be it their social characteristics, their interests, their votes, their opinions or their wishes.

Representation as composition is not a concept of representation: it aggregates many different views of representation among which there may be real conceptual differences (such as those between descriptive and substantive representation, for example). It is, on the one hand, exemplified by the electoral procedure: the fact that a representative is elected by his or her constituents necessarily goes with the idea that this representative is legitimate because he or she is the expression of (and thus expresses) the will of the majority – although the represented are not necessarily the voters themselves, as in Burke's virtual interest or Mansbridge's surrogate representation.[3] Selection by lot is another variant of this category of representation despite having nothing in common procedurally with election, as the representative body is composed of a random selection of citizens along characteristics that are said to be representative (Dowlen 2008; Sintomer 2011). From both cases, we can construct, as an analytical tool or a Weberian ideal-type, this category of representation as composition to designate any concept, discourse or institution that relies on three elements: (1) there is a pre-existing represented body; (2) there is a procedure to draw a representative body from this represented one; (3) the legitimacy of the representative is based on the fact that it is a composition of some characteristics of the represented, as selected by the procedure.

THE PROBLEMS OF COMPOSITION

The constructivist turn is an attempt to break with this core idea of representation as composition. There is an epistemological break, linked with structuralist theories of language and accounts of social constructivism, with the basic assumption that there are entities that exist and can be known prior to their representation (see Saussure 2013: 75–9; Berger and Luckman 1991). From these epistemological perspectives, representation as composition is based on what Iris Young, following Deleuze and Derrida, calls the 'metaphysics of presence' (Young 2000: 126). In the political realm, this epistemological critique means that the problem of representation is not so much the relation between the represented and their representative (the focus of most theories of representation), but the competing processes that construct both the representative and the represented. The proliferation of regional and international organisations and the empowerment of NGOs multiply both the scenes of political discourse and the voices heard in those scenes (Kröger 2014). When global governance becomes more relevant than state-centred government as a pattern to describe the political system, representation as composition becomes less relevant: with governance, there are

undoubtedly representative *claims*, but with no pre-existing constituencies (Mulieri 2014: 169–89). The metaphysics of presence has
not simply disappeared; it remains very much in use, especially in
the discourse of state political actors, but it is now in competition
with a new constructivist narrative, both in the political realm and
in academic analyses.

These epistemological and factual reasons for the critique of representation as composition also have political and normative implications. According to its more radical critics, the metaphysics of
presence does not simply obfuscate the reality of representation; it
is also a tool for dominant classes and groups to ascribe their own
actions to those who are subjected to them. Hence Pierre Bourdieu's
critique of representation as 'usurpatory ventriloquism, which consists in giving voice to those in whose name one is authorised to
speak' (Bourdieu 1991a: 211): the metaphysics of presence allows
governments to act and speak not only on behalf of the people, but
as if they were the one and only legitimate voice the people have.
Even more importantly, representation as composition suggests that
if a social group is not represented, it means it does not exist as a
group, at least not as a political subject. As such, theories of representation as composition generally fail to take into consideration
two kinds of relations of power. On the one hand, they downplay
the power aspect of the relation between the represented and the
representative, by failing to take into account the fact that representatives can make their own interests and opinions pass for those of
the represented. On the other hand, they do not take into consideration the relations of power between social groups and the subsequent erasure of dominated persons and groups in the very definition
of the represented. The refutation of representation as composition
can thus be justified in reference to a theory of domination, such as
Bourdieu's sociology, that seeks to unveil power relations hidden
behind democratic discourse, both between representatives and represented, and among the represented themselves.

The normative implications of this critique regarding a theory of
democracy are unclear: how can we discuss the norms of a good and
just democratic rule when the basic premise of democracy – the existence of the *demos* – is questioned? The constructivist approach to representation, convincing from a descriptive point of view, deprives us of
the strong normative criterion given by all forms of representation as
composition: a legitimate representative, from a democratic point of
view, must to a certain extent be composed of elements derived from
the pre-existing entity that it represents. This criterion makes it possible
to describe power relations that render some groups invisible or allow

representatives to unjustly ascribe their actions to the represented as forms of unfair misrepresentation. This leaves us with two possibilities: we can either accept this discrepancy between the descriptive and the normative realm by saying that the democratic norm of representation as composition provides us with standards to judge actual representative processes, even though it is based on an erroneous description of these processes,[4] or we can take seriously the constructivist critique of representation as composition and try to frame a new democratic standard to judge representation, one that does not presuppose the existence of the people (and their opinions, interests, identities) prior to representation. I will try to follow the latter option, participating in the project of constructing 'a normative criterion adapted to the "constructivist turn" in theories of representation' (Disch 2014: 25).

Two conceptions of constructivist representation

From a constructivist perspective, the represented is created through the activity of representation. It does not mean that the represented is given its material existence by representation but that representation creates the represented as a *subject*. Assessing the democratic potential of representation requires therefore defining the criteria for a democratic process of *subjectivation* – the process through which a subject is made. According to Michel Foucault, the creation of subjects is deeply linked with the question of power: 'There are two meanings of the word "subject": subject to someone else by control and dependence; and tied to his own identity by a conscience or self-knowledge. Both meanings suggest a form of power which subjugates and makes subject to' (Foucault 1982: 781). This dichotomy between subjectivation as subjection and as conscientisation is crucial to enrich our understanding of the constructivist turn and its normative implications. Indeed, as a process of subjectivation, representation implies power, and from a normative point of view any substantial form of *democratic* representation must guarantee some sort of power to the represented, including power over its representative (Christiano 1996). Thus the democratic potential of representation largely depends on the power relations allowed by the intertwined processes of subjection and conscientisation.

REPRESENTATION AS IMPOSITION

Among all the different conceptions of representation that do not postulate the existence of the represented prior to representation, we can single out those that insist on the subjection aspect of the subjectivation process. Once again, these conceptions of representation are diverse, but we can construct an ideal-type, as an analytical tool, which stresses one aspect of these conceptions: the fact that they consider representation as the *imposition* of an identity on the represented. The famous chapters on representation in Hobbes's *Leviathan* contain elements that can be related to this idea of representation as imposition. For Hobbes, 'A Multitude of men, are made *One* Person, when they are by one man, or one Person, Represented [. . .] For it is the *Unity* of the Representer, not the *Unity* of the Represented that maketh the Person *One*' (Hobbes 1909: 126). In the second part of the book, this definition justifies the *subjection* of the multitude: when the Commonwealth is generated by covenant, it is embodied by one person: 'this Person is called SOVERAIGNE, and said to have *Soveraigne Power*; and everyone besides, his SUBJECT' (Hobbes 1909: 132). Men become subjects, that is members of a polity defined by a common law, through an act of representation.

Though archetypal, Hobbes's conception of representation is by no means isolated in the history of political thought. During the French Revolution, Sieyes defended a conception of representation as imposition to justify the power of the National Assembly (Pasquino 1998). Such a conception is also central in Carl Schmitt's critique of liberal parliamentarism (Kelly 2004) or in Frank Ankersmit's aesthetic theory of representation (Ankersmit 2002). In general, representation as imposition is an important feature of discourses that legitimise the construction of modern states: it can be used during constituent processes, as rhetoric against rebels or secessionists, for nationalist purposes – every time defenders of the state and its unity claim that citizens exist first and foremost as subjects.

However, representation as imposition does not function solely at the national level. It is also a feature of discourses that are made on behalf of more delimited subjects, such as social classes. In his theory of the political field, started in his 1979 book *La Distinction*, Bourdieu stated that social classes could become political subjects only when they were represented by professionals in the political field. Members of the working class, in particular, 'have no choice but to abdicate (*démission*) or hand over their power (*remise de soi*) to the party, a permanent organisation which has to produce the representation of the continuity of the class' (Bourdieu 1991b: 173). A few years later, in a series of articles, Bourdieu radicalised the constructivist aspect of his theory, by conceptualising representation as a 'process of institution, ordinarily perceived and described as a process of delegation, in which the representative receives from the group the power of creating the group' (Bourdieu 1991c: 248). This is what Bourdieu calls the 'mystery of the ministry': representatives exist only inasmuch as they speak on behalf of the group they represent, but they create the group by doing so. It is no surprise then to see Bourdieu use an analogy with Saussure's linguistic theory to explain the process: in the case of dominated groups, at least,

> the act of symbolisation by which the spokesperson is constituted [. . .] happens at the same time as the constituting of the group; the sign creates the thing signified, the signifier is identified with the thing signified, which would not exist without it, and which can be reduced to it. The signifier [. . .] has the power to call into visible existence, by mobilising it, the group that it signifies. (Bourdieu 1991a: 206–7)

In Bourdieu's theory, the process of subjectivation is entirely a process of subjection: representatives give to the represented their existence as subjects – they effectively *subject* them.

REPRESENTATION AS PROPOSITION

As a process of subjectivation, representation creates subjects, but what happens once these subjects exist? Either they simply obey and adhere to the identity that was imposed on them – the option privileged by approaches focusing on representation as imposition; or they develop a consciousness of their identity and formulate judgments about it. In the latter case, the reasoning is still constructivist: the represented are created by representation, but the conscientisation at work in the process of subjectivation opens the space for some *agency* (Davies 1991; Ahearn 2001). As a result, representation appears here not as an *imposition* but as a *proposition*: by claiming to represent a group, the representative institutes this group – but its members can judge, criticise or even reject what is done and said in their name and the *representations* that are given of their identity. *Representation as proposition* can thus be constructed as an ideal-type to describe theories and situations in which the focus is on the response of the represented to the process of representation.

   This understanding of representation is at the core of Michael Saward's ambitious reframing which holds that representation is defined by a discursive activity of claim-making centred on different roles – and thus constructing the actors that play these roles in the process. But there are important differences with representation as imposition. The most important for our purpose is the role that

Saward gives to what he calls the *audience*.[5] Representative claims are only offers by the makers to the audience about a relation between an object and a subject: therefore 'representation is an ongoing process of making and receiving, accepting and rejecting claims', in which 'audiences are not simply passive recipients of claims – they make counterclaims about themselves as subjects, or about the subjects proffered to them by other claims' (Saward 2010: 36–7).[6] This is an important qualification to the constructivist conception of representation as imposition: there is an audience (not necessarily the represented) to any claim made by the maker (not necessarily the representative), and the success of a representative claim depends ultimately on the way it is received and judged by the audience. Representation is a 'performance' and therefore 'representative claims only work if audiences acknowledge them in some way, and are able to absorb, reject, accept, or otherwise engage with them. Processes of claim-making and consequent acceptance or rejection by audiences or parts of audiences produce representation' (Saward 2010: 66–7). Applied to the problem of subjectivation, the conceptualisation of representative claims helps to clarify the relation between subjection and conscientisation: any representative claim creates both an object of representation (the identity of the represented) and a conscience, the audience, which judges if this object is adequate *and* if the subject (the representative) represents it adequately. The agency of the subjectivity created through the representative claim resides then in the capacity it has, as an audience, to accept or refuse claims made about itself as an object.

However, from an epistemological point of view, the problem remains to determine where the agency of the audience comes from. Indeed, if we intend to maintain that in democratic representation there is some sort of power of the represented (being both the object and the audience of the claim) over its representative (the subject and often the maker), then the ways through which the represented can gain some agency must be at the core of our normative reflection. There are important resources for exploring this question in a French sociological school that has not figured into debates over the constructivist turn, which have taken their normative moorings largely from deliberative democracy. This is pragmatic sociology, or sociology of tests (*sociologie des épreuves*), which develops the notion of 'test' to make it possible for social scientists to confront contradictory representations of reality without resorting either to naturalism to affirm certain representations as truer, or to pure relativism to concede that constructions taken as reality are merely the result of relations of power (Lemieux 2013). A test is 'any situation in which actors experience the vulnerability of the social order, for the very reason that they feel a doubt about what reality is' (Lemieux 2013: 174). On this account, constructivism is no longer a rarefied position reserved for the social scientist; it is a common experience to have doubts about the representations of reality, and the testing of those doubts (leading to their reinforcement or their elimination) is the way each one of us constructs social reality. This is not a relativist position. Following Michel Callon and Bruno Latour's anthropology of sciences and techniques, pragmatic sociologists assert that 'the world offers humans resistances and practical refutations to the definitions of reality they can adopt [. . .] Some realities turn out to be more "real" than others, meaning that they resist better to the different tests they are submitted to' (Barthe et al. 2014: 199). As Luc Boltanski, one of the founders of this strand of pragmatic sociology, puts it, one has to distinguish between reality, which is always socially constructed, and the world, defined as everything that happens: the discrepancies between the two explain why reality always needs testing, but also why not all realities are as robust – since there is indeed a world out there (Boltanski 2011: 57).

The representations that constitute social reality, including the social identities of the represented, are always put to the test, because no representation can exhaust the possible representations of the represented. Any representative claim is vulnerable to doubt, judgment, critique, not because the represented pre-exists its representation but because as a social construction it is always simpler than the entirety of the parts of the world it is related to. Conscious subjects that are created by representative claims can always recombine parts or use some other parts, coming from different experiences of the social world, to judge claims, that is, to make these claims succeed or fail. With representation as proposition, understood in the pragmatic sense of the sociology of tests, power does not only flow from the representative to the represented: there is a constant circulation – and this circulation of power, inherent to the tests of representative claims, is what makes both subjection and conscientisation possible.[7]

An example of this process can be found in the history of the working-class movement. Workers constituted one of the first social groups to be the object of competing representative claims on a national and international scale. In France, after the revolution of 1848, the Provisional Government created an official representation of Parisian workers, the *Commission de gouvernement pour les travailleurs,* known as the Luxembourg Commission (Hayat 2014). The purpose of the government was to prevent popular unrest by making workers discuss a social reform to be presented to the Constituent Assembly after its election, instead of demonstrating in the streets. In Saward's terms, the government (maker) claimed in front of Parisian workers (audience) that the Luxembourg Commission (subject) represented them as a peacefully deliberating class (object), an image of actual workers (referent). By doing so, the government gave an official and unified voice to workers, something that organised workers had been asking for since 1830 (Sewell 1980). But contrary to what the government intended, the elected members of the Luxembourg Commission did not settle for a peaceful deliberation. During the first session, they refused to sit if their demands were not satisfied, leading to the enactment of the first social legislation in modern France. Then they proceeded to establish themselves as a labour court by solving conflicts in the workplace and fostered the development of workers' associations and socialist experiments. Finally, after the Commission was dissolved, former delegates constituted the core of new endeavours to build a unified working-class movement, from the *Société des Corporations réunies* in June 1848 to the Parisian section of the First International in the 1860s. So the representative claim made by the 1848 French Provisional Government succeeded in creating a unified representation of Parisian workers. But members of the representative body used other elements present in actual workers (the referent, in Saward's terms), such as their corporative tradition or their former projects to constitute an emancipatory association, to enact another representation of these same workers.

This example illustrates the analytic distinction between imposition and proposition, as two ideal-types of constructivist understandings of representation that stand very differently on the question of power. In representation as imposition, the represented is purely subjected to their representatives. Thus, even when potential representatives have to compete for the capacity to impose their representations of the represented, they only compete against each other. As a process of subjectivation, representation as imposition can sometimes lead to the emergence and the recognition of subjects that were previously invisible and thus contribute to the transformation of power relations in society in a more egalitarian way and even to the development of some agency for the represented. But as a process of subjection, it does not favour the conscientisation of the represented and strictly limits the progress of their agency, especially regarding the relation with their representatives. A theory of representation as imposition is then necessarily a theory of domination and obedience. Whereas it may be an important tool of critique, because it effectively indicts democratic representation as a contradiction in terms, it is of no help in laying the foundations for normative judgments regarding when acts of representation are more or less democratic. With representation as proposition, on the contrary, representation is possible only through a process of testing (and thus judgment, doubt and eventually rejection or acceptation) of representative claims by audiences created through the activity of claim-making itself. These tests open up the possibility, for the represented, as objects, to acquire an existence and thus transform power relations in society, but also, as parts of the possible audience for claims that concern them, to gain agency in the relation of representation itself. The purpose of a constructivist theory of democratic representation is to delineate the ways to maximise such an agency and the desirable forms it should take.

Inclusiveness as a democratic norm for constructivist representation

As long as democratic representation is understood as a proposition, constructivist theorists of representation do not have to give up on the possibility of normatively assessing which acts of representation are more or less democratic. While the constructivist turn questions the validity of norms that depend on the pre-existence of the represented (such as responsiveness), it opens new avenues for normative investigation. At the core of these rests the simple idea that representation is democratic if the represented gains some agency in the process of subjectivation that constitutes it as a subject. To be democratic, this agency should find its expression in two sets of activities. On the one hand, it should empower the subject to act and to be recognised in the broader society, especially when the subject constructed by the representative claim is composed of subaltern and dominated persons and groups.[8] On the other hand, the agency acquired by the represented should lead to a constant activity of *testing* representative claims in the pragmatic sense – this is the distinctive democratic trait of representation as proposition. In the wake of the representative turn of the theory of democracy, it is of paramount importance that the represented *gain* and not only retain some agency in the process, otherwise representative democracy would only be a 'second best' or a 'defective substitute' for direct democracy (Brennan and Hamlin 1999: 111; Urbinati 2006: 4; Mansbridge 2003: 515). Pending a proper constructivist theory of democratic representation, I will just offer two reflections about the possible criteria of good representation in such a theory.

AGAINST CONGRUENCE

The mere acceptance of representative claims by the represented – what David Runciman calls the 'non-objection criterion' (Runciman 2007) – does not constitute in itself the proof that this claim is satisfying from a democratic point of view (Severs 2010). As Pitkin herself argued in discussing the *Addressat* theory, according to which an audience is necessary to representation and 'the existence of representation is to be measured by the state of mind, the condition of satisfaction or belief, of certain people, be they the represented of the audience', such theories transform representation into 'a kind of activity to foster belief, loyalty, satisfaction with their leaders, among the people' – as she noticed provocatively, 'at the extreme, this point of view becomes the fascist theory of representation' (Pitkin 1967: 107). When a representative claim passes the test of reality and is accepted by the constituency it creates, while there is undoubtedly representation, there is no way to know if it is *democratic* representation, that is, if the success of the claim is the expression of the agency of the represented and not of the coercive power of the claim-maker. The discrepancy between the world and reality, the gap between the referent and the object, the vulnerability of the social order, all these signs that a test is actually happening *and that the represented is the tester* must be evident and palpable – even though in the end representative claims can pass the test and be accepted. For this reason, any form of undisputed congruence or accord between the representative and the represented should cast doubt on the democratic aspect of the relation of representation.

Luc Boltanski has argued that disputation should emerge by virtue of the role that institutions play in the constitution of social reality, which he describes as giving rise to the 'hermeneutic contradiction' (Boltanski 2011: 86). In order to avoid a permanent state of doubt, we rely on institutions to state 'the whatness of what is' (*ce qu'il en est de ce qui est*), that is, to confer some robustness and stability to our social reality. But because institutions are 'bodiless beings' that exist only through their spokespersons, there is a discrepancy between reality and account that potentially gives rise to a perpetual suspicion regarding 'whether the spokespersons who enable the institution to express itself clearly convey the will of this bodiless being or, under the guise of lending it their voice, simply impose their own will'. In light of this discrepancy and the 'herme-neutic contradiction' to which it gives rise, representatives should perpetually face suspicion – barring a coercive power that prevents the expression of public doubt. Its absence indicates that institutions do not work properly.

Suspicion should be even more frequent in the case of elected offi-cials because they are doubly representative: they claim to represent the institution they are part of *and* to represent the constituency that elected them. They may betray not only institutions, but the persons who gave them the right to speak on behalf of those institutions in the first place. Representatives then face the choice between embody-ing the unity of the institution before their constituency – and thus betraying its inherent multiplicity – and trying to give way to this multiplicity and thus failing at accomplishing the role of unification inherent to the institution. Bruno Latour calls this dialectics between unity and multiplicity the 'circle of representation' or the 'political circle', which is essentially a circle of mutual betrayal:

> She who talks in the name of all must necessarily betray those she rep-resents, otherwise she will fail to obtain the transformation of the mul-titude into a unit; in turn, those who obey must necessarily transform the order received, otherwise they will simply keep repeating it without implementing it. (Latour 2003: 151)[9]

Perfect representation, that is maximal congruence between the repre-sentative and his or her constituents, goes along with perfect obedience. A democratic conception of representation requires, on the contrary, a continuous public attention to the multiple and ever-renewing discrep-ancies between institutions, elected officials and the people. Hence the relevance of approaches of representation that value the role of public judgment and surveillance and that underline the need for representa-tives to be under permanent scrutiny (Kateb 1981; Rosanvallon 2008; Urbinati 2014).

On a constructivist account, which foregrounds the construction of subjects by means of claims that define the borders of both the representative and the group to be represented, acts of represen-tation should be the most prone to debate and contestation. This point has been dramatised by the history of social movements that claimed rights for dominated groups: these struggles always accom-panied deep reconfigurations of the political subject constructed through these claims and generated discussions and sometimes refus-als of those claims (Laclau and Mouffe 2001). This is particularly clear in the history of feminism: the borders (external and internal) of 'women' as a political subject were constantly questioned as the movement gained momentum.[10] In the United States, from the beginning of the 1970s, some feminist movements contested whether rich women could speak on behalf of the poor, white women on behalf of black women, straight women on behalf of lesbians. bell hooks argued that it was impossible to constitute the object of the claim of the early feminist movement (women as a whole) without making 'the white American woman's experience [. . .] synonymous with the American woman's experience' (hooks 2015: 186). The erasure of the experience of black women could only be stopped through a major reconfiguration of women as a political subject. This reconfiguration did not mean a fragmentation – black feminism did not contradict the existence of a unified feminist movement – but a different way to construct this subject, integrating elements of the world that were considered irrelevant, paying attention to what would be called intersectionality, that is the plurality of sometimes contradictory effects of domination (Crenshaw 1991). The same kind of argument was at the core of the invention of subaltern studies: the majoritarian narrative of decolonisation movements often rested on the monopolisation by indigenous social elites of the right to speak and act on behalf of the majority, thus extending the erasure working-class colonised groups suffered under colonial domination (Guha 1997; Spivak 1988). In any representative claim that concerns a social group, congruence is not necessarily the indication that the group is properly represented in its multiplicity; it can also result from the erasure that the dominated parts of the group suffers – a central concern for theories of group representation (Young 1990; Phillips 1995; Mansbridge 1999; Young 2000; Williams 1998).

INCLUSIVENESS AND INCLUSIVE REPRESENTATION

These limits to the congruence criterion all point to the fact that democratic representation supposes that representative claims should not be usually accepted in the terms they are first made. To use Jacques Rancière's vocabulary, democratic representation should be based on *disagreement* over representative claims, the features and borders of the groups these claims create, and the represented should play the major part in these disagreements (Rancière 1999). Claims should create subjects that become both active in the existing system of power relations and active in their relation to the claims that gave them this agency. There should be a constant disposition of the represented to use their agency to judge, criticise and transform both the social world they live in and the claims made in their name and that contribute to giving them their identity.

I propose to call this state *inclusiveness*, a term that carries a different meaning in the wake of a 'propositional' account of representation than it has done in the context of traditional 'compositional' accounts. Inclusiveness, as I understand it, is the opposite of Pitkin's criterion, responsiveness. To begin with, it is a property of the represented, not of the representative: it describes the ability of the represented to act as subjects by their inclusion in the existing power relations and to react to a representative claim that concerns them by their (often disruptive and agonistic) inclusion in the process of claim-making. Similar to responsiveness, inclusiveness is both a systemic property and something that has to be at least potentially present in any given representative claim. But, contrary to responsiveness, it does not presuppose that the represented pre-exist the relation of representation – it embraces the constructivist idea that before any disagreement, there is a claim made. More importantly, inclusiveness is a truly democratic criterion, while responsiveness is a criterion of good government, which solely relies on the goodmindedness of leaders. Inclusiveness depends on citizens to be actively engaged in discussing and judging both the existing social order and the claims made in their name; hence, it often requires institutions that assist them in acting as subjects and in putting representative claims to the test.[11]

This criterion is not enough in itself to characterise democratic representation, but it may help to delineate ways to reassess the theory of democratic representation in the wake of the constructivist turn. As Catherine Colliot-Thélène has argued, the current pluralisation of powers reveals a feature of democracy that was dissimulated by the idea of popular sovereignty: democracy is essentially the activity of addressing claims for equal rights to institutions that have authority (Colliot-Thélène 2011). Thus it is not the quality of decisions or the legitimacy of ruling institutions that makes a system democratic; a system is democratic when citizens are able to face these institutions that have power over them in order to claim rights. Bryan Garsten has similarly argued that 'a chief purpose of representative government is *to multiply and challenge governmental claims to represent the people*' (Garsten 2010: 91). As a result, democratic representation does not rely on the government's responsiveness or on the congruence between the represented and representatives, but on the dynamics of claim-making and claim-challenging. Lisa Disch also presents such an argument when she defends a mobilisation conception of representation: after having rejected congruence and responsiveness as criteria for democratic representation (for constructivist reasons), she proposes 'reflexivity as the normative standard for evaluating political representation'. Reflexivity in her sense would require that the 'representation process [. . .] encourage contestation' (Disch 2011: 111). Colliot-Thélène, Garsten and Disch propose that what makes representation democratic is not a feature of government: it rests on the pluralisation of institutions and claims, and, more importantly, on the ability of the represented to be included in the representation process through dissenting, protesting, right-claiming, sometimes against their representatives – activities that require that the represented have some agency, but do not contradict the constructivist conception of representation as proposition.

Finally, it is possible to draw on the criterion of inclusiveness to delineate a conception of representation that could function as a regulative ideal. I call *inclusive representation* any form of representative claim or system of representative claims that has as its consequence the increase of direct participation and the proliferation of activities of testing claims by the represented. I distinguish it from *exclusionary representation*, which, on the contrary, limits these (Hayat 2013, 2018). Inclusive representation is realised through the participation of the represented in the discussion of collective outcomes and of representative claims, but also in the pluralisation of these claims. Indeed, some forms of inclusion can be internal to the existing means of representation (politicisation, judgment on elected representatives) or external to them, through the formation of alternate representative claims, in social movements (such as Occupy movements), NGOs, and so on, in order to equip the represented with other means of recognition and action. They can involve citizens as individuals or as social groups – in the latter case, once again it can take internal forms such as quotas, or external forms through movements and associations that claim to represent the social groups in question. Some forms of inclusion can rely on political subjects already recognised, or initiate new processes of subjectivation. But all these forms of inclusion share the same basic feature: they activate political subjects as objects and audiences for representative claims and by doing so accord them agency. By contrast, the devices of exclusionary representation deprive them of agency.

Conclusion: inclusive representation and democratic legitimacy

The constructivist turn poses a real challenge to normative democratic theory. As Dario Castiglione and Mark Warren put it in their chapter in this volume, 'a normative conception of democracy entails *the empowered inclusion of the community of those affected in collective decisions and actions*' (p. 24). Constructivism deprives us of any simple means to make representation adequate to this principle, by highlighting the power relations that underlie the determination of the 'community of the affected'. While the institutions of representative government take for granted the existence of a community of citizens that are represented through elections, the constructivist turn leads us to turn our attention to the processes through which the represented are spoken for, signified, performed and thus created as political subjects – or erased. My conceptualisation of inclusiveness is a way to reformulate this democratic criterion to make it more aligned with constructivism. It builds on the fact that, as Dario Castiglione and Mark Warren state, 'it is distinctive of *democratic* representation that persons are represented on the assumption that they actively participate in asserting, authorising and approving that which is represented on their behalf' (p. 36). Instead of interpreting constructivism as a mere impossibility for the represented to be agents, representation as proposition takes into account the double movement of subjection and conscientisation implied by the processes of subjectivation triggered by representative claims. In this perspective, representation is democratic to the extent that it allows for the inclusion of the represented as conscious agents, able to gain enough visibility and agency through representation to put to the test the power relations that subject them, including the very representative claims that gave them agency.

As a democratic criterion for representation as proposition, inclusiveness may help us reconsider some of the problems about the democratic legitimacy of political representation, such as the ones raised by Nadia Urbinati's chapter in this volume, and to renew the normative critique of representative government from a constructivist perspective. Nadia Urbinati's account of constructivist representation is very pessimistic about its compatibility with democratic legitimacy. According to her, either representative claims are mere forms of advocacy, distinct from government and party politics, and then they only belong to the liberal sphere of free judgment and have nothing to do with democracy legitimacy; or representative claims are intended by their makers to have some democratic legitimacy and then they should accept the rules and procedures of the electoral formation of popular will. While Nadia Urbinati's argument is well founded, it largely deprives constructivism of its epistemological and political relevance. The constructivist critique of the institutions of representative government, as articulated by Bourdieu, is that they obfuscate the power relations between social groups and between representatives and their constituents, allowing elected representatives, through representation as composition, to ascribe their actions to the governed. Thus determining the democratic legitimacy of representative claims by their electoral success (or any other procedure) avoids the normative conundrum raised by the constructivist turn. Inclusive representation is a way to revert this logic. Instead of saying that representative claims should abide by the rules of representative government to acquire democratic legitimacy, I contend that the institutions of representative government should be considered as one (admittedly sophisticated) way to make representative claims, which should be deemed democratic only if they satisfy the norms of inclusive democracy. It means that mere congruence, as measured by electoral success, for example, does not provide any substantial legitimacy to elected representatives as far as inclusiveness is concerned. From this perspective, only the popular agency that results from an electoral success, including the activity of testing and challenging the elected representative's claim, and the way these activities actually affect political outcomes, may render an election democratic.

To be sure, inclusive representative does not equate with democratic representation; it is only one of its features, born from the necessity to reformulate a theory of democratic representation adequate to the epistemological and normative implications of the constructivist turn. It should therefore be completed with further investigations related to other features of democracy, such as equality and the pursuit of common good, in order to delineate a broader theory of democratic representation. In particular, when political subjects are institutionally stabilised and competition between representative claims provisionally loses its intensity, representation as composition undoubtedly has democratic merits. But even in these situations, representative claims will and should be challenged, leading to the emergence of new political subjects willing to circumvent the power relations that both constitute and constraint them. From the perspective of a democratic theory of representation willing to take constructivism seriously, inclusive forms of representation as proposition should be regarded as democratically preferable to both institutionalised representation as composition and exclusionary claims of representation as imposition.

Notes

1. Many arguments in this text were previously exposed in Dutoya and Hayat (2016). I sincerely thank Virginie Dutoya for letting me expand on points we developed together. I also largely drew on debates with Virginie Dutoya, Émilie Frenkiel, Yves Sintomer and Stéphanie Tawa Lama-Rewal in the French Political Science Association research group on representation (GRePo) and in the French and German ANR-DFG research project '(New) Political Representative Claims. A Global View' (CLAIMS). I presented part of this chapter as a paper in Leuven in September 2016 in a workshop organised by Alessandro Mulieri. I also thank Lisa Disch for her invitation to write this chapter, for her advice and for her careful and kindly reading.
2. The theory of representation was first built to describe the relation between elected representatives in legislative bodies. But, as Pierre Rosanvallon notes, the executive branch is now largely prevalent in most democratic polities, displacing the focus from representation to other features in order to maintain and expand democracy (Rosanvallon 2015).
3. On the concept of surrogate representation and its relations with virtual representation, see Mansbridge (2003); Rehfeld (2009); Mansbridge (2011); Rehfeld (2011).
4. An example of this move is the study of congruence between representatives' actions and the constituents' wishes as a way of testing the system's responsiveness to popular influence (Miller and Stokes 1963; Pierce and Converse 1986): the epistemological assumptions are false from a constructivist point of view, since the constituents do not have an opinion as such before it is produced by the activity of their representative or by the study itself (Bourdieu 1979). Still, it can be tested and produces results epistemologically flawed but with acceptable normative implications.
5. The role of the audience in representation is also central in Rehfeld (2006), in which the author argues that 'political representation [. . .] results from an audience's judgment that some individual, rather than some other, stands in for a group in order to perform a specific function' (p. 2). However, as Lisa Disch rightly notes, Rehfeld's conception of the role of the audience is not constructivist (Disch 2015: 499).
6. The word 'subject' can be ambiguous, since in Saward's conceptualisation of representative claims it designates the claimed representative. To avoid confusion, we will not use 'subject' in this sense but will use the word 'representative' instead.

7. This can be compared with Michel Foucault's conceptualisation of power: exerting power over a subject supposes the existence of a subject that can act accordingly with what is expected of him or her, which always leaves open the possibility of resistance. As an 'act upon [. . .] actions', power as a relation requires 'that "the other" (the one over whom power is exercised) be thoroughly recognised and maintained to the very end as a person who acts; and that, faced with a relationship of power, a whole field of responses, reactions, results, and possible inventions may open up' (Foucault 1982: 789).

8. I thank Yves Sintomer who insisted on the importance of this aspect.

9. A similar point is made by Mineur (2010) in a more ontological perspective: the impossible identification between the representative and the represented creates a permanent state of crisis.

10. On feminism and representation I am especially grateful to Virginie Dutoya for the references she provided me with and her authorisation to use them.

11. I tried to analyse how this form of inclusiveness was institutionalised during the revolutionary period of the French 1848 Republic (Hayat 2014, 2015).

9

Don Alejandro's fantasy: radical democracy and the negative concept of representation

Oliver Marchart

Political representation – a magical mystery tour

In 'The Congress', a short story by Jorge Luis Borges, a Uruguayan landowner by the name of don Alejandro arrives at a rather eccentric decision. Frustrated by his failed attempts to be elected to the National Congress of Uruguay, he concludes he has to found a congress of much larger importance. Inspired by the historic example of Anarchasis Cloots, the 'orator of mankind', who at the time of the French Revolution had appeared before the Constituent Assembly as an ambassador of the human race and defender of a World Republic, don Alejandro 'conceived the idea of calling together a Congress of the World that would represent all men of all nations' (Borges 1977: 33). For this purpose he assembles a group of like-minded conspirators in a Buenos Aires *confitería* to engage in the necessary preparations. Very soon, however, the whole enterprise runs into insuperable paradoxes. How to guarantee that all inhabitants of the planet will be represented in the congress? As *what*, that is, in what regard, will they be represented? And who would be entitled to represent them? A member of the secret meeting formulates the philosophical crux of the whole project: 'Planning an assembly to represent all men was like fixing the exact number of platonic types – a puzzle that had taxed the imagination of thinkers for centuries' (Borges 1977: 34). As he suggested, don Alejandro 'might represent not only cattlemen but also Uruguayans, and also human great forerunners and also men with red beards, and also those who are seated in armchairs' (Borges 1977: 34–5). The same problem applied to Nora Erfjord, don Alejandro's Norwegian secretary: 'Would she represent secretaries, Norwegian womanhood,

141

or – more obviously – all beautiful women? Would a single engineer be enough to represent all engineers – including those of New Zealand?' (Borges 1977: 35).

What Borges describes in his story is a fundamental problem of representation – the latter being an occidental, or, as Heidegger would have said, 'onto-theological' concept with a history reaching from theological doctrines of incarnation via political theories of sovereignty to the institutional practice of parliamentary democracies. The Borgesian problem – who represents whom in what respect – appears to be still unresolved. Depending on perspective, answers to the question of representation vary largely. Do parliamentary representatives, to paraphrase Borges, represent the mystical figures of 'the people' or 'the nation'? Or do they represent empirical entities such as the entire population or, more modestly, the electorate? Or, rather than representing the entire electorate, do they merely represent their electoral district, or even only those who actually voted for them? Are they accountable only to their own conscience, or will they have to subordinate their conscience to a higher *raison d'état*, or, perhaps less openly, to the lobby that has financed their campaign? Different political systems, traditions and political cultures will produce diverging views on the nature of representation. As it was to be expected, the preparation committee for don Alejandro's World Congress could not arrive at a definite solution. The plan failed, but not just because representation is a notoriously vague idea. It failed because of the paradoxes produced by the phantasmatic idea of total representation. What kind of congress could ever live up to the task of politically representing the whole of humanity? This enterprise was doomed to end in disaster. But then, don Alejandro was struck by a sudden revelation. Four years after the preparation committee had embarked on the hopeless project, its members were called to don Alejandro's ranch and presented with the solution to the riddle:

'It has taken me four years to understand what I am about to say,' don Alejandro began. 'My friends, the undertaking we have set for ourselves is so vast that it embraces – I now see – the whole world. Our Congress cannot be a group of charlatans deafening each other in the sheds of an out-of-the-way ranch. The Congress of the World began with the first moment of the world and it will go on when we are dust. There's no place on earth where it does not exist. The Congress is the books we've burned. The Congress is Job on the ash heap and Christ on the Cross. The Congress is that worthless boy who squanders my substance on whores.' (Borges 1977: 47)

Don Alejandro had encountered the most elegant solution to his problem: The world is not in need of any congress as the world *is* the congress. The field of representation is coextensive with the field of the represented (analogous to the other famous Borgesian idea of a map coextensive with the territory covered). Consequently, representation as such is rendered obsolete. If everyone represents him- or herself (or itself), then obviously nobody needs to be represented at all. This solution, descending on don Alejandro in an epiphany, would be impeccable were it not entirely phantasmatic. Not by chance the Borgesian story ends in a mystical fantasy of unification when an ecstatic preparation committee becomes one with the universe:

> The mystics invoke a rose, a kiss, a bird that is all birds, a sun that is all the stars and the sun, a jug of wine, a garden, or the sexual act. Of these metaphors, none will serve me for that long, joyous night, which left us, tired out and happy, at the borders of dawn. [. . .] What really matters is having felt that our plan, which more than once we made a joke of, really and secretly existed and was the world and ourselves. (Borges 1977: 49).

The representatives immerse themselves into the world of the represented. The conclusion to be drawn from this fantasy of 'magic realism' can only be as follows: total representability coincides with total irrepresentability. In a world in which representation is all-encompassing, representation will become redundant, if not impossible.

The politically dubious, perhaps dangerous implications of such a view are all too obvious. Isn't a world in which all relations of representation are dissolved – a dissolution that eventually will culminate, as we will see, in the dissolution of the political – strangely reminiscent of regressive utopias?

Doesn't the magic Borgesian world of total (ir-)representability recall, for instance, a certain Marx who, in weak moments, remained attached to those 'utopian socialists' he had attacked vociferously on other occasions? Given that for Marx a finally liberated society was premised on the overcoming of the self-alienated nature of the human species, representation, it follows, will have to be eliminated if humanity is to be reconciled with its true nature. For as long as relations of representation persist, they attest to human alienation. Only in the gracious state of communism will things lose their fetish character as commodities, and people will enter the realm of freedom defined as self-identity rather than self-alienation. Such society will be entirely transparent vis-à-vis itself; that is, it will not be in need of any mediating function of representation. This will mark the end of history; the process of emancipation will come to a halt and we will arrive where everything started – in the pastoral idyll of a humanity reconciled with itself, an idyll not much different from the earliest human stages of so-called primitive communism.

The approach of radical democracy, as defended in this chapter, is antipodal to the nostalgic longing for a pre- or post-historical state of harmony. Radical democracy can be defined as an emancipatory project that is premised upon an unreserved recognition of alien-ation, opacity and representation as constitutive facts of democratic life. Radical democrats, to the extent that they are political realists, cannot afford themselves the luxury of imaginary solutions to real problems. For this reason, one cannot simply inherit the classical discourses of emancipation without re-evaluating and deconstruct-ing them. This will imply that we determine how a non-phantasmatic project of emancipation would avoid traditional leftist adversity against both representation and 'alienation'. On the other side, there would hardly be any reason for speaking about radical democracy without distinguishing the latter from the impoverished notion of representation prevalent in actually existing 'liberal' democracies. We thus have to forge a theoretical path between the phantasmatic idealism of don Alejandro and the cynical 'realism' of actually exist-ing democracy.[1]

To forge this path, it will be unavoidable, given the confused and sometimes contradictory use of the concept, to raise our notion of representation to a more general level of theorisation before applying it to the empirical field of democratic politics. I will, hence, proceed in three steps. In a first step, in discussing two post-foundational the-orists of democratic representation – Frank Ankersmit and Ernesto Laclau – I will point out that we have to extract from their theories what I will call, in an entirely affirmative mode, a negative concept of representation. Such a negative concept is not geared towards an identitarian (or 'positive') relation between constituency and rep-resentative, but, on the contrary, inclines us to redirect our focus towards the very discrepancy that lies at the heart of every represen-tational relation. In a second step, the analytical value of this negative concept of representation will be tested by applying it to an empirical case: the 'state anomaly' of Bosnia where representation is running wild in a strange multiplication of what appears as representational relations but, on closer inspection, turns out to be, as Derrida would say, an *ipsocentric* order of positive representation. In the course of this discussion, I will be criticising the 'liberal' norm of the

Western model of democratic representation by contrasting it with the Bosnian anomaly generated by this norm. In a third and concluding step, and in contrast to any over-enthusiastic endorsement of direct democracy, I will be affirming the necessity of accepting representation as a constitutive feature of democracy. The point, however, will be that recognising the necessity of representation (and, implicit in this, self-alienation) does not in itself constitute a political move. It constitutes, it will be argued, a move pertaining to the ethical rather than the political dimension of democracy.

The negative concept of representation (1): Ankersmit and the 'gap' of representation

In order to lift our commonsensical ideas about representation onto an adequate level of conceptualisation, merely enumerating the positive features of representational procedures, as they are practised in today's liberal democracies, will not suffice. Such an approach would never lead us out of a mere descriptivism. Let us, instead, proceed on the *via negativa* – not only in the sense of distinguishing representation from what 'it is not', but by reflecting upon the peculiarly negative dimension present in what has been variously described as the very gap between the representative and the represented.

Among post-foundational political thinkers,[2] Frank Ankersmit has focused intensely on the negative core of representational relations, which he associates with an ineradicably aesthetic element of all representation, including political representation. While it is customary to distinguish between artistic representation in the sense of what in German is called *Darstellung* and political representation (what in German would be *Vertretung*), Ankersmit insists that both views of representation are present in art *as well as* politics. According to the resemblance view of 'Darstellung', any representation is supposed to mimic as closely as possible what it purports to represent. In art, such an attitude amounts to a mimetic mode of hyper-realism. While, arguably, this would seem slightly outmoded in today's art world, in politics the same view appears still fashionable among critics of representational democracy who would defend the notion that 'the opinions of the electorate's representatives should be exactly the same as those of the electorate itself' (Ankersmit 2002: 109). Defenders of resemblance or, as they are sometimes called, identity theorists of representation typically favour ideas of direct democracy or council democracy. Hence, resemblance theories appear closer to an egalitarian approach associated with the more traditional perspective on democracy.[3] Substitution theorists, on the other hand, cut the 'tie of identity between represented and his representative postulated by the resemblance theory' (Ankersmit 2002: 112). As a result of this separation, a certain degree of autonomy has to be granted to the representative whose opinions will not necessarily overlap with the voters' opinions. In the most formal way the substitution theory of representation can thus be defined as follows: 'Representation is a making present (again) of what is absent. Or, more formally, A is a representation of B when it can take B's place; hence, when it can function as B's substitute or as B's replacement in its absence' (Ankersmit 2002: 109).

Ankersmit himself clearly opts for the substitution view. Siding with Edmund Burke, he holds that it would be a mistake to conceive of the parliament as a congress of ambassadors bound by their constituencies. The parliament, in a democratic sense, is the deliberative assembly of the whole nation; and for this reason the actions of the representative must not be pre-determined by the represented. On the contrary, by substituting for the represented the representative will have to re-articulate the will of his or her constituency within a larger context. He or she therefore re-creates the represented and, thus, re-creates political reality. This is the deeper reason why representation is of supreme importance in democratic politics:

> We need political representation, not so much in order to compensate for the practical impossibility of assembling the whole nation in one national agora so that the whole nation can participate in political decision making. Political representation is much more than that. For without political representation we are without a conception of what political reality – the represented – is like; without it, political reality has neither face nor contours. Without representation there is no represented – *and without political representation there is no nation as a truly political entity*. Hence, to put it provocatively, even if it were possible to get the whole nation together, or to achieve the same effect by some variant of direct democracy such as electronic voting, even then we should prefer representation. Political reality only comes into being after the nation has unfolded itself in a represented and a representation representing the represented. Without representation no democratic politics. (Ankersmit 2002: 115)

There are two ways in which Ankersmit makes use of the notion of aesthetics to grasp this process. In the first sense, 'aesthetics' points at the dimension of creativity involved in artistic as well as political representation: the (partial) construction of reality. In a second and more interesting sense, it is turned into an attribute of what he calls the '*aesthetic* barrier between the represented and its representation' (Ankersmit 1996: 18) – a barrier, or gap, which cannot be removed without immediately regressing into the resemblance view. Of course, in a fundamental sense a gap will always appear in processes of representation. An artist may be mimetically seeking identity between representation ('art') and represented ('reality'), but only at the extreme end of the scale would art become indistinguishable from reality. Such a magical effect of total *trompe l'œil* – as, in Borges, the map which coincides with the territory, or the congress which coincides with the world – is a sheer impossibility. And to avoid such an impasse, we cannot but assume an 'unbridgeable *aesthetic* gap' (Ankersmit 1996: 18) between represented and representative.[4] This also implies that, for Ankersmit, consensus on correct representation is unachievable: the representational gap cannot be bridged by rational consensus. If such consensus – envisioned by those who search for a rational ground of ultimate consensus (such as Habermas or Rawls appear to do) – was ever reached, it would overwrite the aesthetic gap between representative and represented. To the extent to which normative accounts propose a rational bridging of the gap, they turn the latter into a foundation, thus putting an end to representation and politics *tout court*. From this we can conclude that Ankersmit's account, rather than being anti-foundational, is post-foundational in the sense of fully accepting the absence of any ultimate normative foundation to political action without, however, denying the necessity of a constant play between ground and abyss, representative and represented. Precisely because there is no ultimate ground, a gap opens and sets in motion the never-ending process of grounding, that is, representation.

Now, while I gladly subscribe to a post-foundationalism of this kind, and while many of Ankersmit's observations remain highly pertinent to a theory of radical democracy, I am sceptical with regard to some of his political conclusions. It is certainly true that democracy, in the modern sense of the term, is premised upon the absence of an ultimate foundation and that, for this reason, the representational gap will have to be maintained to some degree. This is precisely what is implied in a negative concept of representation. Consequently, one has to be careful to differentiate between political projects which, to some degree, respect the difference between representative and represented, and those collapsing it. In the eyes of Ankersmit, today's most dangerous tendency leading to a collapsing or, at least, a narrowing of the gap is bureaucracy. When bureaucracy starts colonising the democratic dispositive – thus turning the latter into an expertocratic governmental regime – the representational gap narrows. Now, it may arguably be true that bureaucracy is 'what we get when politics attempts to come as close to the citizen as possible' (Ankersmit 2002: 117), but what would Ankersmit's alternative be? Direct democracy, in his eyes, will not count as an appropriate answer to large-scale bureaucratisation as it only functions on a local scale and with regard to questions that can easily be answered with a yes or a no.[5] Unfortunately, the only solution he is prepared to offer rings a conservative bell. The magic word, for Ankersmit, is compromise.

Needless to say, the relation between represented and representative will always have to be negotiated, which will of course involve compromise and an attitude of, as Ankersmit persuasively puts it, 'principled unprincipledness' (Ankersmit 2002: 96). But what he seeks to defend with his notion of compromise is not simply the post-foundational 'an-archic principle' (Schürmann 1987) of 'principled unprincipledness' – it is something much more politically biased. By insisting on representational democracy being the political institutionalisation of compromise, he engages in a defence of the historic *'juste-milieu'* politics of Guizot and other liberal conservatives of French post-Napoleonic parliamentarism as a recommendable model for today's democratic politics. In Ankersmit's eyes, their parliamentary 'democracy' provided a solution to the historical problem of social division that had become pertinent in Europe since the French Revolution:

> The countries of the European continent, having all experienced in a one way or another the upheavals following the French Revolution and the regime of Napoleon, all ended up after 1815 with politically strongly polarized populations, and therefore had to face a kind of major political problem that had no precedent in European history. (Ankersmit 2002: 102)

Coalition governments of the 'centre', the argument goes, had to search for a compromise between inimical political ideologies.

This argument is hardly convincing. The French parliaments between 1815 and 1848 were representative only of the interests of the grand bourgeoisie – that is, they were representative in a resemblance theory sense. Ankersmit's hero Guizot, a declared enemy of universal suffrage, is mostly remembered today as inventor of the capitalist slogan of self-enrichment: *'enrichissez-vous !'*. But in a historical situation in which parliamentary representation means representation of only a minute section of the population (0.3 per cent of the population were entitled under the July Monarchy to represent an electorate of 2 per cent), the democratic strategy of the day is certainly not compromise, but struggle for universal suffrage and political inclusion. Ankersmit, however, holds a different opinion:

> Since parliamentary (continental) democracy, thanks to *juste-milieu* politics, succeeded in finding creative solutions to such potentially dangerous conflicts as those between the *ancien régime* and the revolution or between capital and labour, we have every reason to be deeply grateful for how it guided us through one of Europe's most difficult periods. (Ankersmit 2002: 104).

The regimes Ankersmit refers to as 'parliamentary democracies' were parliamentary indeed, but they were far from being democratic. Political representation alone is not a sufficient criterion for democracy as long as large sectors of the population remain excluded from the sphere of representation. Modern democracy is characterised precisely by an uneasy combination of representation with popular sovereignty, while Ankersmit – without in the least considering the deeply anti-democratic function of a census based on property or taxation – appears to implicitly favour a liberal representational regime without popular sovereignty because only then, he insinuates, can social conflicts be domesticated. He is, no doubt, correct that there is no democratic politics without some degree of compromise – otherwise we would be speaking about outright civil war, not politics. This trivial fact, however, should not seduce us to hypostasise a *juste-milieu* or, in its more contemporary variant, post-democratic 'third way' politics into the only reasonable form of politics. The democratic revolution unfolded through exactly the opposite process of self-radicalisation. It was the struggle between radical democrats and the *ancien régime*, between 'labour' and 'capital', together with subsequent democratic struggles (for instance by the suffragettes and other radical democrats), which led to the expansion of the democratic horizon and the establishment of a legitimate ground for claims for universal suffrage and political as well as social inclusion. To claim, as Ankersmit does, that our 'political problems no longer have the character of setting one part of the electorate against another, as was paradigmatically the case in the struggle between labour and capital' (Ankersmit 2002: 126), is to claim that the democratic revolution is completed – as if struggles for emancipation, liberation and equalisation were outmoded and superfluous. This would amount to nothing other than a claim for a post-political and, eventually, post-democratic order.

The negative concept of representation (2): Laclau and radical negativity

Ankersmit's negative notion of representation has the great advantage of sharpening our sensorium for the gap between represented and representative. At the same time, compromise is given priority over conflictuality. His concept of representation therefore turns out to be not negative enough. We have to account for the fundamental role of what Ernesto Laclau has succinctly described as the logic of social antagonism. A negative theory of representation has to provide us with an account of both dimensions: the discrepancy, or non-self-identity, of the represented/representative as well as the dimension of radical conflictuality, or antagonism. And, as I will try to show in the following, the latter lies at the ground of the former.

Let us first consider the Laclauian version of the representational gap. For Laclau, representation is the process by which a particular content (a particular political demand, a particular social actor, a particular class position or ethnic identity, and so on) assumes a universal function without, however, collapsing with the universal *tout court*. That it is to say, a particularity comes to represent more than what it actually stands for. In order to do so, it has to appeal to other particularities, include them into an equivalential chain and, at the same time, seek to represent this entire chain of particularities. In other words, by representing contents other than its own one, a particular content assumes a universal function. For Laclau, such hegemonic relation, in which a particular content hegemonises the universal function of representation, is the very essence of politics. Politics, in this sense, is essentially representational as 'representation is the process by which somebody else – the representative – "substitutes for" and at the same time "embodies" the represented' (Laclau 1996: 97). There is no politics without the representational play between the universal and the particular.

Given the substitutive function of the representative, the 'dialectics' between universality and particularity amounts to a play, in Heideggerian parlance, between presence and absence, for what is involved in a representational process is 'the *fictio iuris* that somebody is present in a place from which he or she is materially absent'.

And yet, this play will stop at the moment in which the particular comes to coincide with the universal, the represented with the representative. Such a process of perfect representation can only be achieved 'when the representation is a direct process of transmission of the will of the represented, when the act of representation is totally transparent in relation to that will' (Laclau 1996: 97), which, of course, would imply, as Laclau continues, a fully constituted political will on the side of the represented and a merely auxiliary function of the representative. Again we would be taken hostage by don Alejandro's fantasy: the idea of a perfect fusion between represented and representative. This is illusory not only because the conditions of perfect representation will never be met for empirical reasons (it is obvious that the desire for perfect representation will always encounter empirical obstacles), but, what is more, they cannot be met for 'logical' reasons. If the two sides of the representational relation were fused, representation as such would vanish. As Laclau sustains, 'no pure relation of representation is obtainable because it is of the essence of the process of representation that the representative has to contribute to the identity of what is represented' (Laclau 1996: 87). Representation remains indispensable because the identity of the represented is still, in fact, in need of representation:

> So far as the represented is concerned, if he or she needs to be represented at all, this is the result of the fact that his or her basic identity is constituted in a place A and that decisions that can affect this identity will be taken in a place B. But in that case his or her identity is an incomplete identity, and the relation of representation – far from referring to full-fledged identity – is a *supplement* necessary for the constitution of that identity. The crucial problem is to determine whether this supplement can simply be *deduced* from the place A, where the original identity of the represented was constituted, or if it is an entirely *new* addition, in which case, the identity of the represented is transformed and enlarged though the process of representation. (Laclau 1996: 98)

Laclau provides the example of a group of farmers mainly interested in maintaining the prices of their products. The function of a representative of this constituency cannot simply consist in transmitting this demand and nothing else. As a member of parliament, for instance, the representative will have to make the farmers' case by negotiating with a diverse range of political forces. Most of the strategic steps required from him or her to achieve the goal will not simply be deducible from the position of the 'vested interests' of the farmers. There cannot be a direct relation of determination between their interests and political actions on the floor of the parliament. The representative, Laclau holds, '*inscribes* an interest in a complex reality different from that in which the interest was originally formulated and, in doing so, he or she constructs and transforms the interest' (Laclau 1996: 98). This is what Ankersmit would describe as the 'aesthetic' moment of creativity in a representational relation. As in Ankersmit, the electorate, or, with Laclau, 'the people', is not simply given in an empirical sense but has to be created politically in the 'aesthetic' process of representation. The very identity of the represented is thus, to say the least, transformed by the action of the representative. By continuing this line of thought, we could even describe the representative as always being in excess of his or her own role (as a mere delegate) while at the same time he or she can only play such an excessive role of at least partially creating the represented because the latter is in need of a supplement – which amounts to saying that his or her identity is characterised by a lack. What Laclau evidently adds to Ankersmit's picture is a theory of lack, borrowed from Lacan, which helps to account for this peculiar absence that has to be filled in the process of representation. It is because the represented lacks full identity in the first place that a substitutional process is set in motion to fill this lack.

Without elaborating it in this way, Laclau's model of representation appears to involve a 'negative dialectics' between an instance that is always-too-much (compared to the literal demand of the representative) and one that is always-not-enough (in the sense of being in need of a supplement): a play, that is, between a constitutive surplus and a constitutive lack. Were it otherwise, 'we would be left with the nude identities of the represented and the representative as self-sufficient ones' (Laclau 1996: 87). Apart from such quasi-Lacanian addition to the argument, there is a second step which takes Laclau beyond Ankersmit. The negative dimension of representation, as previously indicated, can be fully explained only when put in relation to Laclau's most fundamental political idea: the concept of antagonism (Laclau and Mouffe 1985; Laclau 2014). In a nutshell, antagonism – a term inherited from the Marxian lexicon – describes the negative outer limit necessary for any identity to establish some minimal degree of coherence rather than devolving into a psychotic, un-ordered flow of elements. Only by way of this radically negative instance of antagonism – that is, only by being delineated from what it is not – can identity be established. However, by virtue of being purely negative in comparison with the positivity of internal elements, the same outside serves not only as the constitutive instance for every identity but also as its destitutive or dislocatory instance. Any identity is both constructed and undermined by the instance of antagonism. In a typically deconstructive formula, antagonism serves as both the condition of possibility and the condition of impossibility of every social identity. For this reason, it is antagonism which lies at the ground of the instable and precarious nature of social and political identities which, in turn, need to be partially supplemented and stabilised by a surplus element that takes on the role of the representative.[6]

Don Alejandro's nightmare: Bosnia and the vicissitudes of positive representation

Laclau provides us with a theoretical explanation of the gap between represented and representative as it is also diagnosed, in a much more descriptive fashion, by Ankersmit. The gap, I have argued, results from a mutual play between lack and excess – between the two non-self-identical ends of the representation relation – and can be traced back to what was theoretically elaborated by Laclau as the logics of antagonism. At no point in the representational process will we encounter something of the order of a solid positive ground accounting for the identity of either the represented or the representative. This negative theory of representation has now to be tested on an empirical example in order to prove that it can provide us with a yardstick to judge the democratic legitimacy of a given political order.

Before doing so, I would like to point out three general implications of what has been said so far. Firstly, we have to once more underline the contingency of the relation between the represented and the representative. This relation cannot be deduced from the 'inner nature' of either term. The arbitrary fact that don Alejandro has a red beard does not mean that he is predestined to represent all red-bearded people. His secretary Nora Erfhord, without any natural disposition towards red-beardedness, could equally represent the red-bearded. If, however, it is don Alejandro who comes to represent the red-bearded, then it is because a contingent representational relation has been established between him and his constituency. The second implication is that because of the contingency of this relation, its very construction will by necessity 'distort' the identity of the represented (and that of the representative). To the extent that the identity of the represented is construed through the very act of representation, the latter takes place within a distorted space.[7] To straighten out this space would mean to dissolve the very terrain – the terrain of political discursivity – on which representation unfolds. As Chantal Mouffe, with reference to Lacan, has claimed, 'if we were to subtract from a discursive field its distortion, the field would disintegrate, "de-quilt"' (Mouffe 2009: 138). Distortion is as constitutive for representation as contingency and conflict are. A world without distortion would place us in the mystical state of direct communication with the nature of all things, yet such a world would be a world without politics. And, thirdly, if distortion is indeed the norm, then what presents itself as the 'norm' of representation – so-called Western liberal democracy – is just one more distorted way of constructing the representational relation. To get into view the distorted nature of what presents itself as undistorted norm, it could be recommendable to direct our gaze to what appears as an extreme anomaly, an outright distortion of the liberal-democratic regime, that is, the distortion of a distortion: Bosnia-Herzegovina.

The anomalous case of Bosnia not only illuminates the liberal standard model of representation, it also illustrates the disastrous consequences of a positive and identitarian notion of representation. As a consequence of the Dayton Peace Agreement of 1995, within a single state two states were created which have very little to do with each other but nonetheless are chained to each other. The result is arguably the most complicated institutional system of representation at the present time.[8] Apart from the political institutions (parliaments, cantonal assemblies, municipal governments, and so on) of the Bosnian-Croatian Federation on the one side and the Republika Srpska on the other, the supra-state of Bosnia has few competencies but all the institutions of a regular state (a parliament, a president, a council of ministers, a constitutional court, and so on). The actual nature or 'form' of this state – if it is a state – remains undefined. The Dayton Agreement decrees that the former Yugoslavian republic of Bosnia-Herzegovina will henceforth be called 'Bosnia-Herzegovina' without further specification. Its two composite states are defined, in their own right, as federation and republic respectively, but it remains entirely mysterious what they are in relation to their supra-state. They are officially called 'entities'. This deliberate indeterminacy is thwarted, on the other hand, by a very precise determination of representational functions according to ethnic criteria on the supra-state level. Representational functions are distributed on a basis of parity and all groups are granted generous veto rights the result of which is an institutionally codified particularism and the effective paralysis of democratic institutions. As any composition of institutions along ethnic criteria will, of course, perpetuate cultural and political forms of particularism or identitarianism, it is quite remarkable that the so-called international community remains stupefied in the face of the continuous success of nationalist parties. What else could be the outcome of a system of positive representation in which only the red-bearded represent the red-bearded?

Through an unequalled multiplication and codification of representational relations, Bosnia was thought to be prevented from falling back into a *bellum omnium contra omnes*. Yet what was meant to pacify a deeply divided society turned out to freeze the play of representation and to eradicate the gap between represented and representative, leading to the depoliticisation and de-democratisation of Bosnian society. In other words, with a view to pacifying a state of civil war (and, at the same time, denying the parties the right to separate that was granted to the other republics of the former Yugoslavia), social identities were pinned down into fixed slots of representation, while the actual process of democratic politics – that is, the representational play of creating the identity of constituencies – was brought to a halt. The 'democratisation' of Bosnia, in the way it was imposed by the West, in actual fact made it impossible for the country to develop into a democratic polity. As David Chandler described the case in *Faking Democracy After Dayton*,

> the dynamic of the Dayton process has been to institutionalise fears and insecurities through disempowering Bosnian people and their representatives. The logic of democratisation, that power cannot be given to Bosnian institutions until there is greater political security, has led to a vicious circle. (Chandler 2000: 196)

It is suggested by Chandler 'that this is a problem of the international community's own making and that this circle could be broken by allowing greater levels of political autonomy – more democracy' (Chandler 2000: 196).

However, one question has not been addressed so far. For, if the institutional design of Bosnia tends to rob representatives of the power of democratic decision-making, how, then, are decisions arrived at? The answer is that Bosnian sovereignty is replaced by an outside power. In the thoroughly Hobbesian mindset of the Dayton negotiators, the Bosnians, in order to overcome a state of civil war, had to hand over all their sovereign powers to a single individual who, cynically, was named the 'High Representative'. Whom does the High Representative

represent? The United Nations, which covers the Bosnian protectorate with a thin veil of legitimacy? The Peace Implementation Council (formerly the International Conference on Former Yugoslavia), in
which fifty-five states and organisations were lumped together? The
so-called 'contact group', consisting of France, Germany, Italy, Russia,
Great Britain and the USA? The USA, and increasingly the EU, which
feels most 'responsible' for the protectorate? Or the entirely chimeric
instance of the 'international community'?

One thing is for certain: whatever the High Representative represents, it is not the Bosnian people, as he is not accountable to
any inner-Bosnian institution. This was most laconically expressed
by one of the former High Representatives, Paddy Ashdown, when
asked in an interview whether his office should not be more accountable to Bosnian institutions. He answered that he *was* reporting to
the parliament regularly; but when pressed further whether his decision to report to the parliament sprang from his own will (rather
than being a legal requirement), his answer was 'But of course' (*Der
Standard* 2003: 5). This answer effectively ridiculed the idea of
accountability – which is a legally binding duty, not an act of grace
by a sovereign who could decide differently. In the Bonn meeting
of the Peace Implementation Council in 1997, the High Representative was unilaterally handed unrestricted legislative and executive
authority which officially allows him (or her) to pass and implement
laws by decree. So far, dozens, perhaps hundreds, of elected Bosnian
officials – mayors, regional representatives, members of parliament,
ministers – have been discharged by the High Representatives. That
Bosnia is stripped of its sovereignty is also demonstrated by the fact
that three out of nine supreme judges are appointed by the president
of the European Court of Human Rights on the condition that they
are not of Bosnian nationality. The governor of the Central Bank,
who is appointed by the International Monetary Fund, is not supposed to be a Bosnian citizen either. The absurdity of the situation is
documented even on the symbolic level of national emblems. It was
the office of the High Representative that worked out the design of
the Bosnian flag, the number plates and the banknotes. The Bosnian
currency – which is named 'convertible mark' – in itself attests to the
absence of Bosnian sovereignty, as it remains bound to a foreign currency, the German mark, which no longer exists and only lives on in
a 'backward colony'.

It is evident that Bosnia is not a sovereign state but rather a colony
or protectorate. The function of sovereignty is usurped by a High
Representative who appears to represent the mythical instance of

an 'international community' in the same way in which the Indian viceroy used to represent 'the Crown'. Strictly speaking, however, the High Representative does not represent anything – provided we agree on the negative concept of representation as developed above. He or she might be granted a certain pragmatic leeway in his or her actions, yet there is no functional gap between representative and represented that would allow for a play between these instances. Rather than speaking about representation we should thus speak about delega-tion: the representative is nothing other than a commissar who acts, very much as described by Hobbes in the Chapter 23 of *Leviathan*, as a mere extension of the will of the sovereign wherever the latter cannot personally be present. Hence, the title 'High Representative' is quite misleading and one should consider a more appropriate title for the office, such as 'Supreme Administrator'. Likewise, the Bosnian representatives do not, rigorously speaking, represent their constitu-encies as long as their actions follow a logic of identity. This logic results in a world where, to once more speak Borgesian, only the red-bearded represent the red-bearded, or, in Bosnia, the Serbs represent the Serbs, the Croats the Croats and the Bosniaks the Bosniaks.

Such universe of frozen particularities, from which the play of representation has been banned, can only operate in reality if the political is supplanted by the order of a Supreme Administrator who runs public affairs without engaging in the representational play of politics. This commissar will act in lieu of a sovereign whose power remains, according to Bodin's classical definition, indivisible, unlim-ited and absolute. Such concentration of power in a singularly abso-lute point is irreconcilable with a negative concept of representation. Where all constituencies are incarnated by a single representative, total representability reigns and, for the same reason, the play of rep-resentation is abolished. In the history of occidental onto-theology, sovereignty became a name for the suspension of representation by absolute representation. If we were to venture a definition of this onto-theological notion of sovereignty, it could be the following: Sovereign is he or she who, by virtue of representation, suspends representation. Democracy, on the other hand, requires a decidedly different concept both of sovereignty and of representation.

Conclusion: representation and the ethics of democracy

Some might see in the failed state of Bosnia-Herzegovina a mere distortion of the Western liberal model of democracy. One should not forget, however, that the institutional framework of this state was designed and implemented mostly by Western liberal democracies. How come these democracies, in exporting their own institutional model (or a travesty of it), 'forgot' about exporting two of the defining features of modern democracy: popular sovereignty and the play of political representation? What if truth speaks through distortion? What if Bosnia should therefore be read as a symptom not of post-Yugoslavian nationalism, but of the post-democratic ideology that radiates from and, at the same time, subverts Western democracies? In other words, what if the Bosnian distortion allows us to catch a glimpse of the hidden ideal of the neo-liberal hegemon – the post-democratic ideal, namely of a democracy without the people, and of representation without politics? To criticise this ideal is not to argue for a return to unmediated, non-representative forms of plebiscitary or direct democracy as an alternative. For sure, there cannot be democracy without popular sovereignty, yet within the modern democratic dispositive 'the people' do not assume the function of an absolute sovereign. Popular sovereignty, to the extent to which it is democratic, or even radical democratic, cannot be indivisible, unlimited and absolute: it must be internally divided, limited and subjected to the play between the particular and the universal (rather than being subjected to the singular instance of the absolute). That is to say, the rule of the people in modern democracy has to pass through a representational gap that can only be bridged temporarily and provisionally. Popular sovereignty is then instituted as the rule of a sovereign whose presence is experienced as an absence (which is precisely the meaning of Claude Lefort's famous dictum that in democracy the place of power remains empty), even though this absence may be temporarily substituted through the play of representation.

Bosnia, as a symptom, exemplifies *a contrario* the modern condition of democracy. The state with one of the most complicated representational systems worldwide is also a state without politics and without sovereignty, let alone popular sovereignty. Democratic politics, as we saw, is replaced by an identitarian fixation of constituencies to their 'representatives' while supreme executive and legislative authority is concentrated in the hands of a Supreme Administrator. Given its subjugation into a mere protectorate it is hardly surprising that even the Council of Europe had to acknowledge 'that Bosnia and Herzegovina is not a democracy' (quoted in Chandler 2000: 204). From a post-foundational and radical democratic perspective, though, an important qualification of this verdict is in order. From the dominant liberal perspective, the main shortcoming of Bosnian democracy will be seen in its insufficient implementation of typically liberal institutional precautions: the division of powers and a regime of effective parliamentary representation. The radical democratic view, which I am prepared to defend, goes a step further. It does not deny the necessity of either representation or a division of powers, but it does not subordinate these dimensions of the democratic dispositive to the higher goal of a defence of individual rights. These institutional dimensions of democracy, I submit, rather point to a democratic ethics of self-questioning or self-alienation. As Ernesto Laclau has argued:

> A democratic society is not one in which the 'best' content [which will come to fill the representation gap] dominates unchallenged but, rather, one in which nothing is definitely acquired and there is always the possibility of challenge. If we think, for instance, of the resurgence of nationalism and all kinds of ethnic identities in present-day Eastern Europe, then we can easily see that the danger for democracy lies in the closure of these groups around fully-fledged identities that can only reinforce their most reactionary tendencies and create the conditions for a permanent confrontation with other groups. It is, on the contrary, the integration of these nations into wider ensembles – such as the EU – that can create the bases for a democratic development, and that requires the split from oneself to be a proper self. There is democracy only if there is the recognition of the positive value of a dislocated identity. (Laclau 1996: 100)

Democracy, as Laclau sustains, 'requires the split from oneself to be a proper self'. It puts a demand on us to abandon our phantasmatic beliefs in fully fledged identities. Representational procedures and the division of powers should be understood as institutional devices through which a democratic society affirms the impossibility of ever reaching the moment when it would become identical to itself. In this sense, they serve as symbolic markers – or markers of recognition – of what I have proposed to call democratic self-alienation (Marchart 2007). The reason is easy to see: a universe whose parts coincide with themselves would coincide with itself as a totality. It would be a fully un-alienated 'whole' – a perfect Parmedian sphere – without any need of mediation or relation between its parts: a pure totality à la don Alejandro (hence the mystical orgy of unification in the Borges story). Against such phantasmatic solution to the problem of representation, it is affirmed in a democratic society that total representability remains impossible and full transparency can never be achieved. This, of course, does not preclude the possibility of partial representations. On the contrary, the play between represented and representative becomes constitutive for democracy on the condition only that total representability is deemed impossible and that the gap between the totality and its parts, between the represented and the representative, is fully accepted.

The same considerations will apply *a forteriori* to any politics of radical democracy, if by the latter we understand the political project of deepening and expanding democracy, that is, of democratising democracy (Balibar 2015). All too often the concept of radical democracy is associated with a certain image of Rousseau and the tradition of what could be is presented as a politics of presence and plenitude.[9] Radical democracy, in its ethical aspects, does not presuppose the presence of the people, but quite the reverse, their absence – with the proviso that this absence makes itself felt (thus assuming some form of presence) through a set of procedures and institutions which continuously confront us with the undisciplined nature of the democratic order. To react to such confrontation in an affirmative way and fully accept the self-alienated nature of social identities and the democratic political order requires an ethical rather than a merely political stance. If democracy were a matter of politics only, we could equally go ahead and install an order of popular presence, plenitude and self-identity. If democracy is more than that or, actually, *less* than that, then that is because the political project of democracy is thwarted by an antinomic ethics of questioning the very foundations of the democratic project (that is, the borders drawn, the exclusions produced, the identities fostered through democratic politics). Such an ethics of democracy requires us to recognise and, in fact, affirm the emptiness of the place of power, the impossibility of absolute and limitless sovereignty, the insurmountable gap between the represented and the representative, the irreconcilable division of powers and the unavoidable recurrence of social conflict: in short, the self-alienated nature of the democratic order. It is this ethical dimension that will provide us with a yardstick for judging the legitimacy of democratic politics. In this sense, we can follow Ankersmit for whom the gap of representation is the very source of legitimate democratic power:

> To put it metaphorically, when a population unfolds itself into a group of people that is represented and another group of people representing the former one, legitimate political power wells up, so to speak, in the hollow between the two groups. Hence, the origin of all legitimate political power must be situation in the aesthetic gap between voter and representative (the state). This would justify, to begin with,

the probably amazing and certainly unorthodox conclusion that *in a representative democracy all legitimate political power is essentially aesthetic*. It follows, next, that in a representative democracy legitimated power is possessed by neither voter, representative, nor state. (Ankersmit 2002: 118)

As much as I concur with Ankersmit's conclusions in this paragraph – democratic power is legitimate to the extent to which it remains 'hollow' – his insistence on the 'aesthetic' nature of the representational gap appears misplaced. There certainly is play and creativity involved in democratic politics. Acting democratically means dancing on an abyss. Acceptance of this fact, however, is not so much a matter of aesthetics. It is, first and foremost, an ethical exigency. We have to conceive of radical democracy as an emancipatory project based on an ethical demand, not an aesthetic experience: the demand to accept and recognise the alienated, intransparent and ungrounded nature of democracy. The negative concept of representation is one of the ways in which this ethical demand is registered in democratic theory.

Notes

1. I make use here of the Lacanian concept of fantasy. For the initial and magisterial application of this concept to the study of ideology see Žižek (1989); for a Lacanian critique of the 'fantasy of utopia' see Stavrakakis (1999) and for an integral model of a post-foundational theory of ideology see Marchart (2015).
2. Ankersmit tends to describe his own approach, while modifying Rorty's understanding of the term, as 'anti-foundationalist'. For reasons elaborated elsewhere (Marchart 2007), I remain sceptical with regard to the prefix 'anti' as post-foundational political thinkers do not aim at abandoning *all* foundations, but, rather, question the idea of an ultimate ground while at the same time *fully accepting* the necessity of temporary, contingent, contested, plural and, thus, partial foundations.
3. As Ankersmit recalls, these questions figured prominently in the debates around the American constitution when the anti-Federalists defended a more egalitarian position based on the resemblance theory of representation, while for the Federalists the goal of representation was to select the most competent candidates (Ankersmit 2002: 110). In the latter approach, the representatives inherit the role of the *aristoi*. It is thus not entirely misguided to detect remnants of an aristocratic imaginary in some of the early ideas about democratic representation. However, as will become clear in the course of my argument, the democratic revolution – which was very much initiated by the French Revolution

of the years 1792–4 – entirely changed this picture by politically preparing the ground for the 'negative' concept of representation.

4. And this holds for art *and* for politics: 'The same dividing line runs between person represented and representative as between the real world and the world of art' (Ankersmit 1996: 46).

5. Ankersmit is also worried about the recent trend to what he calls a 'referendum democracy' where periodic elections are seen as an opportunity for protest voting, not for a more nuanced evaluation of government performance.

6. The discursive role of this element was famously theorised by Laclau in his 'empty signifier' paper (see Laclau 1996).

7. Ankersmit appears to shy away from this conclusion when insisting that the representational gap 'is not necessarily an indication of *conflict, distortion* or *incorrectness*' (Ankersmit 2002: 112). *Contra* Ankersmit I would insist that there is nothing to fear from the idea of a 'distorted space', and I would even add that the gap, as a matter of fact, *is* an indication of conflict in the Laclauian sense of social antagonism.

8. For an exact description of this system see Bose (2002).

9. There are attempts, though, to give Rousseau a more post-foundational reading; see Inston (2010).

10

Pinning down representation

Lasse Thomassen

Introduction: deconstructing representation

Work on political representation has taken two turns over the last two decades: first, a representative turn placing representation at the centre of politics and democracy while simultaneously extending the category of representation beyond formal political institutions (Urbinati and Warren 2008); and, within the representative turn, a second constructivist turn where representation is taken as constitutive of what is represented (Disch 2011, 2015). Those two turns reflect recent developments in the politics of representation: from Occupy to Trump, political representation is much more than formal political institutions, and representative claims shape the world they refer to.

Michael Saward's (2006, 2009, 2010, 2014) theory of the representative claim is part of these two turns. According to Saward, political representation takes place not just within formal institutions but across society, and representative claims constitute – that is, construct – what they claim to represent. The theory of the representative claim is the most systematic and sophisticated conceptualisation of the constructivist turn available today, and it has become the most important reference point for current empirical and theoretical research on political representation (Decreus 2013; Disch 2015; Hatherell 2014; Severs 2010, 2012; Tanasescu 2014). Yet, as I shall argue below, there are three areas where Saward does not take the full constructivist turn. They are, first, the notion of the referent, which is not constituted through the representative claim; second, while Saward argues that the representative claim is an event that cannot be pinned down, it remains transparent and stable in some respects; and, third, the normative aspects of the theory remain within the horizon of a future in which we may one day be able to pin down the meaning of the representative claim.

One of Saward's sources for his theory of the representative claim is Jacques Derrida's work on representation (1973, 1978, 2007a, 2016). Derrida puts forward a critique of representation as the reflection of presence, for instance, a representative claim as the reflection of, and the transparent medium for, the intentions of an author or the interests of a social class. While it may at first appear as if Derrida rejects representation, he is critical of a particular conception of representation, and he generalises a deconstructed, and deconstructivist, conception of representation. Derrida's conception of representation is another version of the constructivist turn: there is no outside of representation; representation is constitutive, or performative; it is inherently opaque and unstable, and it is impossible to finally pin down the representative claim, and so it is an event.

In this chapter, I bring Derrida's conception of representation and his deconstructive readings of discourses of representation to bear on Saward's theory of the representative claim. It is with the important caveat, however, that the resources for radicalising the theory of the representative claim are already present in that theory.

Derrida addresses the question of representation through the deconstruction of a number of discourses of representation, above all those of Edmund Husserl, Jean-Jacques Rousseau, Antonin Artaud and Martin Heidegger. He does not treat those discourses as documents of an essence of the concept of representation (Derrida 2016: 163). Instead they are treated as contingent, but privileged examples of wider and prevalent discourses of representation, with the caveat that the privilege does not arise from some congruence between these representations of representation and some conceptual essence of representation. In the following, Derrida's work serves as a road into the question of representation. His conception of representation is also a particular conception of representation that opens the question of representation in a particular way and through a particular vocabulary and particular texts.

If there is no outside of representation, and if representation is constitutive, then all we have are particular representations of representation and no concept or essence of representation behind, or beyond, those representations. Derrida's is just one of them, as is Saward's, and they do not give us access to any non-representational concept of representation. Yet there is also a claim in Derrida's work on representation, and in my use of it, that Derrida's (particular) deconstructions of (particular) discourses of representation tell us something general about representation. This is the justification for translating insights and gestures from Derrida's deconstructions of discourses of representation to other discourses, such as Saward's theory of the representative claim. There is, then, an irresolvable tension between the particularity of Derrida's work on representation and a generalisable conception of representation that, it is claimed, follows from it.

In what follows, I do not try to first establish 'what Derrida says' or 'what Derrida means' as if that could be taken as a ground on which to proceed with a critical and deconstructive engagement with Saward's work. There is no systematic theory of representation in Derrida, even if his writings do lend themselves to a certain degree of systematisation (Thomassen 2007, 2010). What is more, it is not a question of finding the true constructivist conception of representation and then comparing it with Saward's theory of the representative claim; engaging with the constructivist turn can only take place by engaging with a particular, but privileged, discourse such as that of the theory of the representative claim.

The referent

For Saward, '[r]epresentation is an ongoing process of making and receiving, accepting and rejecting claims', and representation is not limited to formal political institutions, but takes place across society (Saward 2010: 36). Saward argues for a constructivist conception of representation as performative, or constructivist, in that representation is constitutive of what is represented. In this sense, representation is dynamic because it does not take identities as given; rather identities are constituted through representation. In addition, representation is not a unidirectional or dyadic relationship between represented and representative as in more traditional accounts of representation, where the movement is from represented to representative, and where the latter is supposed to respond to the former. Instead, Saward's theory of representation is a systemic one. This is evident in the definition of the primary category of this theory, namely the representative claim whose 'general form' is the following: 'A *maker* of representation ("M") puts forward a *subject* ("S") which stands for an *object* ("O") that is related to a *referent* ("R") and is offered to an *audience* ("A")' (Saward 2010: 36). What matters are the relations among the different elements as it is the relations that constitute those elements; and the multi-relational and multidirectional character of representation means that representation must be conceived as systemic; each element is constituted through its relations with the other elements.

For Saward, the representative claim constitutes the object of the claim. If I claim that 'America is falling apart', that claim contributes to the constitution of the object ('America') of the claim. The represented object 'is related to' the referent, which in this case would be the physical entities making up what the claim refers to as America. The referent is the element that Saward pays the least attention to in his theory of the representative claim, and, as Simon Thompson has pointed out, Saward conceives of the referent in various ways (Saward 2010: 36; Thompson 2012: 111). In one version, the referent is 'a materially existing group or entity' (Saward 2010: 79; Saward 2006: 315), for instance 'the actual, flesh-and-blood people of the constituency' when an MP represents and, thus, constructs their interests (Saward 2010: 37, 53). In a second version, the referent 'is all the other things' the object 'is, or might be' (Saward 2010: 36, 116, 121; Saward 2006: 313; Saward 2009: 3, 18), and, in a third version, the referent is 'the thing itself' which is subject to '[c]ompeting significations' (Saward 2010: 74, 36; Saward 2006: 310). In a fourth version, the referent is used interchangeably with 'an original' (Saward 2010: 80).

Whatever the possible different meanings of these different version of the referent (see Thompson 2012: 111), what remains constant across them is the identification of something – the thing itself, material entities, an original, and so on – that is isolated from the effects of representation. The representative claim constructs the object – that is, what is represented – but not the referent. As Saward (2010: 51; also Saward 2006: 313–14) himself writes, 'There is always a *referent*. But the real political work lies in the active constitution of constituencies – the making of representations.' However, in the theory of the representative claim, the referent denotes an element that is not constituted through a (representational) relation with other elements – it simply is. Derrida (2007a: 102) writes of conceptions of representation that take representation as secondary to presence: 'you represent something – a sense, an object, a referent, indeed, already another representation in whatever sense – that is supposed to be *anterior* and *exterior*' to the representative claim. In Saward's theory of the representative claim, the object is no longer anterior and exterior to the claim, but constituted by it; however, something does remain anterior and exterior to the claim: the referent.

Saward (2010: 79) otherwise insists 'that there is no place "beyond representation"'. He may have introduced the referent to meet the criticisms of those who, while taking on board the theory of the representative claim, nonetheless argue for some bedrock of substantive interests in order to counter what they see as the normative vertigo of a theory of representation that takes representation as performative (for example, Severs 2010, 2012). It may also be that Saward introduced the referent to avoid idealism, but if we think of representation as material, there is nothing in the theory of the representative claim that need imply idealism.

Thomas Decreus (2013; Disch 2015: 493) has identified the problems of introducing the notion of the referent into a theory of representation 'built upon the performative and constructivist definition of political representation as the contingent product of "representative claims"' (Saward 2014: 725). Decreus turns to Ernesto Laclau and Chantal Mouffe (1990: 82–4) for a solution and distinguishes between the existence and being of a thing. The thing will have a being for us insofar as it partakes in a meaningful practice (what Laclau and Mouffe call discourse). That is, its being is representational, while its existence is not – for instance 'a constituency' and 'the actual, flesh-and-blood people of the constituency'.

However, the problems remain the same. First, it is not clear why the distinction between existence and being is necessary, that is, what work it is doing. Second, this distinction too posits a beyond representation: the category of existence and the distinction between existence and being are placed beyond representation. There is something – a presence – which is not constituted through a representational relation.[1] This is not to say that there are no limits to representation, but these limits must be understood differently, as a lack or an excess marking representation, not as a border between the play of representation and something beyond it (Thomassen 2007).

This suggests that we must get rid of the referent from the theory of the representative claim (see also Decreus 2013: 38–40). However, it is impossible to think representation without some notion of reference, because a representative claim has the double aspect of bringing the object (the represented) into being and claiming to merely reflect this object (cf. Decreus 2013: 40). A representative claim is also a claim to represent something already there, something prior to the representative claim; representation is always also representation *of* (Colebrook 1999: 107).

Decreus (2013: 38, 40) proposes to think of the referent as another representation: the representative claim gets parts of its force from its resonance with existing representations that are taken as given.

The referent moves inside the play of the representative claim, so to speak, and the representations that function as referents are themselves the result of other representative claims. Here Derrida's notion of iterability is helpful.

A representative claim is a performative act in J. L. Austin's sense that it performs an action rather than constatively describing or representing a state of affairs. As Derrida's (1988) deconstruction of Austin's theory of performatives showed, the performative cannot be completely dissociated from the constative. Take, as an example, the American Declaration of Independence (Derrida 1986). The Declaration declares the will of the people and thereby performatively institutes the people that, in a future anterior tense, will have been the people who declared their independence through their representatives. The Declaration institutes a new object (an independent people), but it is also a constative claim to merely reflect the people and its will. The representative act of the Declaration is both performative and constative. Importantly, the performative aspect of the representative act draws on the constative aspect for its force.

A representative claim is a claim to merely repeat in a constative fashion, thereby hiding the performative behind the constative. The claim appears transparent, and its authority is based in what it reflects and its claim to reflect it accurately. It is authorised by appearing to be authored by what it claims to be a representation of, for instance the intentions of the author of a novel, or the will of the people. In this way, the representation refers backwards towards something that already was before it. This may take many different forms, for instance in the politician's claim to represent his or her constituency, the claim to represent the views of the constituents may be combined with an image of the flesh-and-blood people of the constituency so as to give the constituency some stability and presence beyond the circulation of views and representations.

Derrida's notion of iterability is meant to capture this relationship between the constative (repetition) and the performative (alteration): the representative claim is a performative, but it is also a claim to merely repeat, or reflect, something already there: a people, the will of the people, and so forth. Repetition, or iteration, involves something new each time because meaning is relational, and the repetition always happens in a slightly new context. The repetition stands at a distance from what it repeats, and so representation understood as repetition involves separation. It is already separated from an original, and the original cannot be an absolute origin because it implies the possibility of its repetition as its condition of possibility. The original can only be constituted through a representation of it as origin, and so it becomes involved in a potentially endless and open chain of repetition where the representation always points both backwards (as representation of) and forwards (to ever new re-representations).

If there are referents, they must be conceived as this 'sedimented iterability' that results from the repetition of representative claims, what we might call re-representations (Butler 1995: 134, emphasis removed). Iterability implies an element of 'play' – a play of iterability or representation: a representative claim is a representation of some presence taken to be already there, but there is always the possibility of repeating it in new contexts, thereby introducing new meanings. 'Play' does not mean 'free play' because we are dealing with representative claims in an already partly sedimented terrain of representation. The effects of the representative claim are dispersed in a web of iterability that is both endless and (therefore) never completely, but always somewhat, stable. There is no outside representation because what is 'present' is constituted through representation, but the representative claim refers to something prior to it (or, to be precise, it posits something as prior to itself).

The object is thus not created *ex nihilo*, but through repetition. Here Saward's (2010: 75–7) notion of cultural background codes helps illuminate the way in which a representative claim must resonate with existing representations whose authority is taken for granted by the audience. For instance, the Declaration of Independence has references to God and to existing structures of representation and authority where the signatories are recognised as representatives. The representative and the representative claim must be recognisable as representative (Thomassen 2017: ch. 3); without this recognition of the representation as a representation *of* something, it loses its performative force. Derrida (1988: 18) writes of the performative:

> Could a performative utterance succeed if its formulation did not repeat a 'coded' or iterable utterance, or in other words, if the formula I pronounce in order to open a meeting, launch a ship or a marriage were not identifiable in some way as a 'citation'.

You cannot represent on your own: a representative claim always refers to, or cites, other representations, and its effect depends on how it resonates with other representations. There is no such thing as private representation. The representation gets its authority from repetition: from repeating existing representations and from being repeated through the recognition as authoritative (and, consequently, repetition) by others (Thomassen 2017: ch. 3). The authority of existing representations is reproduced through their repetition in representative claims, that is, their status as taken-as-given, or 'referents', is produced in this way. The individual representative claim can be understood as the production of a referent as its own ground: the representative claim is self-referential (because it performatively constructs the represented), but, at the same time, it must posit something as prior to its performative claim, which will then appear as merely constatively referring to what it posits as a referent. If something appears as a referent in Saward's sense, it is as an effect of representation. The representative claim will take something as given, or posit something as given prior to it, but, *contra* Saward and *contra* some of his critics, the 'presence' of this referent is an effect of the representative claim.

Presence and event

Michael Saward (2010: 39–43) distinguishes between two broad approaches to representation – presence and event:

> In the event approach [. . .] representation is seen as a thing that is done (it still has 'thingness,' but that quality derives from its invocation within, or from being an unstable effect of an event, a practice, or a process). [. . .] 'Representation' is the product of a performance. (Saward 2010: 42)

In other words, representation is an effect of iterability or the play of representation – it is an event, and this makes it impossible to pinpoint it (it is 'unstable'). Saward continues by comparing the presence and the event approach:

> Where the presence approach stipulates meaning, the event approach defers it (or better: deflects it back into the claim-making context). Where the presence approach posits full presence, the event approach is haunted by never-quite-presence(s) [. . .] The presence approach tends to posit a given subject, where the event approach posits an invoked or summoned subjectivity. (Saward 2010: 43)

Representation is an effect of claim-making, and, insofar as there 'is' representation, it is as an uncertain event that is ultimately impossible to pin down. This has implications for the status of Saward's (2010: 15) theory of the representative claim: 'We should not imagine that we can uncover, or discover, the essence of representation, or assume that there is one, superior mode of "representing" the problem of representation.' Therefore, he is 'interested less in locating a correct theory of representation [. . .] My focus instead is on understanding what representation does, rather than what it is; [. . .] to stress its dynamic character rather than its correctly understood forms and types' (Saward 2010: 4). Representation is itself subject to the opacity and instability of the representative claim.

This notion of representation as event is very close, if not identical, to Derrida's notions of representation and iterability. It has implications for how we conceive of the representative claim, as I will show by looking at how Saward treats dog whistle politics and shape-shifting, two issues that bring the 'event-ness' of representation to the fore.

In an article entitled 'Dog Whistles and Democratic Mandates', Robert E. Goodin and Michael Saward (2005) argue that dog whistle politics undermine democratic representation. Their example of dog whistle politics – 'a way of sending a message to certain potential supporters in such a way as to make it inaudible to others' – is the Tory slogan from the 2005 British general election: 'Are you thinking what we're thinking?' (Goodin and Saward 2005: 471; Saward 2010: 46). While (presumably) inaudible to decent Conservative voters, the message was (presumably) audible to xenophobic segments of the population who did not otherwise feel represented. Another example is George W. Bush's reference to the so-called Dred Scott decision during the 2004 campaign. On the face of it, the reference either did not make sense, or may have sounded like Bush was making a case against slavery. However, the reference may have meant something different to a particular subset of the electorate, namely anti-abortion activists. They sometimes see themselves as doing what the antislavery activists were doing, so Bush may have meant this reference as a wink to these groups – part of his core electorate – that, if elected, he would select Supreme Court justices that would overthrow Roe v. Wade in the same way that Dred Scott v. Sandford was eventually overthrown.

For Goodin and Saward (2005: 471), the problem with dog whistle politics is the lack of 'clarity' and 'consistency' of the representative claim and, so, of the relation between represented and representative. The 'mixed messages' of dog whistle claims can be taken up differently by different constituencies or voters (Goodin and Saward 2005: 473), and they thereby undermine democratic representation and the authority of the representative. The problem, then, is the opacity of the representative claim and of the relation between representative and represented. We cannot be sure that representation takes place because (democratic) representation is understood as responsiveness: when voters respond to representative claims, we know whether they are represented or not, but this is impossible to know if the meaning of the representative claim is not transparent, and this is the problem with dog whistle politics.

In their article, Goodin and Saward rely on a view of representation where at least the representative claim can be understood in terms of presence: the literalness of the claim means that it can be identified and individuated and thus be the transparent medium guaranteeing a stable and transparent relation between represented and representative. But what happens when we treat the representative claim as constituted relationally, for instance when the representative claim is constituted through its uptake? The meaning of the claim would be constituted through the re-representations of it, that is, it would be marked by iterability. In that case, we are not just dealing with different interpretations (or uptakes) of the same underlying claim; rather, the claim can no longer be pinned down in a single point but, instead, is dispersed in the play of representations. There never is a stable and transparent representative claim except as the provisional effect of partly arresting the play of representation.

Dog whistle politics raises the question: *was* there representation? The representative claim is a performative, and Derrida (2007b: 446) suggests we can think of performative speech acts as 'speech events'. The new meaning brought about performatively by the representative claim cannot be pinned down, because it only 'is' in the future anterior of what will have been the representative claim, where the future is a future to-come in Derrida's sense of a future that never arrives (Derrida 2005: 86–92; see also Thomassen 2011). This is so because the representative claim is constituted through its uptake – that is, on being re-represented – and these re-representations are also representative claims in their own right. Consequently, they are inherently open-ended. Derrida (2003: 90) writes of the event:

The undergoing of the event [. . .] is [. . .] a certain *unappropriability* of what comes or happens. The event is what comes and, in coming, comes to surprise me, to surprise and to suspend comprehension: the event is first of all *that which* I do not first of all comprehend. Better, the event is first of all *that* I do not comprehend.

We thus have an aporia where, as an event, representation cannot be represented, and yet the event only gains any presence through representation (the event is absolutely singular and so must escape the iterability of representation, but there is no presence outside – and no full presence within – representation). A representative claim must be recognised and, thus, repeated, and not just the content of it but also as a representative claim. The event is always inscribed within iterability (Derrida 2007b: 452–4), and the representative claim only 'is' through its representation. This is why the opacity and instability of representation applies not only to the content of the representative claim, but also to representation itself. Was there representation? The answer can only be given by representing representation, but this immediately creates a distance that cannot be recuperated because it opens up the possibility of iteration.

If representation is not presence, but event, then the problem with dog whistle politics is a general problem of representation: the constitutive instability and opacity of representation (democratic or not). And this is otherwise Saward's (2006: 306) position: 'the representative claim can never be fully redeemed, always contains ambiguities and instabilities. As such, "representation" can be said from this perspective not to exist; what exists are *claims* and their receptions.' Indeed, in *The Representative Claim*, Saward (2010: 58) concludes, 'Arguably [. . .] all representative claims, to some degree, indulge in dog-whistle politics.' However, he still qualifies dog whistle politics as 'perhaps manipulative' and 'strongly manipulative' (Saward 2010: 58, 90). But if the opacity of dog whistle politics is a general feature of the representative claim, then so is manipulation, although with the important caveat that attempts to 'manipulate' always depend for their success on their contingent uptake.

In the case of dog whistle politics, we saw how the representative claim is dispersed in iterability so that it cannot be thought as presence but as event. The representative claim is constituted through iteration – re-representation – in the form of uptake or recognition. In the case of shape-shifting, we are dealing with the same general structure. 'The shape-shifting representative is a political actor who claims (or is claimed) to represent by shaping (or having shaped) strategically his persona and policy positions for certain constituencies and audiences' (Saward 2014: 723). Representation is performance (Saward 2010: 66–70), and shape-shifting occurs when a (would-be) representative takes up different positions at different times or at the same time, thereby representing him- or herself in different ways, while also rearticulating the positions or roles he or she takes up. As Saward (2014: 730) notes, shape-shifting shares with dog whistle politics the deliberate introduction of ambivalence in order to further the success of the representative claim.

As with dog whistle politics, however, shape-shifting lays bare a general structure of representation, what we might sum up with the notion of iterability and the notion of event. The only difference is that, in the case of dog whistle politics and shape-shifting, the opacity and instability of the representative claim is intended, even if the meaning of the claim can never be completely pinned down with reference to the intentions of the claim-maker, because the claim is subject to iterability. The shape-shifting self-representations of a would-be representative are subject to iterability and the play of representation in the same way as any other representative claim. Put differently, the shape depends on the uptake. The self-representations of the shape-shifting representative are constituted through the uptake by the audience, and the effects of this uptake – the potential for rearticulation of the representations – cannot be controlled from the side of the shape-shifter. The representative is an effect of the shape-shifting, but the shape-shifting happens not only through the performances of the would-be representative, but also through the uptake and recognition of the representative as representative and as this or that representative. In this way, shape-shifting is a characteristic of any representative claim, including the sort of representative claim that shape-shifting representatives make about themselves. Shape-shifting is a general characteristic of representation because any representation is subject to iterability and the play of representation through its re-representation. And so the opacity and instability of shape-shifting – which some (but not Saward) may lament – is a general characteristic of representation.

The cases of dog whistle politics and shape-shifting show the full consequences of thinking representation as fully systemic. The representative claim is dispersed in the 'system' of representation, but this system is inherently open – it is marked by iterability or the play of representation. The presence of the representative claim is an effect of the systemic relations of representations, but there is never full presence – hence why we must (also) think of representation as event. As Saward (2010: 145) himself notes, 'Even "presences" take on a more fleeting characteristic because they are first of all "events."' As quoted above, Saward (2006: 306) believes that representation is always ambiguous, unstable and, therefore, does not exist as such. However, when he adds that representative claims and their receptions exist, we must insist that the opacity and instability of representation extends to the claim and its uptake.

Opacity and instability are constitutive, but they are relative rather than absolute; the play of representation is precisely not free play where everything and nothing is possible. One way to conceive of the relative stability and transparency of representation is in terms of the relationship between the individual representative claim and the cultural background codes (Saward 2010), communality (Decreus 2013) or representative repertoire (Hatherell 2014), which serves to pin down the meaning of the representative claim, thus making it possible. The cultural background codes are constituted through performative acts of representation against a background of already existing codes; how certain codes come to persist, and how some come to dominate over others, is a matter of contingency.

Democratic representation and provisional legitimacy

Moving from political to democratic representation, Saward (2010: 144) defines the democratic legitimacy of representation as 'the perception of legitimacy, not legitimacy according to a standard that is posited as independent of the context in which the question arose'. He specifies that 'provisionally acceptable claims to democratic legitimacy across society are those for which there is evidence of sufficient acceptance of claims by appropriate constituencies under reasonable conditions of judgment' (Saward 2010: 145, emphasis removed; see 2014: 733–4 for another formulation). The emphasis on perception places his definition of democratic legitimacy squarely inside the play of representation: 'Democratic legitimation of representation is a contingent product of the complex political play of claim and reception' (Saward 2014: 733).

When Saward emphasises the perception of legitimacy, he is referring to the constituency's perception of the representative claim. He wants to leave the question of legitimacy to 'the constituency and not the theorist or other observer' (Saward 2010: 145); this is the properly democratic approach, he argues, and he also refers to this as the 'citizen standpoint' (Saward 2010: 147). He is therefore interested in the 'actual acceptance (or rejection)' by the constituency (Saward 2010: 152), rather than in hypotheticals or universal yardsticks. This approach pushes the theorist or observer to the background, but not out of the picture altogether: the political theorist is tasked with assessing the conditions under which claims are made and accepted or rejected. For a representative claim to be legitimate, it must be accepted in 'a tolerably open society' (Saward 2010: 151), which is defined in terms of individual and civic liberties (with little mention of economic and social conditions) (Saward 2010: 154–9). It is the role of actual citizens and others to accept or reject the claim, and it is the role of the political theorist to assess whether the acceptance (or rejection) happened under conditions such that we can take it at face value.[2]

Identifying acceptance (or rejection) is a matter of interpretation on the part of the political theorist and can only be provisional because identifying actual acceptance depends on knowing the meaning of the claim accepted and on being able to take the constituency's perspective (Saward 2010: 147–54). Yet, as Saward (2010: 147) seems to acknowledge, the interpretation by 'the theorist or other informed interpreter' is itself a representative claim, and so the two roles of actual acceptance and assessing the conditions of acceptance – citizen and political theorist – cannot be wholly separated. The citizen and the political theorist are both making a representative claim about a representative claim. The observer is herself a participant in the acceptance or rejection of claims, and indeed Saward (2010: 147) rejects the possibility of an objective, universal yardstick of democratic legitimacy.

Since the perception of legitimacy is the basis for democratic legitimacy, it is necessary to consider whose perception – that is, acceptance or rejection – it is. Saward (2010: 148) suggests that 'the appropriate constituency' is the sum of the intended and the actual constituencies of the representative claim. The appropriate constituency is distinguished from 'audiences of other citizens, including, for example, members of the observing media, who are not part of the targeted or intended constituency or are unable or unlikely to see themselves as part of the claim's actual constituency' (Saward 2010: 149–50, emphasis removed). These audiences 'may also have a voice and an impact on the assessment of representative claims' (Saward 2010: 150). It should be clear, though, that constituency is mediated by audience: the meaning of the representative claim that 'the Republican Party is the true defender of blue-collar workers' must first be established before the claim can be accepted or rejected; and for someone to be able and likely to be seen, or to see themselves, as part of the intended or actual constituency, the identity and limits of that constituency must be established. I am a member of an audience before I am a member of a constituency; the latter only exists as the effect of the representative claim and of the mediation of that claim by some audience. There is no constituency without an audience. We thus enter into a complex web of representation and re-representation, where the meaning of the relevant representative claim and the identity of the would-be constituency are never fixed. This is what I referred to above as the 'play' of iterability or representation.

This takes me to what Saward (2010: 152) calls 'acceptance acts', which he also dubs '"acceptance events"' (with quotation marks around the phrase). These are the acts whereby a constituency accepts or rejects a representative claim, and so they are the medium through which to assess the democratic legitimacy of the claim. If we accept the inherent instability and opacity of representation – and there is no reason why, according to Saward, we should not – then these acts are precisely events. They are events because their meaning is, and will always remain, ultimately opaque to both participants and observers. Like events, acceptance acts only exist as represented, and their meaning is forever deferred in a web of iterability.

Saward (2010: 144, 153, 159) introduces the notion of provisionality as a response to this problem: judgements about the democratic legitimacy of representative claims are provisional. Acceptance of a claim must be assessed over time: 'the claim can be respected by observers as long as it receives validation by the relevant proto-constituency at some reasonable future date, and rejected if it does not' (Saward 2010: 159). However, this notion of provisionality, which he takes from Amy Gutmann and Dennis Thompson (see Thomassen 2011), works within the horizon of a not-yet: we are not yet in a position to judge the legitimacy of a claim, but we may be so one day when the conditions are right. Yet, if the acceptance event is inherently opaque, then we will never arrive at this point; with a phrase from Derrida (2005: 86–92), judgement and acceptance will remain to-come, that is, forever postponed and without the possibility of closure. The event of the representative claim is what will have been so, but this future anterior has the character of a future to-come that never arrives.

For the political theorist to be able to judge acceptance acts and legitimacy, they must take place under conditions that Saward summarises with the phrase 'the open society', and which can be summed up as 'openness of criticism, claim and response' (Saward 2010: 154; 2009: 15). We might also sum it up in terms of a general openness and contestability, and this echoes the importance of reflexivity stressed by other authors (Disch 2011: 110–13; 2015: 495–6; Tanasescu 2014: 50–1). While the democratic legitimacy of a representative claim goes through the acceptance or rejection by the potential constituency, this depends on the right conditions being present.[3]

In light of this, consider what Saward (2014: 734) writes about shape-shifting:

> Shape-shifting may obscure or disrupt the basis upon which constituencies may accept or reject representative claims – it may, for example, undermine a clear sense of just what claims are to be accepted or rejected. By the same token, it may make representative claims more difficult to contest, in that shape-shifters may make a slippery, moveable, and complex set of claims that are difficult to 'pin down'.

However, this difficulty in pinning down the meaning of the representative claim is, as we have seen, a general feature of all representation, and we can never be certain what claim someone has accepted or rejected. Saward's (2014: 734) response to what he identifies as a problem with shape-shifting is: 'The difficulties with the first issue may mean that, specifically in cases of shape-shifting, certain systemic conditions may be particularly important to judgements about democratic legitimacy.' That is, in the face of instability and opacity of the representative claim, Saward turns to the conditions of acceptance and rejection, which are identified through the observer perspective of the political theorist. The conditions – the open society – is placed outside the play of representation and its inherent instability and opacity.

When it comes to the democratic legitimacy of a representative claim, Saward assumes the transparency and stability of the claim and of the space for the acceptance and rejection of claims. What is more, he also assumes a certain kind of subject capable of reflecting on the claims made. Citizens and theorists are shaped by the society in which they live, but, under the conditions of the open society, we need not worry how citizens have been shaped:

To the extent that the context is one of pluralism, contestation, and alternative sources of information, the provenance of my preference *does not matter.* From a slightly different angle: in most contexts citizen preferences will be co-constituted in some form, and to some degree, by citizens and elites. This fact is insignificant compared to the conditions of plurality, contestation, and so on. I can accept as *my* preference an idea produced by another so long as I have had sufficient opportunity to do otherwise. (Saward 2014: 734)[4]

Saward is correct that the provenance is less important because the distinction between self- and other-representations is problematic, but this is also the reason why no speech act (or representative claim) is simply 'mine'. I am a subject of representation, and so there is no 'I' behind my acceptance or rejection of a representative claim other than the 'I' constituted through past claims, acceptances and rejections. If I am a subject of representation, the constitutive instability and opacity of representation also applies to my acceptance or rejection of a representative claim. Like dog whistle politics and shape-shifting, the acceptance act depends on its uptake beyond my sovereign control. And so, it does matter where 'I' come from, and genealogies of (incomplete and overlapping) subjectivities are important for understanding the 'quality' of acceptance events and the open society.

Elsewhere, Saward (2006: 304; 2010: 55) uses the phrase 'silencing effects' to refer to a situation where a representative appropriates the voice of the represented, and this may happen even when it is the representative claim that evokes the represented subject (for example, someone claiming that 'feminists vote for Hillary'). This silencing effect is constitutive because we can only speak as particular subject positions which are also defined by people other than ourselves. There is no representation (including self-representation) without silencing. However, as Saward notes, the effect is always uncertain, and silencing requires that the subject is first brought into being through a representative act. The act of silencing also subjectivises, and representation is not the unidirectional imposition of identity (there is always some 'read back').

Conclusion: representation as event

As an event, representation is marked by the structure of the to-come. Opacity and instability are inherent characteristics of representation, and so representation is impossible to pin down. This in turn points beyond responsiveness as a criterion for the legitimacy of representation because, even as contestability and reflexivity, responsiveness tends to rely on the transparency and stability of the meaning of the representative claim: acceptance or rejection of a representative claim can only serve as a basis for assessing the legitimacy of the claim if the acceptance or rejection is indeed acceptance or rejection of the claim being made. The trouble is that the meaning of the claim is inherently opaque and unstable; it is provisional in the sense of a future to-come. It will not even be the claim that was accepted, because there is a constitutive gap between the claim made and the claim judged.

And yet representation happens. Representation may be characterised by opacity and instability, by event-ness and a certain 'play' of representation, but something happens that we call representation. The notion of iterability may help us here. Representation is marked by iterability because any representation must and can be re-represented, and because any representative claim at once constatively re-represents and performatively constructs. That opens representation to a 'play' of iterability and to opacity and instability. However, this 'play' of iterability is not a complete free play. Rather, we are dealing with a 'play' of iterability that happens within a terrain of sedimented iterability (and the sedimentation will sometimes be more, sometimes less). Put differently, a representative claim depends for its success on its resonance with this sedimented iterability, or cultural codes in Saward's terms. The next step is, then, how to conceive of the relationship between the play of iterability and the sedimented iterability, between the performative representative claim that constructs what it represents and the cultural codes it draws upon and is limited by. That relationship can only be analysed in the contexts of representative claims made, but one must also develop a conceptual framework for this analysis. Here Saward's theory of the representative claim is a useful starting point, but only if we accept the full implications of the turns Saward has taken.

Notes

1. Indeed, like Laclau and Mouffe (1987: 82–4), Decreus (2013: 39) himself rejects the discursive/extra-discursive distinction because there is no reality that is not discursive, and so the distinction becomes superfluous. The same, I argue, applies to the existence/being distinction.
2. This division of labour between citizen and political theorist is mirrored in a distinction Saward (2014: 733) makes between the procedural-temporal and the substantive-snapshot views respectively.

3. Contestation is possible because it is always possible to 'read back' representative claims, even when claim-makers try to limit this possibility (Saward 2006: 303–4; 2010: 53–4). Reading back claims is possible because representation is never complete and must be taken up and iterated. Since they are inherently open-ended, all representative claims are read back when recognised and re-represented.

4. Saward (2014: 734) also writes: 'If preferences are endogenous, one might be concerned whether such preferences were "educated" (democratic?) or "manipulated" (undemocratic?) into their current state [. . .]. My approach does not resolve this question so much as dissolve it; if recipients of representative claims accept those claims (contingently or otherwise), then it is the fact of acceptance (or rejection) and not the provenance of the preferences involved that matters.'

11

Representative constructivism's conundrum[1]

Nadia Urbinati

The renaissance of representation and the new terrain of legitimacy

The renaissance of representation in political theory emerges at a time of democratic disenchantment, while citizens' participation in the traditional representative channels – elections and political parties – is facing a serious decline. Whereas citizens desert ballot booths and mistrust parties, political theorists praise representation and indirect democracy. Yet renaissance in a time of disillusionment has some advantage as it presses scholars to be attentive to new forms of representative politics beyond its traditional channels. The theory of representation as claim-making partakes of this fortunate concurrence.

The representative renaissance materialised in two conceptual achievements. The first, which is the older, dates back to the 1960s, before the deliberative turn and as an answer against the conventional conception of representation as a loss of democracy, which was shared for opposite reasons by mainstream liberal-democratic theorists (pluralists, elitists, Schumpeterians) and by proponents of participatory democracy (Walker 1996; Dahl 1996; Barber 1984). Democratic theory showed then no ambiguity in equating representation with electoral appointment and juxtaposing it against participation. To recover it for democratic politics, scholars would have to amend this exclusively institutional conception and acknowledge representation's complexity. This was one of Hanna F. Pitkin's most precious contributions. Pitkin reinstated representation in political theory by interpreting it as a form of political creation, not only against those who deemed it 'by definition' 'anything done after the right kind of authorization', but also against those who regarded it as alienation of the political will to the few (Pitkin 1967: 39).

The second and more recent achievement holds representation to be a process of collective subject construction through the making of claims (Saward 2006, 2010). This approach aims to overcome all residue of pre-political ontology and to question criteria of validation external to political activity itself – thus critically revising both the 'speaking for' approach (as if constituencies existed prior to their representative's appearance) and the normative attitude of deliberative democracy (its taming of claims in the attempt to adapt them to reflexivity and a principled rationality).[2] Representation acquires a new capacity – that of making possible the fully-fledged political appearance of claimants in the forum. Adapting Thomas Hobbes's famous argument for the construction of the sovereign, contemporary constructivists argue that prior to claims' articulation there are no political actors, and no 'people' to begin with (Ochoa 2011; see also Mulieri's chapter in this volume). Iris Marion Young (1997, 2000), Ernesto Laclau and Chantal Mouffe (1985) contributed importantly to this movement, which finds now its most cogent rendering in Michael Saward's theory of representation as claim-making. Saward makes representation synonymous with politics itself as the varied activities that people stage in the sphere of opinion when they stand against or for something, and in so doing express themselves as political actors to modify or affect the overall political discourse of their society. Although it can have an institutional frame and still derives its formal democratic legitimacy from universal suffrage, representation so understood becomes a form of political creativity independent from voting and the representatives' lawmaking function (see Castiglione and Warren's chapter in this volume).

Although connected, 'speaking for' and 'claim-making' diverge as to their relation to democracy and hint at different theoretical implications. The former is naturally sensitive to the question of democratic legitimacy as it does not disconnect the act of 'speaking for' from that of selecting 'standing for' persons through voting. The latter is instead more interested in explaining the phenomenology of advancing issues and constructing claims by a speaker, the potential represented and the audience. The first is open to the quest for normativity. The second mistrusts or downplays issues of normativity such as formal legitimacy because it sees them as external to political representation's expressivity. Representative claim-making celebrates the constructive power of ideology as a discourse that gives reality through interpretations and significations of extant social conditions to groups that re-present themselves before a public which evaluates, judges and reacts to their claims. Representation is not 'speaking for'

as if something pre-existed the speaker and the representative event
and required formal approval by the potential represented; nor is it
reflexive translation of raw claims into ideas that conform with the
basic norms of democratic deliberation. Its reference point is neither
the decision-making domain (formal norms and institutions) nor
the aspiration of amending actual politics of issues that contradict
democracy's principles (moral and epistemic norms). Representative
claim-making becomes an affirmation of realism, the recognition of
the effectiveness of the claim or event by which means a group is created. The group is indeed mobile, wholly artificial, not delimited by
state jurisdiction and potentially borderless. It is the act of claiming
and identifying with claims that makes it; its success in gaining attention is already an evidence of its legitimacy.

The theoretical implications of these two conceptions of representation are also different. A consequence of the 'speaking for'
approach is that representation retains a direct link with democratic
institutions and is based on the electoral consent of constitutionally
free agents, the citizens. Suffrage makes the representatives normatively dependent on the represented and, in addition, it contributes in
enhancing a wave of communication that wraps the entire society –
this speaks for the diarchic nature of representative democracy,
the fact that procedures and the political process are unavoidably
entwined and not autonomous from each other. The claim-making
approach instead holds the link between representation and suffrage,
and representation and institutions, to be peripheral. In *The Representative Claim*, the manifesto of this theory, Saward advances a
conception of representation as enacting citizenship, wherein the latter is not the name of a status (or suffrage and political belonging
in a jurisdiction) but of an event that occurs in public and appeals
to an audience that is not identified necessarily with compatriots
and a national public sphere. 'Representative claims operate across
borders and even across species; they denote shifting power relationships rather than fixed institutions; and they can work democratically and undemocratically' (Saward 2010: 1). Representation is
thus identified with people's activity in concert, and both people and
representative are thought as independent from democracy as a form
of government. Lisa Disch captures quite effectively the ambiguous
relation representative claim-making entertains with democracy: 'it
evacuates the most familiar basis for normative judgments regarding
when representation is democratically legitimate: Is the representative authorized by the represented and accountable to its interests?'
(Disch 2015: 488). Effectively making everything 'representation',

claims-making 'depoliticize[s] the concept' (of representation) whose specificity rested solely on the citizens' voluntary choice of identifying with the claim-maker (Ihalainen et al. 2016: 4).

In this chapter I pursue Disch's line of thought and interrogate representative constructivism from the perspective of democratic legitimacy. If it is true, as Saward writes, that claim-making can be both undemocratic and democratic we would need to know what makes it lean to one side rather than the other, or what makes the phenomenology of representation not simply a political event but moreover an event that complies with democratic norms. Once electoral participation and the ensuing deliberative institutions have been declared peripheral, what makes for democratic legitimacy? The very distinction between the 'audience' and the 'affected' constituency seems to become vague as constructivism entails that there are no 'groups' before they have become 'ideas' and are 'evoked' in the public arena (Saward 2010: 51).

I argue that the tension between claim-making and democratic procedures originates in the remnant of an elitist conceptualisation of proceduralism. Put simply, claim-making falls into the familiar trap that splits democratic politics into two poles: the spontaneous formation of collective subjects (democracy) and the norms regulating it from outside (institutions). Within this pre-deliberative scheme democracy resembles a tale of two cities that border one another but don't mix: the popular and the institutional (Ferejohn 2013; Achen and Bartels 2016). A diarchic conception of democracy offers us a way out of this conundrum as it advances a view of political action that incorporates procedures and amends the dualism between raw masses and a regulated people.

Political activity is free not in the sense of Hobbes's constructivism or as licence and indifference to norms, but because it is an immanently regulated form of public interaction by and among persons who are strangers to each other and have made themselves into equals in authority or as citizens. This holds true also in the case of claim-making outside jurisdictional borders or the institutional system of decision-making within which political representation is embedded. Indeed, although claim-making can group people transnationally and beyond the limits of citizenship as a status, the input moving claimants is that they can influence audiences and activate citizens politically, through the procedures and norms they dispose of (Saffon and Urbinati 2013). Representation as claim-making cannot avoid being tested by a claim of legitimacy, even when it proposes itself as only a creative event that is situated within the domain of opinion and consent.

The basic argument and some preliminary questions

Saward makes two arguments that disentangle political representation from normative criteria of evaluation: that the norm of suffrage is
external to representation; and that any normative theory of democracy risks displacing the actual claims that persons make by priori-
tising some 'would-be' criteria of judgment; yet 'it is the judgments
of appropriate constituencies, not independent theoretical judgment,
that matter to democrats' (Saward 2010: 159). To be political, Saward
invites us to think, representation does not need to be practised in view
of some desirable decisions or be embodied in an institution that is
entitled to make decisions; and to be democratic, representative claims
do not have to be filtered so as to cohere with criteria of impartiality
or reciprocity (as in deliberative democracy) or of security protection
(as in militant democracy).

Both arguments are well posed. As we saw above, they are embedded in a conception of political liberty as political practice, not status. Concerning the former argument, it is true that while elections
designate the representatives they don't make representation, which
is a political process enacted by the represented and the representatives together and that precedes and follows the act of the will or
formal designation (Pitkin 1967; Mansbridge 2003; Urbinati 2006).
Concerning the latter, the filtering of claims in representative democracy is the work of the forum itself, not of some external agents in
the attempt to pre-empt the public sphere of claims that a substantive
conception of democracy deems morally illegitimate. This last point
is part of a complex issue that calls into question two kinds of limits
on political activity and freedom: containment *ex post* and exclusion *ex ante* which would take us to a discussion concerning 'open'
democracy (procedural and pluralist) and 'militant' democracy (substantive and majoritarian).

Containment *ex post*, which is the task of constitutional courts,
intervenes after decisions have been made by elected assemblies,
thus after issues have been discussed freely in the forum as representative claims. Exclusion *ex ante* intervenes instead before the
political game starts by banning from the public arena and the electoral competition as well those claims, groups and parties that a
large majority have deemed risky to the system at the start, in the
moment of designing the constitution. This dualism, which is very
important in order to assess the position of representative claim-
making in relation to democratic government, brings to the fore the
dualism between 'procedural' and 'substantive' democracy, wherein

the former corresponds to a political order that is in theory open to all representative claims and pluralistic, and the latter corresponds to a selective view of democracy that screens in advance the content of claims that are allowed to take part in the formation of the public sphere of opinions (Loewenstein 1937; Müller 2012; Thiel 2013; Kirshner 2014). This dualism reverberates in the two main theories of democratic legitimacy: one that holds the people to be disembodied and not definable before it expresses itself through its procedures and public acts (Lefort 1988; Abizadeh 2002; Ochoa 2011; Näsström 2015), and one that is embedded in a national set of values or a people that pre-exists its constituent political decision and demands an assurance of being protected over time (Miller 1995). It seems that the theory of representation as claim-making finds itself at home quite naturally with the procedural model, which is the perspective in relation to which we are invited to discuss the relationship of representation as claim-making with democracy.

While resting his case on a diarchic premise, Saward breaks with a procedural approach in the attempt to make representation an expression of 'judgment' only. He thinks that, when disconnected from procedural (formally normative) and institutional dimensions, claims can gain in creativity as they state their proximity to people and the public. This is the scheme Saward proposes: political representation is a discursive dynamic by which means 'persons' (not necessarily or not only 'citizens') converge in various ways, thanks to the advocacy of a speaker (the 'maker' of the representative claim) who speaks for them by portraying some specific claims (the 'subject' of representation) that are validated by the judgment of the represented ('constituency') and of the public at large ('audience'). The maker, the claim, the constituency and the audience are the four components of the event of representation, whether or not voting occurs. What makes it 'political' is the free work of rhetorical construction by a speaker and the group of persons he or she represents by making claims. The representative construction is a purely 'ideological' creation and, in this sense, an expression of freedom first and foremost.

Occurring outside state institutions and disconnected from suffrage, representative claim-making is an expression of freedom of association and the formation and open discussion of ideas, yet not necessarily or directly an expression of democratic empowerment, which may or may not occur. It thus complies for sure with a constitutional state based on civil rights and individual liberty, but has less sure a linkage with equal political liberty (and the right to vote), although the latter is an essential condition for the actualisation of claims. I surmise that its democratic legitimacy is evaluated essentially in relation to the free expression of the speakers (the actor, the represented and the audience) and the freedom of association, rather than the self-governing process by the citizens (lawmaking decisions) or the equal share in power between speakers and represented (intra-claim-making democracy).

In relation both to voting and governing institutions and to power relations among political actors that constitute the representative event – the two domains in which questions of democratic legitimacy are pivotal – representation as claim-making is silent. For sure, claim-making is or can be an expression of contestation against conditions of exclusion, injustice and discrimination – in this sense we can consider it a chapter in the negative power of contestation and surveillance that democracy embodies (Rosanvallon 2006; Pettit 2012). But its discursive and judging nature does not require that representative claim-making enter the electoral competition and translate claims into new laws. Hence, the only source of authority or legitimacy that claim-making presumes and demands is informal consent or the expression of political judgment by the people who identify with the claims and by the audience that approves or disproves them. Power in government and political equal power are peripheral while power of opinion and power as symbolic presence are central.

An issue of freedom and success

If representation is made independent from institutions, the evaluation of its democratic credentials seems to be marginal, although not completely so. If we set aside the typical normative democratic test ('free and fair elections' and control and limitation of power), we are left with *two acts of consent* that work as a test and lie outside any formal validation, although they are within the democratic modality of adjudication: 'acceptance' by the represented, and the 'success' of the representative claim with the public at large. The skill of the 'maker', the rejoinder of the 'represented' and the reception by the 'audience' define the triangulation of a successful representative claim as well as the climate of freedom it breeds and contributes to expressing.

This triangulation puts in motion a kind of democratic legitimacy as *voluntary participation* in the forum or the creation of partisan movements or claim movements with no criterion of discrimination between kinds of movement and claims (White and Ypi 2016). To cite a provocative example from Italian history: in liberal pre-Fascist years, when the public expression of political ideas was guaranteed by civil rights but there was not yet universal suffrage, a charismatic Benito Mussolini became a successful 'maker' of the movement of the veterans of World War One, who voiced their social distress against the existing government. The fact that Mussolini strategised the veterans' claims to woo a national audience to a cause that would prove detrimental to constitutional government is external to the evaluation of his success as a representative. As said before, representative claim-making rejects substantive views of democracy and containments *ex ante*. All in all, Mussolini's veterans' movement was a case of claim-making and in this sense a democratic expression of people's active presence in the public sphere, although its proposal would not necessarily advance democracy. Their claim-making had a democratic character as an event. The same can be said of any other movement that relies upon informal consent and the factual identification of diverse persons through issues that a leader articulates successfully. Representative claim-making does not make any promise except for acting in a climate of freedom of speech and association.

Reception or 'adhesion' by a potential constituency and by a larger audience (the two acts of consent) is the basic 'adjudicator' of the success or failure of a claim and its maker. Relying upon a similar phenomenology, Laclau maintained that politics and democracy are interchangeable insofar as they both denote one identical way of proceeding: creating a political narrative that can make sense of the many voices, expectations and claims existing in a given society; and devising a hegemonic ideology that is capable of unifying and mobilising them towards an objective a leader defines. Similarly, the representative work consists in devising common interests and prescribing common objectives to make one strong collective actor out of many individuals and groups (Laclau 2005). But the similarity between Laclau's constructivism and claim-making constructivism ends here.

Indeed, Laclau was not simply interested in the making of claims or constructing a representative event. His interest in representation was in view of achieving power at the state level; for this reason, he did not discard elections, party politics and the winning of a majority; he did not content himself with raising issues and alerting an audience. Seen from the angle of giving words and credibility to a represented unity (a group), the work of the maker was to Laclau a chapter in rhetoric and performed in view of achieving a goal that lay beyond it. Hence he suggested we interpret the act of representing as expressive of a kind of rationality that belongs only to politics – a rhetorical rationality made of myths, imagination and a narrative that would allow the speaker to convince many different persons and one-issue groups to focus only on the equivalences unifying them in order to make their political action effective collectively against proponents of opposite interests, and in view of winning the political competition for power and making decisions consistent with their interests and claims (Laclau 1996: 87–98). This ideological construction of a collective actor or 'the people', Laclau agreed, is embedded in the foundation of modern representative government and not limited to making claims public and winning consent to a cause (Laclau 2014). The ideological or rhetorical character of representation is to him unavoidably connected to issues of power and government. To restate the diarchic argument, Laclau thought that the two levels together – that of the will and that of judgment – defined the political world of representation, not each of them separately.

Mark A. Kishlansky, in his analysis of the birth of the electoral process in seventeenth-century England, has offered an important confirmation of the diarchic character of representative government. He showed there was a chronological and functional link between the adoption of the electoral method to appoint lawmakers; the transformation of the delegates from speakers chosen by ascriptive classes of unequal subjects in political representatives of equal electors; and the emergence of ideologically constructed forms of grouping (Kishlansky 1986: 12–21). Although elections have always been considered an aristocratic institution, in modern states the electoral process stimulated two movements that became crucial to the birth of democracy. On the one hand, it touched off a separation between society and politics, or, better said, a transition from *symbiotic* relationships between the delegates and their communities to forms of unification that were thoroughly *symbolic* or *politically constructed*. On the other hand, the disassociation of the candidates from their social class foregrounded the role of speech and ideas in politics and finally the unifying and partisan function of representation. A similar process took place in France with the revolution of 1789. There, too, elections gave birth to entirely new cleavages and identifications made according to ideological criteria by deliberation and voluntary associations among legally equal voters. Clubs and political aggregations took over the whole country, binding people who lived far away and severing neighbours (Cochin 1979: 33–47).

Within that diarchic political context in which representation was unavoidably both claim-making and an institution, it happened that Emmanuel-Joseph Sieyès and Immanuel Kant translated what was then factual constructivism into a theory that posited representation as the legitimate form of political presence as a practice that pertained to all human relations insofar as they are artificially constructed (Urbinati 2016: chs 4 and 5). Representation became the name of a process for making political subjectivity and the public world, at the very same time unifying citizens according to interpreted and chosen issues and pluralising their belongings and partisan allegiances. Hence Disch makes constructivism start with the representative turn of the eighteenth century, a revolutionary shift from the social determination (ascriptive estates or classes or identities) to a wholly political determination (political representation); from 'topographical [social] categories' to representation as a 'hegemonic practice' or making politics as a grand process by which means the identity of the represented is wholly made by the citizens in their political conflicting struggle for power (Disch 2015: 490). Disch adds:

> The idea is not that the representative makes up the represented from scratch. [. . .] The idea is that the subject of democratic politics –what we understood as a people, a constituency, or a group – becomes recognizable as a unified and not merely aggregated entity only by means of representation. (Disch 2015: 490)

Seen from outside its institutionalised form, representation consists in free vindication of claims and their free acceptance (or contestation and refusal) by the addressees and the audience at large. This extra-institutional rendering confirms its competitive nature and the celebration of freedom associated with it. Saward is thus right when he argues that questions of democratic legitimacy are out of place here; but he should add they are out of place *at this stage* since claim-making configures a movement of opinions with not yet a direct role in authoritative decisions. In conclusion, representative claim-making in the pre- or not-institutional stage relies solely upon civil rights; it is associated with the construction of opinions and claimants in the public sphere and the freedom of speech and association to advocate and organise for or against. It complies in all respect with liberal legitimacy. As anticipated above with the case of Mussolini, all representative claims, regardless of their content, participate in the free atmosphere created by the open and public arena of contestation and communication. This is essential to a representative government which can have a vivid echo outside the national community and even in countries that are not themselves democratic. The global communication of ideas and the system of information define the *borderless public* within which representative claim-making occurs and becomes influential (as the well-known cases of Bono, Al Gore, Angelina Jolie and their representative struggles show). However, issues of indirect power make the quest of democratic legitimacy not truly out of place or peripheral insofar as claim-making is not simply an expression of freedom but more precisely an expression of freedom that influences a given institutional system and has an impact in the decision-making activity (Mulieri 2013). Representative claim-making helps us understand how democratic legitimacy is more complex and richer than formal authorisation through voting although it cannot be wholly dissociated from it.

Exit, voice and loyalty

Albert O. Hirschman's (1970) three-part division of civil and political freedom as expressing the individual's propensity to 'exit' a game, to 'voice' their opinions and to state or change their 'loyalty' is an excellent paradigm to explain the kind of legitimacy representation as claim-making invokes. The former two are central to our case. As an expression of exit and voice, claim-making presumes an open and free public sphere; it denotes a democratic practice that is projected towards consent and enhances communication among people; it is a form of interpellation to the public in the name of commonly shared principles that justify the making of those claims. As for 'loyalty', this is certainly dependent on the maker's persuasiveness and the success of the claim but does not require any factual or ascriptive identity of the constituency. Since judgment by the represented and by the audience at large is crucial in the adjudication of the success of the maker and the claim, loyalty is not blind faith or acritical partisan adhesion to a claim.

Representative claim-making has an unavoidable pragmatic character as it elaborates and gives voice to issues that some addressees recognise as objective and reasonable. Thus it is primed to generate a movement that is less tied to loyalty than a political party and more interested in attracting attention to the claim (in this sense being successful). Representative claim-making is defined by 'voice' and 'exit' (or its threat) even more than by 'loyalty'. This is what makes it different from a political party, which is also a representative group united by some claims or projects and personated by some leaders or maskers. While a party entails a certain degree of faithful adhesion by its members or a partisan identification, a claim-making phenomenon of identification is more directly connected to the practice of advocacy and its efficacy (in publicising, influencing and obtaining results).

Representative claim-making is a chapter in 'single issue' movements that Moisei Ostrogorski opposed early on against organised political parties as examples of a truly liberal attitude towards political association and the freedom of the constituency from the imposition of an irrational trust to a doctrine or a platform or a 'we' pre-existing it:

> The object of each movement was the redress of a grievance; its aim was specified and limited; and the combination formed was consequently a provisional organization destined to come to an end with the triumph of the particular cause which had called it into life. (Ostrogorski 1902, vol. 1: 133).

In addition, unlike representative claim-making, the political party has an organisation that makes it not directly or solely dependent on a skilful leader (although it may need such a leader) and not directly subjected to the verdict of its sympathisers and the audience at large and even votes (although it seeks success with both of them, not only with the electors). The party retains a kind of existential autonomy from claims, claimants and the makers that a claiming movement doesn't because the party is supposed to last beyond the satisfaction of a claim. In addition, the party is primed to include several different claims and not to speak for one specific group because its goal is that of attracting many votes or as much consent as possible.

In a representative democracy both parties and one-issue movements are vital and needed, but their character is very different: while the former entails democratic diarchy, the latter wants for sure and essentially to be an affirmation of judgment (that is to say of political views and opinions). This difference casts some light on the relationship of representative claim-making with democracy.

The movement that representative claim-making engenders is an exquisite example of informal consent formation, vindication and mobilisation. Consent does not, at this stage, need to pass through voting and can very much remain what it is: a free process of 'invocation' (Saward 2010: 4) in the name of some issues and in front of the public that judges them. Acceptance versus refusal (of a subject) and reception versus refutation (of a maker) by the persons who recognise themselves in the claim made by the maker, and moreover by the public at large (local, national and global): these stages confirm that claim-making aims at a strong manifestation of consent and belongs in the domain of opinion movements.

The question is that although not endowed with authoritative power in and by itself, consent is no weak power, and the maker who seeks and impersonates it may have a strong impact on people's imaginary, state institutions, and finally voters and decision-makers. A claim-making movement may actually have more impact on the opinion at large than a political party; it may induce decisions by electors or institutions even if is not intentionally organised in view of partaking in the decision-making process. It is thus precisely its informality that challenges us to interrogate it from the point of view of democratic legitimacy, because we assume that not only voting procedures are a form of power but also the extra-institutional world of opinion and claim-making.

Informal power and the challenge to equality

The main objection to the claim-making theory of representation raised in scholarship so far points to the traditional form of democratic legitimacy as voting authorisation. Sofia Näsström has posed this problem clearly: 'to act in the name of the people does not in itself qualify as a democratic form of representation. What is required is that the act is committed to the principle of equality' (Näsström 2015: 2). Saward would agree with this objection but would conclude that the issue of democratic legitimacy is misplaced here. In effect, the issue of political equality collides with the role of leadership because although all people involved are free to speak and in this sense legally and morally equal, it is a fact that representation, whether electoral or not, projects the speaking ability of one, not the many. Representation has both a democratic and an elitist side: the qualities of a candidate are judged by the constituency in relation to both the articulated claims and their efficacy on the field (Pitkin 1967: 90). Thus although every citizen can become a representative in theory and *de jure* and speak for a cause that many people share, citizens tend to select, formally or not, those whom they judge to be better advocates. They do not choose randomly; they feel it is not enough that the candidate belongs to their group (they, in fact, discriminate within their own group); they do not want someone who holds ideas opposite to theirs. A maker is an advocate who needs to share the claim they advance in order to perform more effectively yet not to the point of being an uncritical partisan. Their adhesion to the cause is not blind trust. Concerning the constituency, it is made of followers yet not blind followers either, as they have to retain some critical autonomy from the leader in order to be able to judge the leader's performance and contribute in recalibrating their strategy, if needed. This process of advocacy shows how complex is equality in politics and why political representation can be hardly descriptive, as said above.

As the maker and the constituency need each other in order to exist, representation is a form of interdependence, not straight equality. It entails that the represented are not passive recipients of the maker's rhetoric as they look for some commonalities between themselves and with their speaker, and in this way cooperate in the representative claim-making (Disch 2015). But clearly, representative claim-making is not more democratic than representation terminating in voting: both have a complex relationship with equality as both configure a form of politics that is exposed to leadership and power verticalisation. Thus Bernard Manin has defined representation as an aristocratic emendation of democratic equality that cannot exist outside a competitive mood and without leadership. Elections set some limits on both of them and induce some accountability. In their absence, what kind of democratic limits can be envisaged on competition among claims and on leadership that is capable of rebalancing the unequal power internal to the representative phenomenon? Claims of political equality have been made to solve this problem. Yet political equality is not a clear-cut concept.

Political equality is complex, particularly when analysed outside the normative context of suffrage. Charles Beitz has argued that the issue of inequality of political influence in the domain of opinion is open to interpretative controversies first of all because of the complexity of the principles of 'political equality' and 'political influence' and, second, because it takes different manifestations in representative politics or when considered in relation to the citizens who want to express their voices and the candidates who claim for an equal condition of competition (Beitz 1989: 194–5).[3] Beitz asks the important question of whether we should retain the expression 'political equality' or abandon it when we talk of extra-electoral participation (which is precisely the case with representative claim-making) since 'it confuses matters of institutional design with deeper questions' about the actual distribution of performative skills and material resources to make it effective. Thus, Beitz proposes to interpret political equality in the informal domain of opinion as *fairness* or the *stipulation* of treating citizens equally – equality of condition and opportunity to have voice and be heard; equality of people's practice and personal engagement. This stipulation stresses moral commitment but imports no certain command as it rests on the subjective will, character and disposition of the maker or the leader.

This rendering, which stresses the moral more than the institutional aspect, takes us back to the point where we started – namely the exigency of recovering the procedural interpretation of political equality although within a diarchic conception, which makes room for norms regulating how participation in opinion-making translates into decisions. Besides, when representation as claim-making is involved, we do not vindicate an equal distribution of the basic political power of making decisions (normative argument) but call for a non-futile participation by people who freely express their mind, try to influence the speaker and in this sense impose responsiveness on the speaker and make him or her somehow accountable. Absent the threat of elections, the only control that the represented can effectively exert on the maker is the threat of 'exit', of withdrawing consent, as we saw above. In substance, the protection of basic rights of liberty is essential to a meaningful political equality within non-electoral representation.

Representation synthesises two claims: that of control, which can be performed by institutions and constitutional provisos but also by public forms of monitoring through the press and the information system; and that of direct action by the citizens, wherein 'action' can be validated through formal contestation, petitions, movements of protest all of which can be phenomena of representative claim-making. Clearly, political equality is the ruling criterion in both instances: that of distributing the power to make decisions *and* that of forming opinions, advancing proposals and advocating for or against a cause in the name of rights that all citizens and persons should enjoy. These two claims together entail that a democratic form of representation does not merely require popular control of government (classical electoral proviso) but also that such control be conducted on equal terms (Urbinati 2010). This is the kind of democratic legitimacy within which we interrogate political representation, as both claim-making and institution lawmaking.

Political equality can be better assured by formal instances like elections, while it is less securely assessable when spontaneous participation is concerned, which retains a broad level of imprecision and informality as with claim-making. For sure, political liberty lives also in this spontaneity and imprecision, no less fundamental to democracy than elections. Thus, Saward writes, correctly, that it is an open question whether 'the language of "legitimacy" is appropriate in this context' (Saward 2010: 144). Since the events of representation are or may be 'sporadic' and 'multisided' and since they do not need to be instantiated in electoral representation or voting, Saward is right to propose a broad and elastic notion of democratic legitimacy: 'provisionally acceptable claims to democratic legitimacy across society are those for which there is evidence of sufficient acceptance of claims by appropriate consistencies under reasonable conditions of judgment' (Saward 2010: 145).

Within this informal world of sporadic representative claim-making, freedom and civil liberty are more central conditions than democratic equality insofar as the represented or would-be represented must be free to accept or refuse the claim(s) made by the maker and express their views publicly. The same holds true for the self-appointed speakers, who speak about and for a portion of humanity (for instance, people who suffer torture or poverty or the exploitation of natural resources and the like) and may or may not be accepted by their hypothetical constituency. It is up to the constituents' moral responsibility and political freedom to speak back to claim-makers or declare their adhesion to them or to simply desert them and be indifferent to their speaking performance. It is up to the audience to magnify or demote claims and press institutional actors to take initiative. Thus Saward is right that the relationship between the maker and the represented can hardly be an issue measurable in terms of democratic legitimacy.

In conclusion, claim-making is a case of opinion-making and freedom of speech and association, of advocacy and denunciation. It is not directly related to equal power in decision-making (although its final goal might be a change in decisions or influencing elected representatives in their decision-making power). It is an expression of informal participation, not yet of a fully-fledged democratic participation that aims directly at decision-making institutions (although decisions can follow that reflect those claims). Representation as claim-making belongs in the domain of opinion or political judgment only; it entails first of all acts of freedom in the form of discourse in public, acceptance, refusal or indifference. Exit and voice are its two performative manifestations, which make it an exercise of civil liberty.

Which legitimacy?

Claim-making's liberal character and its weak democratic legitimacy raise the question of the kind of legitimacy it involves or mobilises. Max Weber proposed a distinction that can be helpful here, between legitimacy in relation to value and legitimacy in relation to goal. The former is connected to belief and trust and applies to the impact of the leader on people's imagination – charisma is within this scope, which involves a view of legitimacy that relies entirely on the emotional identification (embodiment) of the subjects with the image, the words and the person of the maker (Laclau's populist leader exemplifies it). The second kind of legitimacy is linked to institutional functioning – in this case, legitimacy is projected onto institutions as embodying the sovereign (the president), guarding the unity of the bodies politic (state bureaucracy, justice, police and the army), expressing the will of the sovereign in legislating (the parliament or Congress) and in administering (the Executive). All these institutions entail forms of representation (of the sovereign) and their function that laws and rules regulate and that define their normative legitimacy. Of the two, the first one seems the domain within which we can situate claim-making because the central role is played by the maker and by consent while no electoral choice is presumed. The kind of legitimacy that better fits it is associated with the power of the maker to affect people's imagination and emotion and that of the people to make the leader feel the impact of their opinion. Charisma is thus the highest form of claim-making legitimacy, which is democratic only in the sense that it relies on people's free consent and voice, but without regulating the way in which consent is extracted, calculated and checked.

However, we are here talking of a charismatic power that is not blind identification or adhesion because, as said above, representative claim-making has a pragmatic nature that makes it subjected also to a functional kind of legitimacy. Nonetheless the maker achieves strong ascendancy over the people in whose name she speaks and on the audience she alerts; the audience's voluntary 'acceptance' of the maker suggests that consent makes here a kind of democratic leader. Acceptance is a manifestation of power – both of the makers (with their influence on the represented and the larger audience) and of the represented and the audience (with their acceptance or rejection of the maker) – and the event that makes the claim of legitimacy pertinent. Let us investigate briefly the implication coming from 'acceptance'.

Representative claim-making can involve a quest of emancipation from subjection and in this sense a quest of power that seeks decisions and is not only symbolic. Laclau and Mouffe have thus rendered representative politics as the making of hegemonic equivalence out of different claims thanks to which a maker (an individual Caesar or a collective 'new Prince') creates an effective strategy – 'effective' insofar as capable of unifying scattered individuals in one collective actor with the goal of achieving state power. The quest of democratic legitimacy is in this case well posed. Yet, as we have anticipated, Saward's view of representative construction is not connected directly to state power and is not identifiable with so strong a notion of constructivism. His claim-making remains an opinion movement and this means that it can enjoy much more freedom from formal norms of designation and accountability.

It seems we have thus *two kinds of constructivism* – one aiming at creating the people as an institutional reality and one remaining on the terrain of opinion. The latter, which concerns us here, is democratic in the sense in which all movements of opinion or contestation are democratic – for sure they mobilise people and are not purely elitist as the maker has to cooperate with the referent (the group) in order for the claim to be effective. Thus Disch writes: 'the representative (or "subject") comes to be seen *as* representative not simply by acting for a constituency by means of a "construction or portrayal of himself (subject) and [the] constituency (object)." Claim making is strategic' because the work of the maker must pass the test of people's receptivity (Disch 2015: 492). *Proximity* is what makes it pass the test and thus gives it legitimacy, the closeness of the speaker to the represented insofar as both share the same claims and identify with them. As we said above, this renders claim-makings more similar to one-issue movements than political parties.

Legitimacy via proximity brings us back to where we started: if claim-making wants to be simply a form of discourse that gives strength to one issue then its credential is primarily liberal as rights-based; if it aims instead at being a strategy for conquering the decision-making power then the question of democratic legitimacy cannot be evacuated and proximity is not sufficient for justification. Like any movement of opinion, claim-making can figure in democratic diarchy. However, if we break all links that connect judgment and the will, and if we assume that judgment is what makes for representation, we confine legitimacy to 'efficacy' and give the audience (succeeding in getting support) and thus charisma (the power of the maker) a pivotal role in adjudicating the rightness of the claim. The success of the strategy adopted by the maker and testified by the favourable reception of an audience is not of course a test of democratic legitimacy unless we identify the latter with the mere fact of consent, any kind of consent. But the criteria that regulate consent (for instance whether the people are involved and how) are not irrelevant or merely optional for democracy although they may be so if the goal of the actors is simply that of making a statement or alerting

an audience to certain issues. The reference point for political success does not need to be the suffrage if the aim of representation is
not institutional. In this case reference to the question of democratic
legitimacy can be held peripheral.

Thus Saward has a good reason to resist the argument of democratic legitimacy and avoid making procedures ('free and fair elections') play a role in validating the event of representation. The
problem is that once claim-making breaks with the diarchic perspective of democracy and states the creative autonomy of the ideological work and its independence from norms and voting, we are left
with no democratic norm of judgment *apart from* the factual success of claims with an audience and the constituency (both of which
are a construction of discourse). It may be interesting at this point
to understand why the diarchic criterion is unsatisfactory to claim-
making. Constructivist theorists question democratic diarchy in the
name of a more radical democratic construction of the political subject as a process that does not need to rely on norms (elections)
which are, they think, external to the participatory process of claim-
making. In suggesting that the democratic norms constrain participation from outside they seem to share a vision of liberty that echoes
Hobbes's state of nature, where freedom is indeed before and outside norms and the law. Claim-making deems norms and free action
mutually exclusive presumably because it embraces a narrow notion
of 'procedures' and institutions as limits that tame the expression of
claims from outside. This leaves it no choice but to rely only on the
reception by the audience and the constituency – its success is identified with public receptivity.

Claim-making's dissatisfaction with a 'merely normative' and
procedural democracy originates in a view of the legitimacy normativity as external to the process of political participation (representative claim), or 'context-independent' (Disch 2015: 496). Yet
the conundrum of siding either with the audience (internal criterion) or with voting (external norm) cannot be solved unless we
transcend this dual image of politics through a vision of 'democratic procedures' as immanent to democratic doing rather than
a set of rules imposed on it. It can be solved by overcoming the
Schumpeterian paradigm of proceduralism, the vessel of the traditional conception of democratic procedures as a realistic claim of
functionality versus 'pure democracy'. Democracy would be highly
inconceivable without procedures shaping languages and actions
toward discussion and decisions, which means that there is no
'the people themselves' outside the constructing work of the entire

panoply of rights, rules and procedures that compose the universe we call 'democracy'.

Claim-making constructivism would need to make two essential moves in order to reinstate the role of ideology and consent in politics *without* falling into the trap of either bowing to a factual success (the audience as the verdict) or reducing representation to formalistic procedural doing (to the electoral act). A tentative solution would follow Claude Lefort, who redefined the meaning of procedures when he depicted representative democracy as 'institutionalised uncertainty' because it is 'founded upon the legitimacy of a *debate* as to what is legitimate and what is illegitimate – a debate which is necessarily without any guarantor and without any end' (Lefort 1988: 17). To attain the full status of legitimacy, a constructivist theory of representation as claim-making would need to emancipate itself fully from the elitist hold over democratic proceduralism and criticise the dualism of 'action' and 'procedures' coming with it. Democratic action, even when informal and not conducted directly in view of a decision, is a proceduralised behaviour as it embodies norms and involves free and autonomous subjects that are mentally disposed to make others attentive to (although not necessarily in agreement with) their claims and ultimately ready to stimulate discussion and achieve a decision. Actors who make claims and talk to an audience do not describe a situation in which unruled masses are transformed into public actors by some straitjacket procedures. There is no public activity or collective process (no matter how informal) without immanent procedures to begin with (Kelsen 2013; Bobbio 1987; Habermas 1996). The game of politics is a game between claims in view of achieving a broader audience yet also reaching goals that are very concrete, like promoting or blocking a political project, changing or making laws, imagining new institutions, or removing the conditions that have provoked a claim-making process. In this sense, norms, procedures and institutions are always the horizon in which claims are made and recognised as representative.

Notes

1. I would like to thank Lisa Disch, whose inspiration has been an invaluable source of reflection through the years and her comments on a first draft of this paper have been precious.
2. As Bernard Manin pointed out, in Jürgen Habermas's theory of democracy, inclusion in the deliberative process is justified for developing 'rationally motivated' forms of participation (Manin 1987: 367). In

the Preface to the new German edition of his *The Structural Transformation of the Public Sphere: An Inquiry into a Category of Bourgeois Society* (Habermas 1990), Habermas expressed his agreement with Manin's criticism of the argument he had made in his 1973 book *Legitimationsprobleme im Spätkapitalismus* (translated into English in 1975 by Thomas McCarthy with the title *Legitimation Crisis*). The English translation of Habermas's new Preface was published with the title 'Further Reflections on the Public Sphere' in 1992.

3. Beitz dissected in detail the implications coming from two different approaches to the protection of equality of political influence: one that is consistent with the 'insulation' of institutions from social interests and one that wants to contrast the formation of social inequality so as to block at the start the potential for an unequal political influence. A procedural conception of democracy, he rightly concludes, is more consistent with the former than the latter. Yet once we follow the former, we have to choose between establishing an equilibrium between the candidates so that they can compete on a fair base and giving the voters the chance to enter the competition if they so choose. The debate over electoral campaign finance in the United States focuses on the former, although a more radical conception of political equality in representative government is interested also in the latter (Beitz 1989: 196–7).

Part III

Constructivist representation: critique and reproduction of power

12

Exploring the Semantics of
Constructivist Representation

Alessandro Mulieri

Introduction

In this chapter, I present an analysis of the semantics of an increasingly popular view of representation in today's Anglophone political theory: constructivist representation. I propose to distinguish between two different versions of constructivism: a moderate and a radical version. I argue that there are important conceptual and semantic differences between these two views that become evident upon specifying the role that different meanings of representation play in configuring constructivist accounts of representation. I begin with a description of three ideal-typical meanings of representation, which are the building blocks for various accounts of political representation. Within constructivist approaches, I demonstrate that a distinction between a radical and a moderate version emerges due to the different meanings of representation that a constructivist theorist prioritises.

There are important 'normative' implications to providing a semantic account of the constructivist approach, and to parsing its different versions thereby. Clarity on which meanings of representation are politicised in a specific model of political representation also tells us something about the narrative of political legitimacy that is bound to this model. Indeed, the linguistic meanings that we use to define someone as a representative also affect whether people are likely to accept that person as their political representative. This means that the question 'what is the meaning of political representation?' is always bound to the question 'what makes someone who claims to be a representative politically legitimate in this role?'. I am particularly interested in the political implications that arise from the appropriation by scholars of global governance of radical linguistic constructivism, whom I argue mobilise this specifically radical meaning of constructivist representation to lend their vision of governance democratic legitimacy.

Three meanings of representation

To explore the ways in which 'semantic' meanings of representation shape different views of political representation, this section presents and describes three ideal-typical meanings of representation that will be used in the analysis. If there is a *leitmotif* in the philosophical and historical literature on representation, it is the idea that representation is polysemic; it is a word to which different meanings attach depending on the specific contexts in which it is used (Chartier 1989; Ginzburg 2001; Hofmann 1974; Mulieri 2016; Podlech 2004; Sintomer 2013).

In his book *Repräsentation: Studien zur Wort- und Begriffsgeschichte von der Antike bis ins 19. Jahrhundert* published in 1974, the German philosopher Hasso Hofmann provides a conceptual, historical analysis of the semantics of representation. Hofmann argues that, when talking about representation (and by this, he means the Latin word *repraesentatio* and its derivative meanings in English, French, German, Italian and so on), we have to keep in mind that 'in the beginning was the word, not the concept' (Hofmann 1974: 35).[1] Examining the history of representation through this interpretive lens helps Hofmann show that the problem of understanding representation was semantic and linguistic before it became conceptual. The meanings of representation presented here are inspired by Hofmann's conceptual history of *repraesentatio*. They are not universal or trans-historical concepts but rather semantic clusters of meanings that help us understand the different 'logics' in which we can say that someone represents something or someone else.[2]

The first ideal-type is that of a *mandate*, modelled on Hofmann's notion of *Stellvertretung*, which sees representation as a juridical form of substitution in which a representative stands for a represented. Hofmann (1974) argues that the meaning of representation as *Stellvertretung* does not originate in classical Roman law but in the Middle Ages when the development of a society in which commerce and trade played a key role made necessary the invention of a new sense of *repraesentatio* – specifically, one that could account for stipulations regarding certain specific economic activities. Representation as *mandate* aims at an almost perfect correspondence between the wills of two people and is a form of identity between the represented and the representative that is objective insofar as it can be legally regulated.

The second ideal-type of representation that we will consider is the notion of *mimetic representation*, which is one way of explaining Hofmann's concept of *Urbild-Abbild Dialektic*. This meaning of representation holds that there must be a relationship between an original and its copy, something that makes it very similar to a form of *mimesis*. Hofmann explains that the first use of representation in the meaning of *Urbild-Abbild Dialektik* can be found in the eleventh-century debate over the way in which Christ's body is supposed to be present in the Eucharistic host.[3] This meaning of *repraesentatio* then spilled over to the epistemological, theological and artistic worlds. The core idea of *mimetic representation* is that there must be a relationship between an original source and its copy. This relationship takes the shape of an aesthetic relationship with a mimetic character, namely it is based on the idea of a perfect correspondence between an original image and its copy.[4]

The third idea-type of representation considered in this contribution is that of *symbolic representation*, which translates the German word *Darstellung*.[5] In contrast to *mimetic representation*, likeness is not a typical characteristic of *symbolic representation*. In the latter, the represented-representative relationship is more complex and requires a more dynamic interpretation than *mimetic representation*. In the case of *symbolic representation*, the task of the representative, far from being limited to the etymological notion of representation of making something present, is aimed at conveying a broader meaning. In this way, it explicates what is only implicit in *mimetic representation*; namely, that the link between the representative and the represented is open to interpretation. Even the clearest example of *symbolic representation* requires additional reflection in order to explain the nature of its symbolism.

The voluntaristic view

A longstanding conception, which can be named voluntaristic, has identified the practice of democratic representation exclusively with elections, arguing that there is a qualitative difference between delegated sovereignty through representation and a genuine and spontaneous expression of popular sovereignty in direct participatory assemblies.[6] On this interpretation, which is most thoroughly criticised by Nadia Urbinati's work on representation (Urbinati 2006), the concept of popular sovereignty is synonymous with 'the will of

the people' and cannot be alienated or transferred through representation to anyone else because it is seen in terms of a pre-existing
will, as a source of indivisible and absolute power. According to
Urbinati, Rousseau is a famous advocate of this view because, as he
writes, 'sovereignty cannot be represented for the same reason that
it cannot be alienated. It consists essentially of the general will and
the will cannot be represented' (Rousseau and May 2002: 198). In
Urbinati's view, Rousseau glorifies an anti-deliberative strong conception of participatory democracy in his idea of the general will.
Moreover, this view of the fundamental incompatibility of democratic
popular sovereignty and representation has had a huge influence in
democratic theory.

In Urbinati's opinion, the voluntaristic understanding of sovereignty has also indirectly served the cause of the critics of the 'ideology
of democracy', above all Schumpeter and the democratic elitists. As
she explains, these theorists of democracy make Rousseau's conception of sovereignty

> the norm of modern democracy discourse in order to trap democracy in
> the cul-de-sac dualism of the 'unrealistic' 'classic doctrine' of the general
> will or the realistic rendering of the will of the people as the factual will
> of an elected class. (Urbinati 2006: 52–3)

The most prominent advocate of the voluntaristic interpretation of representation in the contemporary debate on democratic theory is probably Bernard Manin in his *Principles of Representative Government*.[7]
Manin sees representation in two ways. On one hand, representation
can be seen as a formalistic procedure exclusively equated with elections (Manin 1997: 161–92). In this way, representation is a concept
based on formalistic procedures of authorisation and accountability.
On the other hand, the aristocratic nature of elections also means that
representation is a form of deliberative activity with elitist outcomes.
Indeed, the inherent advantage of representative government is that
it is able to select the wisest and most capable people. Likewise, it
allows for the possibility that these people are better than the average citizen at discussing and deliberating over laws that express the
common good.

In Manin's view, however, elections guarantee the democratic
nature of popular government because they connect the representative's preferences to the consensus of the represented, or what he
calls the 'verdict of the people'. On this view, representation is seen
as a formal instrument for guaranteeing the 'indirect' presence of the

people in the representative's decisions, insofar as the representative can be sanctioned at the next election if he or she does not properly respond to the 'will' of the represented (Manin 1997: 175–83). While contrasting his own position with Schumpeter's, Manin explains that the 'democratic' function of elections lies in their power of sanction of the representative based on the retrospective judgement of the represented (Manin 1997: 200). However, apart from this power of sanction at the time of the vote, Manin is very sceptical of the role that the people can have in the intra-electoral periods or outside the channels of parliamentary politics. As he puts it:

> [T]he electorate as a whole rarely expresses itself outside elections, though this can happen. Most of the time, then, the expression of public opinion remains partial in the sense that it is only the point of view of a particular group, however large. (Manin 1997: 171)

The voluntaristic view mostly relies on the two meanings of *mandate* and *mimetic representation* in order to outline its model of political representation. As a result, this view tends to erase, diminish or underestimate the political relevance of *symbolic representation*. The starting point of this view of democratic representation is the belief that it is impossible for modern representative democracies to have the same 'authentic' democratic form of political legitimacy that ancient democracies had. The argument works as follows. We can't have true ancient popular government because of the social and economic conditions of the modern world. Accordingly, we have to rely on a second-best form of popular government, representative democracy, hoping to come as close as possible to ancient virtuous popular government. Accordingly, as Madison and Constant stress in their writings, we have to adopt representation in order to make popular government possible in modern states.

But which meanings of representation do we make politically relevant in order to approximate as much as possible the democratic credentials of popular governments? The answer of voluntaristic democratic theorists is that we have to get as close as possible (or at least we have to give the impression that we are getting as close as possible) to the idea of democratic legitimacy that was at work in ancient popular government. This is the idea that the people directly participate in the common decisions that concern it in the public assembly.[8]

Among the meanings of representation that best serve the purpose of creating a narrative of democratic legitimacy as social consensus, is representation as *mandate*. Indeed, we saw that the main characteristic of representation as *mandate* is the idea that there is an objective and legally regulated correspondence between the wills and views of represented and representative. The completeness of this correspondence serves the goal of seeing democratically elected representatives as approximating to the highest possible degree the practice of direct rule in popular government. It is on the basis of this same claim that Rousseau rejects representation. He says that representation alienates the sovereignty of the will. However, in rejecting representation for political purposes, Rousseau ends up confirming the same narrative that he wants to criticise. He argues that it is not possible to have a perfect correspondence between the people and its representative, and so we should just rely on a pure will of the people that cannot be represented. But this implicitly means that Rousseau and the elitist advocates of the voluntaristic view do not think that symbolic meanings of representation should play any role in the formation of the concept of political representation. It seems implicit in Rousseau's view that, by politicising *symbolic representation*, we would lose contact with the will of the people as such.

Voluntaristic views of democratic representation answer the question of which meanings of representation should be politicised in a second and related way. They implicitly claim that the only meaning of aesthetic representation that should be relevant to political life is *mimetic representation*. Indeed, in promoting the idea that representative democracy is a second best, voluntaristic theorists suggest that representative assemblies are perfect substitutes for the ancient democratic assembly. This is because these assemblies reflect in the best possible way all the different views and opinions that are present in a society. Stressing the political dimension of *mimetic representation* and the resemblance between the will of the people in a society and those who are their representative has a specific political purpose. This purpose is to discourage or diminish the importance of extra-parliamentary and societal forms of politics that take place outside the representative assemblies. There is an implicit elitist dimension in claiming that, since all the views of civil society are already reflected in an elected parliament, it is useless to value any participatory and societal forms of politics outside parliaments. To support this latter claim, the politicisation of meanings of *mimetic representation* plays a crucial role.

As a normative view of democratic representation, the voluntaristic view achieves two main purposes. First, it aims to give the impression that representative government is as friendly to popular sovereignty as to ancient democracy. However, and this is its second characteristic, at the same time it downplays this participatory dimension of ancient popular government. To reject the embodiment mechanisms of the people contained in any extra-institutional and extra-parliamentarian forms of participatory politics, the voluntaristic view of democratic representation rejects any politicisation of *symbolic representation*. On this view, we can claim that someone is a legitimate democratic representative when (1) there is a high correspondence between his or her views and those of the represented and (2) there are legal and institutional mechanisms that can regulate the correspondence between the wills of the representative and the represented. In other words, a representative is democratically legitimate if it sticks to the powers delegated to it.

Constructivist representation

The politicisation of the meanings of representation works differently in constructivism. Lisa Disch calls constructivism an approach to representation that refutes the assumption that representation is a 'descriptive and mimetic process, one that merely transmits something preexisting' (Disch 2011: 104). On a general level, constructivist representation wants to enrich and broaden the democratic vocabulary of political representation. It is thought of as a way of showing how variegated and complex the notion of sovereignty that we associate with democratic representation actually is. Constructivist representation enriches the vectors of political activity that make representation democratically legitimate by including many different meanings of representation in democratic representation. Broadly speaking, we can argue that the constructivist interpretation of democratic representation re-discovers the political relevance of *symbolic representation* and puts it centre stage in order to present its specific concept of democratic legitimacy. Let us then look more in detail at how these symbolic meanings of representation function within constructivist representation.

In a very interesting analysis of Rosanvallon's work on representation, Disch describes the theoretical insights coming from the constructivist idea of democratic representation. She explains that both Rosanvallon and Urbinati advance an anti-foundationalist conception of popular sovereignty that questions our ordinary understanding of democratic legitimacy – the idea that 'representation is democratic only when legislators and other public spokespersons keep the promises they make to their constituencies, and respond to their already-formed preferences' (Disch 2008: 48). Disch argues that constructivists 'hold that the people is an effect of democratic representation, not the ground of democratic legitimacy' (Disch 2008: 48). Of course, one implication of such a view is that there is a void before the representative relationship is instituted. This could lead us to think that the people are just an indeterminate construction that arises completely *ex novo* during the representative process. However, is this really the case? Interestingly, Disch answers this problem by distinguishing between two different models of constructivist representation, a radical and a moderate version. For the radical version of constructivist representation, which Disch thinks can be found in the work of Sieyes, 'the will of the collectivity cannot exist except through an organ that gives it form (the people being constituted as political subject only through representation' (Disch 2008: 51). This approach entails a view of representation that is process-oriented rather than substantialist in nature. In other words, even the idea of a political reality in its simplest form, the people in this case, cannot exist except insofar as it is represented. The entire setting and development of the political as well as the democratic world depend completely on representation.

In contrast to this radical constructivism, Disch argues that scholars such as Rosanvallon and Iris Young defend a moderate version of constructivism. They argue that political contestation or struggles define the identity of groups, and they deny that 'political constituencies are given prior to politics' (Disch 2008: 59). For example, for Disch, Iris Young proposes a shift from an identity-oriented understanding of representation to a process-oriented one in which 'constituency preferences emerge only over time and by the mediation of deliberative political institutions' (Disch 2008: 59). In both Rosanvallon and Iris Young, this anti-essentialist and organicist process of group-formation presupposes the existence of individuals that enter into the representative process. Thus, the difference between a moderate and radical interpretation of constructivist representation is that the moderate treats the idea of the people as the result of a temporal process, though something still needs to be presupposed prior to the process, while the radical does away with any idea of political reality prior to the representative process.

The difference between these two positions results in two different conceptions of democratic representation. The moderate version of constructivism contributes to democratic politics by identifying a set of rules or institutions that can be used to frame the democratic representative process. According to these rules and formal institutions, the moderate view maintains that the struggle of alternating viewpoints and conceptions occurs between people. In other words, rules are put into place, according to the moderate interpretation, because individuals or political subjects have agreed upon certain common and shared rules or institutions prior to the representative relationship. For the radical version of constructivism, everything is reduced to the constitutive role of representation, meaning that the need to highlight some basic rules or procedures that structure the representative relationship is far less important for the world of politics. Indeed, according to this perspective, there is no political reality as such prior to the process of representation.

As we have already observed, the starting point for understanding the particular nature of democratic representation that is defended by constructivists in contrast to the voluntaristic view is their rediscovery of the crucial role of *symbolic representation*. There are two questions that we must ask concerning the way in which constructivists use *symbolic representation*. First, how do constructivists politicise *symbolic representation*? Moreover, in light of the constructivist critique of the voluntaristic view, how do constructivists look at representation as a *mandate* and as *mimetic representation*? In dealing with the two models of constructivist representation presented in the remaining part of this chapter, it will be argued that the difference between moderate and radical constructivism depends on the different answers that they provide to these two main questions.

Moderate constructivism

Urbinati's critique of the voluntaristic view of sovereignty is a good example of the constructivist critique; it touches upon some fundamental aspects of the voluntaristic approach and it constitutes an example *par excellence* of the moderate constructivist view. First of all, Urbinati argues that the voluntaristic view reifies the concepts of sovereignty and of the people. By attributing a sovereign will to the people, the voluntaristic view claims that democratic politics is always a question of decision *hic et nunc*. Idealising the notion of direct democracy as based upon the gathering of people in the *ekklesia* of ancient democracy cannot keep pace with the modern world nor with the necessary temporal gap between the will and judgment in the politics of representative democracy. This critique of the voluntaristic view amounts to an implicit critique of the politicisation of *mimetic representation*.

Second, Urbinati criticises the voluntaristic view for having a limited concept of representation that only grounds this notion in elections. She argues that this dismisses any representative dynamics that take place in between electoral votes and in the deliberative public space of a democratic polity. Urbinati maintains that this view dismisses the intra- and non-electoral dimension of representational politics. This second critique of the voluntaristic view suggests a politicisation of *symbolic representation*. In the period between elections, formalistic and legal forms of representation (that result from a politicisation of *mandate*) are difficult to implement, meaning that political representation must be understood mostly along aesthetic and symbolic lines. Urbinati's purpose is to put forward a normative defence of representation that follows the rediscovery of the inherently 'democratic' aspect of representation. To achieve this aim, she needs to start from some assumptions about the definition and description of democracy as a polity regime and the type of representation her theory must be concerned with. Public discourse is the first factor to consider; the role of voice and speech as public means of interaction constitutes an essential part of democracy. Urbinati argues that representation, when democratic, is both 'advocacy' and 'representativity'. In a representative democracy, representatives are advocates insofar as they have a two-fold relationship with their electors. On the one hand, representatives are linked to the electors in an almost passionate way, as they maintain beliefs that are driven by the electorate's needs and interests. On the other hand, representatives have a great deal of autonomy, meaning that their goal is to 'steer partisan convictions down the path of deliberation and, ultimately, toward decision' (Urbinati 2006: 47).

However, as she clarifies even further in her latest book on democracy, the 'democratic' re-discovery of representation does not have to forget the importance of elections, procedures and rules in a representative democracy. In her book *Democracy Disfigured* (2014), this idea is clearly explained through the concept of the will, which constitutes the legal and institutional frameworks of a representative democracy.

In a representative democracy, the logic of representation always entails two different meanings of representation. First, it always has to politicise *symbolic representation*, the different ideas of the people that emerge out of elective politics but also out of extra-parliamentary and extra-institutional forms of politics. When Urbinati talks about political representation, she suggests that there is no representative politics in a democracy if we do not politicise *symbolic representation*. Second Urbinati is clear in stressing the necessity of a politicisation of the meaning of representation as *mandate*. However the type of politicisation of representation as *mandate* that she seems to advocate is completely different from the one that we find in the voluntaristic view. In the latter, the idea of democratic legitimacy that we see in representative democracy makes use of representation as *mandate* in combination with *mimetic representation*. Using Rousseauian language, we could say that the elective process is an idealised moment in which the will of the people emerges in all its strength through the election of some representatives. That is identified as the key time for the construction of a truly democratic narrative of political legitimacy. In moderate constructivism, things work differently. The politicisation of *mandate*, the idea of the 'will', is always seen in combination with the politicisation of *symbolic representation*. One of them cannot be imagined without the other.

When we look at the crucial characteristic of moderate constructivism through the lens of the relationship between the meanings of representation and their politicisation, it is clear, at least in Urbinati's version of moderate constructivism, that the two meanings of representation as *mandate* and *symbolic representation* must cohabitate normatively while remaining distinguished analytically. The only meaning of representation that is left out of the picture of political representation is then *mimetic representation*. This of course tells us something about the idea of democratic legitimacy that is linked to Urbinati's moderate form of constructivism. If we ask what makes Urbinati's moderate model of constructivist representation democratically legitimate, we have to consider two factors that are implicit in the two main meanings that make representation political in such a model: *mandate* and *symbolic representation*. In Urbinati's theory, when someone claims to represent someone else, it is because (1) they are delegated authority within a specific legal and institutional framework and (2) they 'stand for' someone else not because of any likeness with the represented but because they are able to bear a symbolic relationship to the represented. What makes Urbinati's representative democratically legitimate is then a mix of symbolic claims (something like 'I as a representative am able to symbolise who you are politically') and compliance with legal and institutional rules that regulate how someone serves as a representative.[9] Within such criteria of democratic legitimacy, there is no space for claims that make someone a representative because he resembles the represented. This is why moderate constructivism rejects any politicisation of *mimetic representation*.

Radical constructivism

Just how differently radical constructivists conceive of democratic legitimacy can be seen in the work of Dutch cultural historian Frank Ankersmit, who is recognised as an important representative of the second strand of constructivism.[10] Following an intuition already explained by Pitkin, Ankersmit uses the example of the relationship between an object and its artistic representation in order to explain the nature of political representation. When an artist decides to represent a landscape or an object, this form of representation can never entirely coincide with the reality that it is supposed to represent. In other words, even artistic representation, when used to represent something accurately, can never be a complete form of mimetic representation. If it was, it would stop being a form of representation and become a form of identification. For Ankersmit, the very same logic applies to the concept of representation. He explains that 'representation finds its purpose and meaning in the indeterminate and interpretable character of the "reality" that is to be represented' (Ankersmit 1996: 47).

A similar argument applies to the concept of political representation. There is no political reality without political representation. As Ankersmit puts it, 'political reality is not first given to us and subsequently represented; political reality only comes into being after and due to representation' (Ankersmit 1996: 47). It is worth mentioning Ankersmit's view of this aspect:

> There is no identity of the representative and the person represented in political representation. Hence there is no identity either of the political will of the representative and that of the person represented; yet the former is binding for the latter. The political reality created by aesthetic representation is therefore essentially political power. The aesthetic difference or gap between the represented and his or her representative is the origin of (legitimate) political power, and we are therefore justified in assigning to political power an aesthetic rather than ethical nature. (Ankersmit 1996: 47)

In Ankersmit's view, the gap between the wills of the represented and the representative eventually creates the normative space of political power. In *Political Representation* (2002), the Dutch scholar argues that political representation is an aesthetic category, which allows us to understand political reality since in a representative democracy 'all legitimate power is essentially aesthetic' (Ankersmit 2002: 118). The aesthetic nature of power in democracy comes from the permanent gap created between the always-changing preferences of voters and the representative's opinions. This results in a productive and constitutive effort within the representative structure to attempt to fill this never-ending gap. As a result, there are no 'people', no represented, prior to representation. The first is constituted through the second as a constitutive act, and its content is always provisional. Ankersmit claims that representation is a never-ending aesthetic process that is essential to democracy.

This means that democratic politics is impossible without representation. The notion of representation also transforms our understanding of the notions of the representative and the represented. If we assume that the represented is the political reality that representation is supposed to produce, then we need political representation in order to conceive of the represented as such. In Ankersmit's words, 'without representation there is no represented – *and without political representation there is no nation as a truly political entity*' (Ankersmit 2002: 115). To state this, the Dutch theorist downplays the role of *mimetic representation* (indicating that since it aims for a complete identification between the representative and the represented, it is no longer a form of representation) and argues that political representation coincides with *symbolic representation*. Sofia Näsström effectively characterises this position by saying that, for Ankersmit, representative democracy is a 'tautology' in which representation forms the essence of democracy (Näsström 2006: 329).

The question that arises with Ankersmit's radical constructivist perspective is the following: how does radical constructivism politicise the different meanings of representation? As in moderate constructivism, Ankersmit's critique of *mimesis* points to a strong rejection of any political relevance of *mimetic representation*. For Ankersmit, the latter does not have any appeal in the modern world. The mimetic theory of representation was prevalent from the Middle Ages (which saw the origin of representation) until about 1800, when the aesthetic theory of representation came to dominance. Ankersmit's idea is that the roots of the mimetic concept of representation lie in the Middle Ages, where representation was conceived as 'representing before' rather than 'representing by'.

This is because the representative relationship always took place within an all-encompassing order or structure in which both the person represented and the representative participated. Ankersmit contends that this understanding of the representative relationship (as a mimetic process that comes from a shared order and structure of things), both in the Middle Ages and in early modernity, came from the influence of Stoicism. According to this view, political representation was essentially transformed into the *parousia* of political truth, making it a static (in fact mimetic) concept that had to guarantee the correspondence between represented and representative. Indeed, the latter both belonged to the same natural order. In the mimetic model, the theory of representation was always based on what Ankersmit calls a *tertium comparationis*, namely a third entity according to which it was possible to draw a comparison between the person represented and the representative. The Stoic doctrine turned this *tertium comparationis* into a political reality grounded in the idea of cosmic harmony.

For Ankersmit, this notion of *mimetic representation* started to lose its significance at the same time as neo-Stoic philosophy started to become less relevant. From the nineteenth century onwards, things began to change. The identity between 'is' and 'ought' was definitely challenged and the idea of the harmonious cosmos that was behind the notion of mimetic representation came into crisis. The identity between representative and represented gradually disappeared and an alternative idea of representation started to emerge: what Ankersmit calls aesthetic representation.

Radical constructivism and democratic legitimacy

This strong critique of *mimetic representation*, which Urbinati shares, comes with a critique of representation as *mandate*. This latter aspect marks a disagreement between Ankersmit's radical constructivism and Urbinati's moderate constructivism. It would be a mistake to think that representation as *mandate* disappears from Ankersmit's model. For example, the latter retains a role in the political process insofar as there must be something that binds the representative to the represented. Also, for Ankersmit, elections are part of political representation. However, these elements do not tell us the most important part of the representative relationship, which arises from the aesthetic power emerging from the gap between the representative and the represented. One aspect that is absolutely necessary for representation as *mandate* is missing in Ankersmit's account: that both the represented and the representative are supposed to have a pre-determined will before the representation relationship takes place. It seems that, in Ankersmit's model, both the will of the representative and that of the represented are so radically transformed through the representative relationship that it makes no sense to talk about them before this relationship takes place. This point marks a significant difference between the radical and moderate constructivist accounts of political representation. Ankersmit claims that there is no political reality without the representative process as such. This means that, for him, political representation results from the politicisation of *symbolic representation* only and, if it entails a form of representation as *mandate* (because it virtually requires elections), this is definitely not what gives political meaning to the act of political representation. *Symbolic representation* remains the only politicised meaning of representation.

Ankersmit's treatment of political representation is a radical challenge to the idea that voting can act as a tool to measure social consensus in society.[11] Voting of course remains crucial in moderate constructivism by virtue of its attachment to the idea that *mandate* defines political representation. In the radical constructivist understanding of political representation, the meaning of representation as *mandate* dissolves into *symbolic representation*. The political implications of this move are radical because they make it possible to claim that a representative should be considered democratically legitimate only because he is able to incarnate a group of people, a collectivity, an interest or a specific narrative. In other words, for radical constructivism political representation can be exclusively identified with embodiment or, in the worst case, with decisionistic form of politics.

Elections are far from being a perfect instrument of social legitimacy in today's democracies. However they presuppose two different meanings of representation, *mandate* and *symbolic representation*, which together contribute to building up a relatively effective way to measure consensus in democratic societies. We saw that moderate constructivism à la Urbinati struck a good balance between the politicisations of these two meanings of representation. However if we do without *mandate*, what can act as a valid substitute for this combination in radical constructivism? There is an element of democratic legitimacy that theorists of radical constructivism will have to do without. This is the claim that there must be institutional and juridical mechanisms for the views of the represented to be carefully and faithfully taken into consideration by the representative.

More important are the consequences of radical constructivism in the context of global governance. Governance network scholars perceive a theoretical convergence with the radical constructivist account of representation because networks lack a defined territory and enact policies in the absence of hierarchical institutions and legally binding frameworks. As they invoke them, however, radical constructivist accounts risk lending democratic legitimacy to what amounts to technocratic, top-down management strategies (Mulieri 2013).

For example, in an article assessing the relationship between network governance and democratic theory Sørensen argues that a constitutive notion of representation supports 'the recognition of the autonomous and productive nature of representation' and challenges 'the traditional image of democratic representation' (Sørensen 2002: 698).[12] Sørensen's debt to a radical form of constructivism is evident when she claims that 'the interest of the people should therefore be seen as an outcome of representation and not a pre-given object of representation' (Sørensen 2002: 698). However, Sørensen seems to apply her radical constructivist account of representation to both governance arrangements and representative democracy indifferently. As she writes:

> The fragmentation of the political system into many layers and self-governing units has initiated a still more intense political battle between elected or otherwise appointed political elites about the right to represent 'a people'. Parliamentary bodies on different levels compete with each other and with self-governing public and semi-public institutions, and even with private organizations such as firms and voluntary organizations about the right to speak on behalf of a 'people'. (Sørensen 2002: 698)

These words take no account of the fact that a radically constructivist practice of representation cannot deliver democratic legitimacy as it is typically understood. In an effort to deal with this, the scholar acknowledges that elections are no longer the best instrument of social legitimacy and proposes 'competition' as a possible substitute of 'elections'. In her view, competition is crucial to determine 'the process of constructing the identity and the interests of the represented' because it 'takes place every time an actor – public or private – claims that s/he represents someone' (Sørensen 2002: 698). 'Competition' is enacted through representative claims and allows us to assess and, possibly, enhance the democratic credentials of specific policies or decisions. This is just an example of how a radical form of constructivist representation, with its productive notion of the demos, becomes a *viaticum* for the democratic legitimacy of the governance network and, eventually, for representative democracy as well.[13]

Conclusion

Today, the constructivist view has become an increasingly popular way of looking at democratic representation. I have shown that there exist two distinct versions of constructivism, one a 'moderate' and the other a 'radical' account. Both versions share a rejection of the politicisation of *mimetic representation* and propose a politicisation of *symbolic representation*. However while moderate constructivists accept the politicisation of *mandate*, radical constructivists fully reject it. A question arises when we consider this semantic shift of political representation in radical constructivism: can an exclusive politicisation of the symbolic meaning of representation still guarantee that social consensus is the basic foundation of any principle of political legitimacy? I have suggested that radical constructivism does not – and possibly cannot – respond to this question. In the introduction to this volume, Lisa Disch maintains that such radical versions of constructivism have no purchase on politics. I argue that she might be too quick to dismiss the political implications of linguistic constructivism. In governance, experts or leaders increasingly aim to create from scratch linguistic frameworks presented as full expressions of the interests or desires of the people.[14] These narratives are often presented as ready-made and offered to their audiences as given truths without contestation or debate and, more importantly, they unfold in the absence of any electoral accountability. The actual consequences of this radical linguistic constructivism could be the disempowerment of the people and the institution of something similar to the Hobbesian sovereign. In *Leviathan*, after the institution of the Commonwealth, the sovereign becomes the exclusive bearer of the meanings of his subjects' words.

Notes

1. 'In Anfang das Wort und nicht der Begriff war'. All English quotations from Hofmann's text are mine as there is no English translation of the book.
2. Partly relying on Hofmann's work, Yves Sintomer has proposed a similar polysemantic perspective to approach the problem of political representation. He distinguishes aesthetico-symbolic and juridical-political logics of representation in order to analyse the different implications of these logics in the political usages of the word *représentation* (Sintomer 2013).
3. One side, which included Berengar of Tours, claimed that the ritual of the Eucharist is symbolic and that the bread and wine are simply symbols or signs of Christ's sacrifice. This doctrine was considered heretical by the advocates of Catholic orthodoxy, such as Popes Gregorius VII and Niccolò II, who claimed that the priest actually transforms the bread and wine into the 'real' blood and body of Christ. See full treatment in Hofmann (Hofmann 1974: 24 and following).

4. It could be argued that Hofmann's meaning of *Urbild-Abbild Dialektik* should not be reduced to mimetic representation as it entails a more dynamic relationship between representative and represented. However the logic of *Urbild-Abbild Dialektik* has a strong 'mimetic' component insofar as it aims to achieve as much as possible a resemblance or complete correspondence between an image and its copy.
5. The last part of Hofmann's chapter 2 is particularly useful for understanding this particular shift in the meaning of representation from *Urbild-Abbild Dialektik* to *Darstellung*. However Hofmann's analysis of *Darstellung* is not particularly detailed in comparison to the other two meanings of *Stellvertretung* and *Urbild-Abbild Dialektik*.
6. Urbinati (Urbinati 2006) uses the label 'voluntaristic' to characterise a 'poor' understanding of democratic representation that treats it as entrenched in the will of the people.
7. Manin does not identify himself as an elitist. Indeed, he clearly rejects this label in Landemore (Landemore 2008: 9). Moreover, in his book on representative government, he criticises Schumpeter and the classical elitist view for ignoring the retrospective judgement of the represented during elections.
8. As is well known, the interpretation of this criterion among the founding fathers of democracy is not historically accurate as the ideal of political legitimacy that was at work in ancient democracy is based on rotation in office and not social consent (Manin 1997), which is the legitimacy criterion of modern democracies.
9. In her contribution to this volume, Urbinati defends a 'moderate' view of constructivism that follows a similar path. She also explains that the strategy of representation as claim-making should not be a test of democratic legitimacy.
10. Several scholars consider Ankersmit's theory of political representation a form of radical constructivism (Disch 2015: 4; Näsström 2006: 330–1). Disch distinguishes Ankersmit's radical linguistic constructivism from a radical democratic constructivism, underlining the democratic components of the latter. I am fully sympathetic to this distinction, and my critique is actually aimed at the unintended consequences of what she calls radical linguistic constructivism, whereas, sticking to Disch's previous work (Disch 2008), I think that a better label for radical democratic constructivism would be 'moderate constructivism'. In this contribution, I consider Urbinati's notion of democratic representation as an example of the latter.
11. My analysis of Ankersmit's theory of political representation is partly similar to that provided by Marchart in this volume. While Marchart welcomes Ankersmit's post-foundationalist view because it is 'highly pertinent' to radical democracy, he rejects what he thinks are its political implications because they end up legitimising compromise and an idea of the parliamentary regime which is hardly democratic. I fully

agree with Marchart that Ankersmit does not explore the full political implications of his radical constructivism. However my analysis of the semantics of Ankersmit's radical constructivist theory of political representation focuses especially on its possible unintended consequences, which do not necessarily overlap with Ankersmit's self-proclaimed normative political agenda.

12. Sørensen quotes Laclau but she does not fully develop this reference to the Argentian thinker.

13. Studies on private regulatory governance emphasise the need for more representation of all the regions and interests of the globe in the managing units of governance initiatives such as Global Gap, and they call for a reflection on 'the representation of groups and interests in the normative debate' (Hachez and Wouters 2011: 693). However, the underlying narrative of the theoretical convergence between the governance network and radical constructivist representation is that they cannot rely on the classical instruments of representative democracy because they lack a defined territory and are enacted in the absence of hierarchical institutions and legally binding frameworks.

14. A typical example in governance is when some experts, policy-makers or politicians give us an exact idea of the composition of society on the basis of statistical datasets (dividing people into pensioners, socially disadvantaged, middle class and so on) and claim to be a representative of some portion of society on the basis of these statistics. On the increasing importance of symbolic representation in populism there is already quite a lot of literature, for example Urbinati (2014) or Rosanvallon (2011).

13

The improper politics of representation

Mark Devenney

Introduction

Recent debates about representative democracy pose two key arguments. First, they contend that the represented do not pre-exist their articulation, putting into question the notion that the represented have pre-constituted interests. Second, they contend that representative claims are wider ranging than is normally assumed. They may 'be formal and informal, electoral and non-electoral, national and trans-national and manifest in multiple guises and spaces' (Saward 2016: 246). These arguments demand a rethinking of how representative democracy is understood and justified.[1] I contend that the constructivist turn inadequately accounts for the relationship between inequality and representation. Unlike classic critics of representative democracy, constructivist theorists fail to think the intrinsic relation between property, the proper and representation.[2] While they maintain an agonistic public sphere at the centre of democratic contestation and opinion formation, they underemphasise the disjuncture between democratic equality and representative politics. In short, these attempts to radicalise representative democracy inadequately address the sedimented forms of inequality which structure representation. In the first section of this chapter I set out the main tenets of the constructivist turn. In the second section I set out three objections to this account, recalling without vindicating the Marxist critique of representative democracy. Last, I distinguish democratic politics as improper from representative claim-making.

The constructivist turn: key arguments

Constructivists argue that those represented are constituted by multiple forms of representation and do not pre-exist their representation.

Representing might be thought of as an ongoing process of negotiation, a war of position, in which 'representative and represented
[are] linked not by a static correspondence but in a dynamic process of mutual constitution' (Disch 2015: 488). Democracy on this
account cannot be legitimised with reference to a pre-existing rational
will or with reference to the 'real' interests of constituents. Rather a
political will is constructed through rhetorical acts of representation
which aesthetically remake, and *in part* establish, what is represented
(Saward 2012: 124). Recognition of the complexity of these many
forms of constituency replicated through reiterative claim-making is
important. Moreover, existing constituted claims are vulnerable to
re-articulation in terms of different imagined communities (Anderson
1991) as they are maintained through performative reiteration – a
reiteration which may fail.

Constructivists then extend the notion of representation to
include claims and the mobilisations of constituencies beyond traditional forms of electoral democracy. In doing so they raise a set
of questions about the relationship between democracy, equality
and representation, as noted by Näsström (2006).[3] Perhaps most
important is how we might distinguish claims that are democratic
in the sense of actuating equality, as opposed to those that are dis-
criminatory. Disch proposes that the representative process may 'be
judged more or less democratic insofar as it [. . .] mobilise[s] both
express and implicit objections from the represented' (Disch 2011:
111). This weak criterion encourages contestation, dissent and the
recognition that there is no one sovereign voice. However, all sorts
of contestations may be mobilised. Witness for example how the
Trump campaign mobilised dissent, claiming to represent a squan-
dered American greatness in the name of democracy. On this criterion we cannot distinguish these racist forms of mobilisation from
mobilisations which instantiate equality.

Where Disch and Saward begin to address these normative
questions they run up against a set of difficulties. In a close reading
of Saward's *The Representative Claim* Disch notes his uncertainty
about normativity: on the one hand he proposes a normative criterion of open, uncoerced choice. Yet he simultaneously insists that
citizen standpoints, the agonistic politics of argument and claim-
making, are where judgements should be generated. Disch argues
that he betrays his own rejection of first-order judgments proposing
instead that 'the citizen standpoint opens up an option that is reso-
lutely constructivist, democratic and enabled by empirical research'
(Disch 2015: 496). What is unclear is why Disch turns to citizenship

given the exclusionary ends to which it is often deployed? In a recent article Saward seems to accept Disch's critique, yet he still holds onto a qualified normativity. Rather than deploy first-order judgments he asks if representative claims enact democratic equality. However, this is only given meaning and texture in the process of its enactment (Saward 2016: 247). For Saward, equality as one of a range of political principles deployed in democratic contestation 'is dynamic and performatively produced' (Saward 2016: 248). He acknowledges that equality is the final resting place of almost every attempt to defend democratic politics. Yet he too has questions to answer. If equality is only given its meaning in practice at what point does a claim no longer instantiate equality? Saward invokes equality yet gives it no content other than what it has become through practice. Disch assumes that the citizen standpoint is both constructivist and democratic, but fails to recognise that the history of citizenship presupposes undemocratic and unequal practices, in every instance.

Urbinati (2006, 2010, 2014) in contrast defends a strongly normative account of representation as democratic. The indirectness of representation shields the political community from the 'harassment of words and passions'. Representatives can advocate for particular, excluded or marginalised sectors in the name of democratic equality. Representation activates the sovereign people which is not presupposed, as in ontological versions of sovereignty, but produced. Proceduralism, she argues, presupposes no other ideal than equal liberty for all. It admits of a process of constant emendation and protects minorities who may later become the majority. The key normative principle for Urbinati is political equality. With Mill she argues that in practice what equality means is the liberty to participate as equals in political debate. Unlike Mill she does not think that economic equality is a condition for political equality.[4] She does acknowledge that procedural rules in a democratic society are meaningless if trivial (Saffon and Urbinati 2013: 462). The problem for her is that in the absence of a more broadly conceived practice of equality they are meaningless.

All three of these theorists, then, either explicitly or implicitly, invoke political equality. However, only Urbinati deploys it as a criterion to judge the politics of representation. For Disch and Saward the content of equality cannot be given in advance. In contrast to these theorists an older critique of representative democracy contends that representation is inequality in its quintessentially political form. The constructivist turn suggests that representation activates a politics of equality. However it fails to consider the relationship between representation and inequality. In summary I have identified two initial problems with these accounts: first, they do not give an account of the materially configured lifeworld which limits who can make a claim, and the nature of the claims that may be heard; second, their account of equality is too limited. In what follows I focus on the politics of property and propriety. The link between property, representation and civil society is forgotten by these theorists. Representation, I will argue, is presented as conceptually abstract rather than as overdetermined by the social and political conditions within which it is found. There can be no easy return to Marxist critiques of property, linked as they were to a philosophy of history, to an expressivist account of the social totality and to a privileging of the proletariat as the subject-object of history. Yet in returning improperly to Marx's critique of representative democracy we can rethink the relationship between inequality and representation.

The limits of representative democracy

The standard critique of representative democracy pointed to the exclusions and inequalities intrinsic to representative democracies. The constructivist account seems to sidestep this critique – it allows that representative mobilisations and claims can challenge existing forms of political inequality. However, it does not account for the fact that the 'properties' historically deployed as the basis for exclusion – race, sex, property and reason (all themselves sedimented forms of representation) – structure the terms on which those historically excluded are forced to engage with the political system. We should not essentialise properties. Race and gender are historically constituted, contested and open to resignification. Identity-based forms of politics are always double edged: to mobilise in the name of women, black people or the working class simultaneously reinforces the very categories which racist, sexist and capitalist logics constitute. Yet centuries-old forms of inequality are structured around 'race', 'sex' and property. A politics of equality plays to a double drumbeat: on the one hand it engages with the established forms of domination; on the other, it challenges those same categories insofar as they police identity.[5] The same is true of representation. Representative democracy and representative claims presuppose a certain type of political agent. Subjects are construed in terms of this implicit or explicit ideal, presenting it as if universal, when it is in fact culturally specific.[6]

Historical forms of exclusion from representative systems structure
the distribution of wealth and opportunity today, thus shaping the
very possibility of making and mobilising representative claims. The
constructivist turn tends to underplay these prior conditions, over-
emphasising the potential to mobilise constituencies against inequality, and thus reproducing those very inequalities that representative
claim-makers might challenge. What is not considered is that some
may be constitutionally impaired by these prior systems of exclusion.
If this is the case then the constructivist account of representation,
in reifying the possibility of representative claim-making, lends suc-
cour to these orders of propriety and property. Marx's critique of the
extension of the franchise in 'On the Jewish Question' is emblematic.
He writes:

> the political annulment of private property does not mean the abolition
> of private property: on the contrary it even presupposes it. The state in
> its own way abolishes distinctions based on birth, rank, education and
> occupation, when it declares birth, social rank, education and occupa-
> tion to be non-political distinctions, when it proclaims, without regard to
> these distinction, that every member of the nation is an *equal* participant
> in national sovereignty, when it treats all elements of the real life of the
> nation from the standpoint of the state. Nevertheless, the state allows
> private property, education, occupation, to *act* and assert *their* particular
> nature in their own way – *i.e.*, as private property, as education, as occu-
> pation. Far from abolishing these real distinctions, the state only exists
> on the presupposition of their existence; it feels itself to be a political
> state and asserts its universality only in opposition to these elements of
> its being. (Marx 1984: 219)

The standard interpretation of this text is well known. Representative
democracies are complicit in legitimising a system of economic and
political inequality. Political representation as a formal bourgeois right
betrays the substantive equality it simultaneously promises. However,
like the money form, political equality is abstract, not real. The logic
of the market requires that individuals act as self-regarding actors.[7]
Representative democracies thus sustain the separation between the
(abstractly equal) political community and the private community of
economic interests in civil society, where inequality reigns. The het-
erogeneous rationality of the market gives the lie to political equality.[8]
Note that for Marx electoral representation is constituted as intrinsic to the reproduction of systemic inequality. Marx anticipates the
constructivist turn but with a twist. He gives an account of the system of political representation, as constituted, or on some readings,

determined by socio-economic conditions. He recognises that representatives may constitute new claims, but argues that such claims are constitutionally impaired by the substantive inequalities which structure socio-political order. The system of political representation separates the citizen from active participation in determining the fate of the community and belies the substantive inequalities which structure social life.

However, there is more to this quote than the traditional reading allows. For Marx the terms of equality are bounded by nation-states which police the separation between civil and political society, the system of property relations which order inequality within the state and the territorial bounds of the nation. In *Nomos of the Earth* (1950) Schmitt extends this argument. He suggests an intrinsic relation between the normative and legal order, ontology and appropriation. A normative and legal order is always related to the organisation of appropriation, the drawing and maintenance of boundaries, and the forms taken by legal property. Schmitt contends that one can only ask ontological questions in light of their relation to legal normativity and forms of property and appropriation (Schmitt 2003: 45). The intrinsic but contingent links between ontology and particular modalities of appropriation suggest the terms on which any politics of representation might be conceptualised. The constructivist turn does not escape this critique, in part because it does not ask the question. Representation, in its different forms, always concerns who counts and how political claims relate to dominant forms of appropriation, division and inequality. Saward does acknowledge that representative claims cannot be conjured out of thin air. They are made from existing terms; in his words, the 'ready mades [. . .] which must tap in to familiar contextual frameworks' (Saward 2006: 303) and can produce silencing effects. The constituencies evoked may be silenced as their voices are appropriated by elites (Saward 2006: 303). Representative claims are neither good nor bad – the identities constituted through representative claims may act as the basis for future dissent, or indeed as conservative restraints on the present. Yet he does not note that the very possibility of a claim becoming effective is constrained (though not determined) by hegemonic forms of order. Furthermore, the very notion of a representative claim already presupposes particular notions of hegemonic order and forms of subjectivity. While I concur with the constructivist argument that the represented are made, I want to insist with Schmitt that the terms of this making relate to particular orders of appropriation, within historically specific hegemonic configurations. A simple example, to which I will return, makes the point.

The legal reformulation of property law since the early 1970s is a key moment in the realignment of the relations between production, reproduction and politics in the globalised nation-state. Two key processes complement each other: first, property rights are now enforced through global property regimes; second, what can be deemed property has been extended to include the immaterial: the genetic code of life, data and information systems. Ownership of genetic technologies of reproduction allows for the development of products, including medicines, food, and new stem cells which are sold on the market. Yet markets in reproductive techniques and in genetic resources are skewed. They are dominated by a relatively small number of governments and private companies, which make undemocratic decisions about the development of medical technologies. The properties over which representative polities supposedly exercise their jurisdiction are now the subjects of patent and property rights which extend beyond these publics. The privatisation of the code of life, and the internationalisation of the legal framework which regulates this privatisation, alters the appropriate terrain of political contestation. Representative claims which challenge this configuration must conjure publics which are transnational. The legal and political infrastructures already configured mean that only certain types of claim might be heard. Likewise, the property rights exercised are often so abstract as to escape any easy framing in political terms. I return to this example later.

There is one last aspect of Marx's argument too often ignored. He equates the role of private property with those of education and occupation. These are not strictly about property, but are central to what I elsewhere term 'proprietary order'. The state exists, Marx writes, on the presupposition of the distinctions that follow from property, education and occupation. Representative democracies determine in advance the appropriate ways of being, doing and saying, to use Rancière's terms (Rancière 1999: 29), and thus the types of representative claim which have resonance. They place certain issues off limits. The representation of the democratic state as an imaginary with which all can identify relies upon general acceptance of these norms of education, occupation and nation. Marx's critique of political representation then concerns both ownership and control over resources and lives, and the ordering of the social world, the allocation of things and subjects to their proper places. The constructivist account of representation outflanks aspects of these criticisms, but not, as we will see, all of them.

Because they emphasise the constitutive aspects of representation constructivists recognise the importance of mobilising and challenging different forms of political exclusion. The recognition that representation extends beyond electoral politics complements a politics aimed at making visible forms of historical exclusion, often occluded from public perception. One can envision both Disch and Saward accepting that elections are (as Charles Taylor argued in 1971) politically and culturally specific, presupposing certain notions of subject, object and reason, a certain nomos we might say. The acts which political scientists characterise as brute data are not simply given: they are institutionally bound and bound up with particularistic notions of identity and autonomy. The same is true, though, of representative claims: they cannot be identified independently of the language used to describe them, a language constitutive of reality. Representative claims are intersubjective practices, modes of social relation, which presuppose a certain set of logics: that claims might be heard; that the world is divided between subjects and objects; that humans can understand what is constituted in the claim made. The notions of constituency mobilisation (Disch) and representative claim (Saward) already presuppose accepted modes of social relation. These prior conditions are not explicitly thematised by the constructivist turn (Taylor 1971: 35).

Let me summarise three main points. First, in failing to thematise the conditions which make representative claims possible, constructivists too quickly assume that the extension of representation is good for democratic politics. Democracy, however, is not the same as representation, and nor is representation its necessary prerequisite (see below). These theorists fail to ask if representative claims, and constituency mobilisations which cut across established boundaries, are themselves overdetermined by global forms of hegemonic order. In failing to thematise these prior conditions they do not address the inequalities which relate back to established proprietary orders. Second, the very notion of representation – as establishing a relation between subject, object and voice – already presupposes certain established notions about human beings. Representation in both its constitutional and symbolic registers presupposes certain ways of being which are neither abstract nor universal. Third, representative claims always aim to establish the limits of their object. Democracy, I argue, is always improper – out of time, and out of place – enacting an equality at odds with dominant modalities of the proper, with the forms of appropriation – of the self, of objects, of what is deemed proper, and thus open to becoming property.

Democracy versus representation

I have already argued that representation is skewed in part by the terms on which time and space, wealth and property are structured and maintained. The claims of representative democracies to represent are undermined by contemporary regimes of property in three fundamentally different respects: first, the globalisation of property laws; second, the articulation of ever-new realms, for example genetic information, as private assets; and last, the hollowing out of the public-private distinction. Signatories to the World Trade Organization, for example, must remove 'restrictive' barriers to trade, to services (including banking, insurance, transport, communications and health) and to intellectual property (trademarks, industrial designs, genetic resources, medicines and the like). The reframing of the public life-world as a private asset from which value may be derived radically forecloses democratic representation within national boundaries (see Honig 2016). When the demos is defined in national terms it cannot make democratic decisions about a range of issues regulated by international treaties. The extension of representative claim-making, and mobilisations, in the ways suggested by Disch and Saward presupposes this reconfiguration of the proper bounds of political and representative power. In concluding I mount a dual critique: first, Disch and Saward have not adequately thought through the sedimented terrain on which representative claims may be mounted; second, they have not adequately conceptualised democratic politics, or equality, in relation to representation.

REPRESENTATION AND SEDIMENTATION

For Disch the standard notion of political representation is theoretically incoherent: 'claims to represent are quasi-peformative: such claims and the functions that follow from them are not just responsive to their constituents but responsible for them'. This notion of responsibility becomes the nub of the normative case in defence of representation which Disch will make. She continues:

> [Representations] constitute and mobilise [. . .] by the biases they tap; the identifications they activate, the conflicts they prioritise, and even the stereotypes they call forth. From this perspective *it is as crucial to examine how bias forecloses serious challenge to the interest of dominant groups* [my emphasis] [. . .] as it is to analyse the conflicts that the system permits. (Disch 2012: 608)

Disch maintains that dominant groups have interests. She recognises that the existing terms of representation shape the expression of conflict. Representatives often mobilise stereotypes, or exercise bias, and foreclose challenges to dominant interests. Yet if dominant groups have interests then those excluded at the very least do not share those same interests. One implication of her precise identification of the bias of representation is that certain claims cannot represent the interests of those excluded or marginalised. Her notion of responsibility in some sense acknowledges this. Claims which entrench inequality, yet which were made in the past, structure the existing representative terrain. Those constituted by prior mobilisations do not simply vanish – prior claims also have ontological effects which later exercise a centripetal weight, limiting other claims. However, these effects are rarely, if ever, wholly new. They always negotiate an order configured by a set of perceived interests with residual weight. Here we get back to the distinction raised by Saward, between object effects and the referent. The referent on Saward's own terms 'expresses the sheer materiality of people and things, versus the constructions of meaning that different actors, perspectives and claims may place upon them', the object effects (Saward 2012: 124). What status do we give to this sheer materiality which constitutes the terrain on which representative claims are made? Surely this limits the forms of representative claim that may be made, constraining the language and descriptions that have a purchase on the world? Is so called sheer materiality not already delimited and demarcated, most often as a form of property?

Why is this important? Let me return to Disch's normativity. Disch identifies systemic effects which privilege the wealthy. How do these structure representative democracy – most obviously through the disproportionate financial influence wielded by wealthy corporate lobbyists? Perhaps more subtle is the indirect influence exerted through what Saward terms the irreducibly material world. The material world of people and things (to use his words) is already partitioned and apportioned. Property is not a natural phenomenon but requires the human mapping and drawing of the world, a cartographic imaginary, in which parts of the physical world are partitioned, allocated and given value. Let me return to the example of the genetic code. Genetic sequences had no existence as property claims before they were legally recognised as entities over which property claims could be exercised. Naturalised in international property regimes such claims act as constraints on the present. When indigenous communities claim ownership of seeds developed over centuries of agricultural practice, they make the claim against companies who

legally own the genetic sequence of the seeds. The existing proprietary regime requires that even counter claims are made in terms of
property. Unless framed in the language of property they cannot be
heard. Farming communities are thus forced to rearticulate the terms
on which they conceptualise the means used for the reproduction
of their lives and communities. Property regimes – often contested,
but always invoked in the name of law and order – place severe
constraints on the types of claim that may be heard. Property in this
example is a form of representation and constitution. It is a performative claim maintained by violence and law. Profound inequality in
the social world is founded on these legal institutions with material
effects. Such relations are represented back to citizens as the natural
order within which any claims they make should be framed. What
Saward terms representative claims are always made on this pre-
constituted terrain, a political imaginary in which the world appears
ontologically secure. Disch and Saward lack a vocabulary allowing
them to distinguish sedimented interests and established patterns of
inequality, from the particular claims made about them.

DEMOCRATIC EQUALITY

Let me turn to the specificity of democratic equality. Inequalities
have their origin in established histories of exploitation, discrimination and exclusion. Saward and Disch invoke equality but are worried that a normative stance in defence of equality in the abstract is
not itself subject to agreement within political communities. It thus
abstracts from interpretive disputes which are the core of representative claim-making, and in so doing undermines the equality it aims
to represent. Yet they simultaneously rely on an implicit or explicit
commitment to political equality. With Rancière I contend that they
are right: democratic enactment presupposes a commitment to equality, which is verified in practice. However, representation is not a necessary condition for the enactment of equality. In fact representative
claims presuppose a structural inequality – they distinguish between
the one making the claim and those in whose name the claim is made.
As noted above this may all too quickly result in elites taking advantage of claims made in the names of others. Democratic equality may
be invoked in order to assess the limits of representative claims – but
representation in itself is not, and nor is it a condition of, democratic
equality. The enactment of equality is always improper in relation to
existing forms of order and their particular configurations of property and propriety. What distinguishes Rancière's account from that

of Saward is the conjunction of two elements: equality is presupposed, while its content is worked out when it is verified.[9]

Democratic equality will always push beyond the established terms of representation. Representative claims constitute bounded communities of interest, and claims are structured in such a way that subjects are constituted in terms of the claim made. Any attempt to represent the world, a polity, any attempt to give borders or number to a represented community, is confronted by democratic claims which do not recognise these limits. This account of democratic equality is in part a working out of what the word means. The word democracy means power of the demos. It does not delimit in advance who is of the people, yet all forms of political representation determine who counts. Democratic enactment challenges the ways in which equality is limited – through unequal access to property and wealth or through forms of propriety which delimit who can do what, when, where and how. A similar point may be made about *kratos*. *Kratos* is generally translated as power – but, as Ober argues, it is better thought of as capability. Democracy presupposes the equal capability of all. On this reading, democracy is not a regime but is a practice in which the equality of all is presupposed. Such practices are manifold. They range from the most banal everyday occurrences through to certain acts carried out by regimes. No regime in itself however embodies democracy (Ober 2008: 6).

This belies the common assumption that democracy is a regime. Political theorists tend to assume that democratic regimes occupy a defined space (the city, the nation-state, the globe); that they include some and exclude others; that they distribute rights and privileges to those deemed members of the people. In contrast I concur with Rancière that 'democracy is irreducible to either a form of government or a mode of social life' (2011: 76). Democracy is 'the wrench of equality jammed [. . .] into the gears of domination, it's what keeps politics from simply turning into law enforcement' (Rancière 2011: 79). On this account democracy disorders existent hierarchies. Rather than seeking a prior principle of legitimation it is the presupposition of equality enacted in the here and now seeking neither future vindication nor a mythical past when the demos was supposedly founded. Democracy cannot be equated with a proper order. Theorists of democracy vainly seek principles to give order to the unruly people. An example makes this point. On 24 August 2015 Germany opened its borders to all refugees fleeing the Syrian war. At a stroke the Berlin government suspended the longstanding convention which held that refugees should remain in the country of arrival. Angela Merkel's government is hardly democratic – in many respects it undermines democratic equality. Yet for this brief moment it enacted an equality without precedent in the history of the European Union. She was widely condemned in Germany and in the rest of Europe. Representative regimes sometimes act democratically. But representation is not intrinsic to democratic enactment.

Democratic enactment, then, always breaks with one or more proprietary regimes. A proprietary regime may be analysed across at least three dimensions. First, it establishes and maintains relations of the proper. This includes the demarcation of proper behaviour and actions. It supports what might, following Foucault, be termed a regime of the sayable. It allocates to certain subjects words which have significance, to others words without significance. A proprietary regime is second, supported by relations of property. Property, in all its forms, entails enclosure, the drawing and the maintenance of boundaries of exclusion and inclusion. Enclosure is not simply the putting up of fences around that which is ontologically prior to the enclosure. Rather it defines the proper, in the very act of enclosing, securing certain ways of being. If democracy's premise is an axiomatic equality, property relations are inherently undemocratic. Third, relations of property are always articulated to practices of propriety. The definition of certain actions as criminal establishes a violation of the use of resources 'rightfully' limited to some; where bodies are entitled to be (which country, which property, which premises and the like); and what one is entitled to do with one's own body during certain times. It establishes when it is improper to transgress not only territorial or legal boundaries but also behavioural boundaries. The exclusivity of any proprietary order requires the exercise of violence over and against others. Democracy is an impropriety which disrupts consensus in attacking unequal wealth in all of its forms.

The attempt to define a demos through restrictive membership and other forms of belonging always invokes what might be deemed a proper politics. The demos is an unruly excess, the mob disruptive of the forms of propriety and sovereignty. This tension was present even in the Athenian polis. One could only be counted a citizen of Athens if already listed as a member of one of the ten demes established by Cleisthenes, against the inherited power of wealthy families. The democratic citizen was a divided subject, first defined in terms of membership of a particular deme – and marked out as such during debates – but second, the subject of a demos which entailed a universalising moment in excess of these particulars. The relationship between deme and demos is not an incidental problem to be overcome once democracy is properly realised. Rather it points to a problem inherent to the very idea of the people as the democratic agent. There is no principle adequate to the people, no qualification which allows us to name the people. Urbinati is correct, then, to distinguish the formation of opinion and will from judgment. She is correct to insist that the demos is never finally realised in the forms in which it is represented and that judgment is best exercised at a distance from the expression of democratic will. However, she is correct for the wrong reasons: the demos is always in excess of any proper representation, and it is not constituted as the complement to liberal representative institutions. Instead, it avows one claim, repeatedly, which does not require institutional form to find an expression, which is in fact constantly violated by these terms of representation: we are equal.

Notes

1. In the past decade justifications for representative democracy have received a new lease of life, most notably in the works of Urbinati (2006), Saward (2010) and Disch (2011, 2012 and 2015). These authors draw, in different ways, on post-structuralist theorisation of representation to rethink political representation. Urbinati argues that representation is integral to democracy, and that attempts to establish government without representation betray the democratic promise. Representatives exercise judgment and advocacy in an ongoing negotiation which also constitutes the represented. Saward (2010) argues that representation is not only about elections. Rather representative claims, which establish represented groups, interests or communities, are limited neither to territorial states nor to electoral politics. Most recently Lisa Disch draws on the work of Laclau and Mouffe to develop a constructivist account of representation. These authors rethink representative democracy in light of the perceived fall in electoral interest and concern that national governments no longer represent their constituents because of global and local challenges to the authority of nation-states.

2. This notion of the proper is central to a text I am completing at present, provisionally entitled *Towards an Improper Politics*. It attempts to integrate classical critique of property, and the proper, into a discursive account of democratic politics. See Devenney (2011).

3. Sofia Näsström (2006) has argued that for all three of these authors it is often difficult to distinguish diagnostic from normative work in their accounts of representative democracy. I think the reference to normativity is a red herring. No normative position can finally be justified. It will always run up against objections. Instead we should simply assert that democrats are committed to the enactment of equality. Those

who disagree are not worth arguing with. They have to be persuaded through hegemonic argument, and accorded the equality which we presuppose. Justification always comes too late, and is an attempt to escape the politics which equality introduces to unequal orders.

4. It is notable that for Urbinati one of her key reference points is John Stuart Mill's *On Liberty*. What Urbinati does not acknowledge however is that Mill altered his views on liberal democracy and representative government. As Medearis (2005) demonstrates already in his *Considerations on Representative Government*, Mill recognises that political representation is skewed in favour of wealth. He suggests that a system of proportional representation may remedy this. In his later works he develops a critique of the distortions caused by the system of private property, celebrates collective ownership and control over property, explicitly recognising that the principle of Utility currently best serves those who exercise control over property.

5. As Achille Mbembe (2017) argues in respect of blackness, to reject the argument that there is anything essential about race does not mean that we should not attack in the name of blackness existing and historic forms of oppression. Likewise, contemporary feminist debates have to address a dual logic of on the one hand recognising that the category women names those who differentially experience sexism, but trans activists note that the name women may itself act as an oppressive category. Last, debates in Marxist theory revolve around the recognition that the working class constituted by capitalism in effect abolishes not only capitalism but itself, in the case of a successful revolution.

6. Charles Taylor develops this critique in his 'Interpretation and the Sciences of Man' (1971) focusing on the constitutive rules of political community.

7. Marx developed his most sustained critique of representative democracy in a series of texts published in 1843 and 1844, responding to Hegel's *Philosophy of Right* and to Bauer's critique of the so-called 'Jewish Question'.

8. For Marx, true universality would transcend the individual defined in terms of self-interest and any system of political representation as conventionally understood. Representatives would be more like functionaries, equivalent to a cobbler, who repairs your shoes but does not change their size while doing so. In representative democracies the citizen is treated as if sovereign in the political realm, but his or her contingent existence constantly betrays this universality.

9. Clare Woodford and I have developed these arguments in an as-yet unpublished article, 'Democratic Theory: Beyond the Pale'.

14

The constructivist paradox: contemporary protest movements and (their) representation

Mathijs van de Sande

Introduction[1]

In these days of austerity, climate change, privatisation, persisting police brutality – and the violent repression of whoever dares to oppose any of the abovementioned – the sufficiency or desirability of representative democracy is increasingly contested. Over the past few years we have witnessed a global emergence of new protest movements which typically questioned the relation between democracy and representation. From the Spanish M15 or *Indignados* movement and its prominent slogan '*¡Democracia Real Ya!*' to Occupy and its claim to embody 'the 99%', it would be an understatement to argue that these protesters felt unrepresented by their respective governments and their democratic institutions. Marina Sitrin and Dario Azzellini argue that

> 'They don't represent us' has emerged as a powerful slogan in mobilizations all over the world. We hear it in the US, Spain, Greece, Brazil, Turkey, Slovenia, and even Russia [. . .] The slogans are not phrased as rejections of specific political representatives, but as expressions of a general rejection of the logic of representation. (Sitrin and Azzellini 2014: 41).

Thus, rather than turning to these very institutions and demanding their reform, these 'prefigurative' activists aimed to remain distant from – and avoid engagement with – the existing public institutions and bodies of representation (Tormey 2015: 32–5). Through the occupation and recomposition of public space and the experimental realisation of alternative, horizontalist forms of organisation and decision-making, they instead sought to present a wholly different image of what 'real' democracy could look like.

It is somewhat ironic that this recent emergence of anti-represen-
tational, direct democratic repertoires of protest coincides with a
revived interest, among theorists, in political representation (Urbinati
and Warren 2008). Whereas previously, representation was broadly
considered to limit or even minimise the democratic potential of a
political regime, today many seem to agree that modern conceptions
of democracy and institutional representation emerged correlatively,
and are in fact hard – if not impossible – to disentangle. Although
initially presented as a minority position (Urbinati 2006: 4), Nadia
Urbinati's claim that 'democratization and the representative process
share a genealogy and are not antithetical' (Urbinati 2006: 225) today
appears to be more widely accepted among political theorists. What
is more, this 'representative turn' also evinces a more profound, constructivist concept of political representation. Democracy, the argument goes, cannot be conceived without an account of representation
precisely because the latter has important constitutive functions.
There is, in other words, no political 'reality' out there independent
of, or prior to, its representations – and, hence, articulations – within
a discursive reality. Without the formulation of representative claims
(Saward 2010), no such thing could exist as a 'people' or a political
community in the name of which such representations could be performed in the first place.

We thus observe two different trends that contradict each other.
On the one hand, throughout the past decades the world has witnessed a global wave of new social movements that are outspokenly
critical of the existing representative institutions and promote a more
horizontalist and participatory form of democracy in their stead. But,
on the other hand, in the academic debate we also notice a revived
interest precisely in political representation and its constructivist
qualities.

One prominent exponent of this constructivist turn in representation theory is Chantal Mouffe. In her recent *Agonistics* (2013),
Mouffe seeks to criticise the abovementioned prefigurative protest
movements. These tent camp movements and their advocates, she
argues, 'interpreted recent mobilizations as a manifestation of the
power of the multitude constructing new forms of social relations
outside traditional institutions. They [. . .] present their encampments
as a pre-figuration of "absolute democracy"' (Mouffe 2013: 111).
But according to Mouffe these movements' refusal to engage with
the existing public sphere and its representative institutions evinces a
fundamental misconception of democratic politics. 'A pluralist democratic society,' she stresses, 'cannot exist without representation',

as 'identities are never already given, but always produced through discursive construction; this process of construction *is* a process of representation' (Mouffe 2013: 126). This constructivist account of representation inevitably implies a context of competition and struggle. Ultimately, these movements' iconic 'General Assemblies' and consensus-oriented decision-making procedures testify to a 'flawed understanding of politics, one that does not acknowledge "the political" with its ineradicable dimension of antagonism' (Mouffe 2013: 78).

My central claim in this chapter is that a fallacy underlies this critique of contemporary protest movements. The constructivist argument in defence of political representation evinces a certain paradox. According to the constructivist advocates of political representation, any political reality is discursively constituted. But at the same time, when it is applied in concrete discussions, this constructivist approach also presupposes an extra-discursive position from which the political theorist can assess political practices and their rate of success or sufficiency. This 'constructivist paradox', as I will call it, testifies to a systematic prioritisation of political ontology over a more practically embedded understanding of political action and thus is at risk of reducing the latter to a mere symptom of the former. This precludes us from truly grasping what was at stake for many of the abovementioned protest movements and its participants, and from understanding their dismissive use of the term 'representation'. If we want to appreciate the gains and merits of the constructivist turn in contemporary political theory, we need to rethink how constructivism should be informed and constituted by political practice, rather than the other way around. Our understanding of 'the political' and its underlying logic, after all, should first and foremost be derived from a critical engagement with the concrete phenomena that it seeks to explain.

Although this is essentially a critique of the constructivist turn in representative theory as such, I will here focus on Chantal Mouffe as one of its most prominent exponents. Mouffe has also provided the most elaborate and fundamental constructivist critique of said protest movements. Through an engagement with her work, I aim to reconstruct and criticise the paradox that seems to underlie the contemporary, constructivist argument for political representation. I will start by fleshing out Mouffe's position in the following section, and counterpoise it to Michael Hardt's and Antonio Negri's defence of these recent protest movements in the subsequent section. After I have reconstructed the constructivist paradox, I will finally return to the context of recent protest movements, such as Occupy and the *Indignados*, and propose an alternative reading of their refusal to engage with the existing representative institutions.

A constructivist account of representation: Chantal Mouffe

Mouffe's constructivist understanding of political representation rests on two theoretical premises that are substantiated throughout her *œuvre*. First, her radically pluralist and 'post-foundational' point of departure leads her to reject any universalist view of human or social nature, or the good life. This means that any concept of a political community or collective identity (a 'people', 'nation', 'class', 'race', and so on) must be discursively constructed. Her second, related, premise is therefore that the relation between a signifier and its referent is mutually constitutive (or interpellative): neither precedes, as such, the relation of representation. Thus, it is only through representative relations that any account of a collective identity can be given.

In order to grasp this first premise, Mouffe's post-foundational critique of essentialism and universalism, we need to return to *Hegemony and Socialist Strategy*, her collaborative work with Ernesto Laclau. The point of departure for this eminent study is a perceived crisis of the left, which, only a few years before the collapse of the Soviet Union, had not only lost much of its appeal and mobilising potential, but also appeared to be lacking a thorough understanding of the political. How, the authors ask themselves, are we to form a new left that on the one hand is capable of acknowledging the successes as well as the failures of preceding Marxist movements, whilst at the same time preserving those particular, radical aspects of a liberal-democratic hegemonic discourse that are still worth fighting for? The answer to both questions, so it seems, lies in the recognition of a non-correspondence or 'gap between political space and society as an empirical referent' (Laclau and Mouffe 2001: 133). That is to say that any representation of a society given in a dominant political discourse inevitably fails to fully correspond with an 'objective' social order outside of it. It is impossible, Laclau and Mouffe hold, to give full political account of the social, even though every hegemonic discourse will aim to do precisely this. The idea of a society that is able to present a full and transparent image of itself to itself, is deluded and potentially dangerous.

Why so? Laclau and Mouffe's reason is simple: the 'social' is, if anything, fundamentally pluralist and divided. This plurality, they state, 'is not the phenomenon to be explained, but the starting point of the analysis' (Laclau and Mouffe 2001: 140). Any sense of collectivity or shared identity hence cannot be taken for given, and must always and continuously be constructed. What is more, no ground or basis for such a constitutive process can be found in a neutral or pre-political society. There is no 'social order' that can be 'understood as an underlying principle' (Laclau and Mouffe 2001: 95–6). For this would presuppose the possibility of finding a collective identity that is able to sufficiently and fully grasp the social from which it is abstracted. Such an identity, in other words, would have to coincide completely with its referent. This is a sheer impossibility, however: if the social is characterised only by its multiformity, *any* representation of its totality is inevitably going to leave out a number of perspectives and identities – as much as it will amplify and centralise others. Hence Laclau and Mouffe conclude that the distance between the representation of a society and its referent – between the ontological and the ontic – can never be closed. 'The incomplete character of every totality', they state, 'necessarily leads us to abandon, as a terrain of analysis, the premise of "*society*" as a sutured and self-defined totality' (Laclau and Mouffe 2001: 111; see also Warren Breckman's chapter in this volume).

This basic point of departure leads Laclau and Mouffe 'to go beyond the theoretical and political horizon of Marxism' (Laclau and Mouffe 1990: 129), and to endorse what Oliver Marchart calls 'post-foundationalism': 'a constant interrogation of metaphysical figures of foundation – such as totality, universality, essence, and ground' (Marchart 2007: 2). Our social reality, Laclau and Mouffe argue, is discursively constructed by human beings, and 'not grounded on any metaphysical "necessity" external to it – neither God, nor "essential forms", nor the "necessary laws of history"' (Laclau and Mouffe 1990: 129). The sustenance and further radicalisation of this liberating principle, which first acquired hegemonic dominance in the liberal-democratic discourse, is what, according to Mouffe, should be at the centre of a contemporary left agenda:

[W]e have to break with rationalism, individualism and universalism. Only on that condition will it be possible to apprehend the multiplicity of forms of subordination that exist in social relations and to provide a framework for the articulation of the different democratic struggles – around gender, race, class, sexuality, environment and others. This does not imply the rejection of any idea of rationality, individuality or universality, but affirms that they are necessarily plural, discursively constructed and entangled with power relations. (Mouffe 2005a: 7)

At this point, we can recognise how Mouffe's first premise is presupposed in her eventual, constructivist argument for representation. For if no 'objective' ground for our social reality can be given, this means that it must ultimately be based on discursive constructions. What is more, no rational legitimisation can be given to favour one of these constructions over any other. '[E]very society is the product of a series of practices attempting to establish order in a context of contingency' (Mouffe 2005b: 17). It is precisely this non-essentialist representativeness of identity that renders Laclau and Mouffe's pluralism radical – not only ontologically, but also politically. No subject position can be retraced to a unitary founding principle, and no 'underlying positive ground' can be established by which to hierarchise its meaning or guarantee its legitimacy (Laclau and Mouffe 2001: 167). The only vertical order that is to be found between different identifications must thus be acquired through competition and struggle.

This brings us back to the abovementioned 'gap' between the political self-imagination of a community on the one hand, and its social 'referent' on the other. For if no extra-discursive 'existence' could be ascribed to the latter (and the 'gap' between political fiction and objective 'reality' thus can never be fully closed), there can be no pre-political social, composed of independently existing and self-identifying individuals. There is no such thing as a Rousseauian moment of contractual engagement between free natural beings, who thus 'enter' a newly constituted political space. The reason for that – and this brings us to Mouffe's second premise – is that the representative relation between a signifier (such as 'people' or 'proletariat') and its referent is *mutually* constitutive.

Any sense of a 'we', in other words, does not merely result from a rational process of negotiation or mediation between different interests that are given as such (Mouffe 2005a: 70). Political identities have no neutral 'starting ground' – no natural or social point of departure from which to engage with other identities. Nor can they remain unaltered by such an engagement. Every form of identification presupposes and produces a range of representative claims that help to constitute 'who' a political collectivity – a 'we' – is. As Mouffe formulates it in a recent discussion with *Podemos*-ideologist Íñigo Errejón, '[t]he way in which the idea or representation is generally understood, as a representation of already existing identities, is completely wrong, because representation is also a process of identity construction' (Errejón and Mouffe 2016: 112). Representative claims thus express and give rise to a course of continuous modification and articulation between different positions that will eventually start to perceive a 'logical' coincidence among themselves. This entails the construction of what Laclau and Mouffe call 'signifiers': 'empty' concepts, symbols and ideas – discursive 'containers', so to speak – which on the one hand inscribe a particular content into different positions and perspectives, and on the other hand, at the same time, help to articulate them as part of an encompassing, discursive set of relations.[2]

Yet what makes this process of articulation inherently *political* is that it always already takes place in a conflictual, complex context of many competing representations. Political representations, after all, only function to the extent that they succeed in presenting themselves as the most obvious or accurate – not to say the *only* – full representation of a social reality. As collective representations seek to establish themselves as hegemonic, they must therefore, inevitably, do this at the cost of others, and seek to 'dominate the field of discursivity, to arrest the flow of differences, to construct a centre' (Laclau and Mouffe 2001: 112). This means that no signifier could ever function independently, but must always be fixed and implied in a larger whole of identifications and demands – a 'chain of equivalence', as Laclau and Mouffe call it – whose mutual correspondence is based not only on what inherently binds them together, but also on a shared, 'constituent outside'. A chain of equivalence, in other words, draws a division between what a representation (within its more encompassing discursive context) *is* or refers to on the one hand, and that which it *is not*, on the other. Thus, rather than merely signifying or identifying, equivalence also *demarcates*:

> [A] formation manages to *signify itself* (that is, to constitute itself as such) only by transforming the limits into frontiers, by constituting a chain of equivalence which constructs what is beyond the limits as that which it is *not*. It is only through negativity, division and antagonism that a formation can constitute itself as a totalizing horizon (Laclau and Mouffe 2001: 143–4).

As far as Mouffe is concerned, representation – and, thus, politics – always implies this negative aspect of articulation. Mouffe therefore has devoted considerable part of her *œuvre* to debunking the possibility of a non-conflictual politics – be it in the form of a deliberative, a communitarian, or, for that matter, an agonistic model. Division and conflict, in her eyes, 'are not to be seen as disturbances that unfortunately cannot be completely eliminated' (Mouffe 2009: 33). Instead, she argues that conflict is the very precondition for any form of politics – and, thus, also for any sense of collective identity – to exist

(Mouffe 2005a: 141). Within a liberal-democratic order, however, such conflicts are facilitated by a public sphere and its corresponding institutions, where contestations and conflicts over discursive identities can be staged. What prevents any discursive articulation from fully arresting the discursive field and enforcing a closed representation of the social, in other words, is the unavoidable dividedness of any discursive reality and the resulting factuality of representative competition.

In summary, we have reconstructed Mouffe's defence of representation and its inevitability for politics in three argumentative steps. First, we saw how a radically pluralist and post-foundationalist ontology leads her to articulate a concept of 'the social' that must always be discursively constituted. Second, this implies a constructivist concept of representation, in which both the signifier of a representative relation and its referent are mutually constructed (and continuously reconstructed) throughout the process: neither can pre-exist the other. Finally, as such representative constructions always intervene in a conflictual context of many competing representations, this process is inherently political: it presupposes antagonism, contestation and exclusion. We can thus conclude that no intervention whatsoever in this political reality could be made without the articulation of a competitive representative claim at the expense of others – or, as Mouffe calls it, without hegemonic struggle.

This brings us, finally, to Mouffe's critique of recent prefigurative protest movements such as Occupy or the *Indignados*. As we have seen, their failure to establish any concrete political successes is, according to Mouffe, due precisely to their systematic neglect of this important lesson: political action *always* and of necessity entails a certain extent of representative claim-making. But before critically challenging this assessment further below, let us briefly look into Mouffe's argument.

'Exodus' and representation

Mouffe's critique of recent protest movements largely revolves around a discussion not of Occupy's or the *Indignados'* practices, but rather of a body of literature that she one-sidedly identifies with these movements: the 'post-operaist' or autonomist Marxism of Michael Hardt and Antonio Negri (and, to a much lesser extent, Paulo Virno). In this body of theoretical literature – which, according to Mouffe, proposes an 'exodus' approach, or a political strategy of withdrawal (Mouffe 2013: 70) – the political potential of social movements such as Occupy or the *Indignados* is ultimately grounded in a range of closely intertwined, technological-economic developments, such as the re-emergence of 'commons' and the 'immaterialisation of labour' (Hardt and Negri 2012). The rise of these new, horizontal and networked forms of production, exchange and communication, Hardt and Negri argue, provides the 'solid building blocks for democratic political organization' (Hardt and Negri 2009: 353). The potential for 'real democracy' is *implied* in newly emerging 'forms of social life' (Hardt and Negri 2009: 354, italics added), and surfaces most visibly in the practices of contemporary social movements. Any attempt to recuperate or mediate this potential within an institutionalised public space should be regarded as an attempt to separate these movements from their own inherent power (Hardt and Negri 2012: 27). Hardt and Negri therefore wholeheartedly endorse the 'refusals of representation and representative governmental structures [that] have been pronounced by millions' during the recent global uprisings (Hardt and Negri 2012: 43–4). Instead of engaging with the public sphere and its corresponding apparatus, the autonomists opt for a strategy of withdrawal or subtraction from any capitalist relations of power and process of production (Hardt and Negri 2009: 152–3; Virno 1996; Virno 2004: 70; Mouffe 2013: 70). Mouffe clearly exaggerates the influence that Hardt and Negri possibly could have had on these newly emerging movements. But they all indeed seem to share a particular imagination of political struggle that could more accurately be described as a prefigurative, bottom-up process of 'building a new society within the shell of the old' (Graeber 2013: 232–3; Hardt and Negri 2000: 207; Hardt and Negri 2009: 8, 301; van de Sande 2015).

Although Hardt and Negri do not categorically dismiss any form of collaboration or exchange between social movements and representative organisations, they are inclined to the view that social movements should better 'maintain an external relationship to the government [. . .] and defend their autonomy, often through actions against the government' (Hardt and Negri 2012: 82–3). Mouffe, however, objects that they thus ignore the antagonism and discursive dividedness that inheres in *any* social and political context. Their analysis evinces a simplified view of the state and its institution as a 'monolithic entity instead of a complex set of relations, dynamic and traversed by contradictions' (Mouffe 2013: 118–19). Advocates of 'exodus' as a political strategy, Mouffe claims, neglect to exploit the many tensions and divisions that inhere even within the state and its representative bodies. In short, Mouffe blames

Hardt and Negri for having a 'flawed' understanding of politics, power, and the negative or conflictual aspects that it inevitably entails (Mouffe 2013: 77–8). Their preoccupation with the multiplicity, immanentism and horizontality of new networked forms of organisation, and their rejection of representation and any form of engagement with the state, Mouffe holds, merely evinces a more widespread 'current incapacity to think and act politically' (Mouffe 2005b: 107). Recent protest movements' refusal to address public, representative institutions with concrete demands would testify to this very incapacity.

Upon closer inspection it strikes me that Mouffe's methodology shares at least one implicit, though rather problematic, characteristic with Hardt and Negri's. For in both cases the ontological – 'the very way in which society is instituted' (Mouffe 2005b: 9) – is systematically prioritised over a discussion of the ontic, of political practice. Hardt and Negri seek to embed a broad set of economical-technological developments in an ontology of 'plenitude' and affirmation (Hardt and Negri 2012: 33). This 'ontology of the present indicated by the bio-politics of production', they then argue, 'needs to be *complemented* [. . .] by a radically democratic structure' (Hardt and Negri 2009: 321, italics added). Movements like Occupy or the *Indignados* could thus be read as 'preparations' or 'manuals' for such complementary structuring (Hardt and Negri 2012: 103–4) – their platforms of communication and organisation as 'symptoms, not causes' of a broader potential (Hardt and Negri 2011). Rather than playing any significant articulatory role, these movements and organisations are thus reduced to the symbolic exponents or symptoms of a more systematic, economically and technologically determined dynamic.

Mouffe, of course, defends the opposite position. It follows from her constructivist view of representation that these recent protest movements *could* and *should* have played such an articulatory role. Their refusal to engage with the existing public institutions and to articulate representative claims, Mouffe suggests, symptomise a more widespread (not to say ideological) misconception of the political (Mouffe 2013: 77). As Nadia Urbinati argues in the present volume, Laclau and Mouffe's concept of representation and hegemony implies that one must seek to acquire political power – which, in turn, requires engagement with representative democracy and its electoral institutions and procedures. Thus perceived, recent protest movements such as Occupy are the manifestations of a fundamental misconception of politics: they symptomise the typically 'post-political perspective

[that] defines the common sense in our post-democracies' (Mouffe 2005b: 109).

What these two analyses have in common, therefore, is that in both cases, the practices of contemporary protest movements are approached as the ontic manifestations of a more fundamental political ontology. Whether the occupations of Tahrir Square, Zuccotti Park or Puerta del Sol are conceived as successes or as failures does not matter much, in this respect. They are either the symptoms of a more encompassing political potential, or they precisely evince a complete lack thereof. Rather than to inform our understanding of politics, these protest movements are employed to confirm a theoretical framework that existed well before their emergence.

Whereas Hardt, and Negri and Mouffe might all be criticised for treating politics as secondary to theory, in Mouffe's case it is particularly problematic. Her assessment of the protest movements in question, after all, is negative – which means that any inconsistencies between political practice and its theoretical analysis lead her to critically reject the former, rather than to adjust the latter. A more fundamental problem, however, is that this prioritisation of ontology discords with its very content. A certain paradox is at play between her constructivist account of political representation on the one hand, and the way it is critically employed in a discussion of Occupy and other protest movements, on the other.

The constructivist paradox

What is this paradox? As we have seen above, Mouffe's constructivist argument for political representation depends on two basic premises: first, a post-foundational ontology that acknowledges only radical pluralism (and no further social grounding) as its point of departure; and, second, the mutual interpellation between a signifier and its referent.

This first premise is somewhat paradoxical in its own right, of course, to the extent that every social 'foundation' eventually must and will be politically constructed. But this paradox can be consistently endorsed. As Oliver Marchart stresses, in a post-foundational ontology the political serves as 'a *ground* that can never be reached and still has the status of a foundation' (Marchart 2007: 176). More problematic, however, is that Mouffe's post-foundational constructivism appears to be limited to the very *content* of this paradoxical relation between the political and the impossible ground that it gives rise to. Whereas the reconstruction of a qualitative social/political divide is continuously at stake in politics, the same does not apply, for Mouffe, to its very *procedure* of reconstruction. Mouffe's political ontology, in other words, presupposes the continuous re-articulation of our discursive reality, but it does not allow us to challenge the very ways in which this re-articulation will – and, thus, *must* – be performed in and through representative claim-making.

A similar critique applies to Mouffe's second premise. As we have seen, in any relation of political representation, both the signifier and its referent are mutually constituted. Neither precedes or remains 'untouched' by the other, so to speak. But this should also mean that not only the *content* of this mutual articulation but also its *form* are continuously renegotiated. As the relation between signifier and referent changes, after all, it would follow that the same goes for the very criteria or standards by which this relation is appreciated. In other words, as much as the discursive articulation of a representative relation changes, so do the terms in which this relation is deemed (un)successful, (in)accurate, (un)fulfilling, (un)worthy, and so on. It is not only the content of a discourse that is subject to continuous re-articulation, but also the way in which it understands and appreciates itself.

In Mouffe's assessment, however, movements such as Occupy and the *Indignados* upheld a 'flawed understanding of politics, one that does not acknowledge "the political" with its ineradicable dimension of antagonism' (Mouffe 2013: 78). These movements' practices, in other words, were not sufficiently political, as they failed to understand how politics, objectively, 'functions'. They naively ignored the negativity and exclusivity that unavoidably inheres in the political, and as a consequence neglected the necessity of representative claim-making. But there is no consideration of the possibility that precisely such meta-political, methodological and strategic questions – what it means to be successful or not; how politics should, in fact, be 'done'; how and to what extent representative claim-making indeed is necessary, and so on – were precisely what was fundamentally at stake for these movements and their practices. Mouffe's political-ontological framework allows us to formulate a comprehensive critique of recent protest movements. Yet it fails to grasp the relevance and meaning of important strategic questions that these movements raised about themselves.

This, in short, is the constructivist paradox. In order to assess particular political practices from a constructivist perspective, one still has to assume a theoretical position that remains 'immune', so to speak, to its own post-foundational presuppositions. This 'immune', extra-discursive position is anchored in particular concepts of 'the political' and of political action; a limited set of 'objective rules' for it to abide by; and a certain standard of 'success', 'failure' or 'sufficiency' by which to evaluate it. To be more precise (for obviously, no such thing exists as extra-discursivity or 'immunity'), these are to be determined from a theoretical position that *precedes*, and remains unaffected by, the concrete political and discursive interventions under scrutiny. Constructivist discourse analysis departs from the assertion that no concept can be ascribed a fixed, objective and/or exhaustive meaning. But it follows precisely from this prioritisation of the theorist's position that there must always be a number of notions or signifiers, whose meaning and relevance are taken as given. They serve as the 'objective' criteria by which political practices can be evaluated. In Mouffe's analysis of contemporary protest movements, her – very specific – concept of 'representation' can be seen to fulfil such a role.

The meaning of 'representation'

Let me make this a bit more concrete. Mouffe's critique of recent protest movements – as much as Hardt and Negri's appraisal, for that matter – testifies to the following implicit assumption: given that movements such as Occupy and the *Indignados* refuse to speak of themselves in terms of representational politics, it follows that they *de facto* refuse to play any significant representative role. Mouffe, as we have seen, counters that a politics without representation is inconceivable. Given its important, constitutive function, no popular mobilisation could possibly succeed without representative claim-making. And from this also follows that these movements sooner or later must 'engage with the existing institutions in order to transform them' (Errejón and Mouffe 2016: 112).

But Mouffe fails to take into account that *her* concept of 'representation' differs significantly from how these movements used the term. It is far from given, after all, what 'representation' exactly means. In her eminent *The Concept of Representation*, Hanna Pitkin distinguishes between representation as a symbolic and descriptive relation – which she describes as a relation of 'standing for' – on the one hand, and representation 'as an acting for others, an activity in behalf of, in the interest of, as the agent of, someone else' (Pitkin 1967: 113), on the other. In many European languages, but not in English or French, this conceptual difference translates into a corresponding terminological distinction: the former, symbolic, concept of representation is called *Darstellung* in German, *rappresentazione* in Italian, *representatie* in Dutch. The latter – more institutional – form is referred to as, respectively, *Vertretung, rappresentanza* or *vertegenwoordiging.*[3]

This distinction between two different uses of the term 'representation' may have significant consequences for our appreciation of recent protest movements and their refusal to engage in representative politics. Take, for example, a slogan like '¡*Que no nos representan!*', which was prominently used by the Spanish M15 or *Indignados* movement. It is evident that the word '*representan*' refers to one concept of representation (*Vertretung*, or 'acting for'), and not necessarily to the other. After all, this would render the slogan self-contradictory, as 'They don't represent us!' could as well be considered a representative claim in its own right (in the sense of *Darstellung,* or 'standing for'). By means of this slogan, the *Indignados* denounced the institutions that claim to 'act for', or on behalf of, the people. But at the same time, the very same slogan also served to constitute the notion of an 'us', for which the movement claimed to stand. Something similar could be said of the Occupy movement. Its prominent slogan 'we are the 99%' and its attempt to provide in its activist tent camp a 'model' for a future society (Graeber 2013: 233) could both be regarded as representative claims in the symbolic sense of the word (see Decreus et al. 2014).

Mouffe appears to overlook the difference between these two concepts of representation. She contends that today's protest movements should engage with the formal and institutional channels of representation (*Vertretung*), but the main argument that she presents in defence of this position – namely, that representation fulfils an important, constitutive function – rather appeals to the second, symbolic concept of representation (*Darstellung*). From the fact that many of these protest movements refused to engage in institutional representation, she derives that they also neglected or failed to appreciate symbolic representation. Their attempt to create 'new social relations outside the existing institutional framework' (Mouffe 2013: 100) is taken to imply a dismissal of 'the very *idea* of representation' – that is: the idea that 'identities are never already given, but always produced through discursive construction' (Mouffe 2013: 126, italics added). But as soon as we, unlike Mouffe, distinguish between representation as 'standing for' and representation as 'acting for', this argument breaks down. It is established by virtue of a very particular notion of representation that is never properly compared to that of the protest movements in question. Mouffe's own terminology, in other words, is assumed to have an 'objective' meaning that remains 'immune' to the discursive interventions of said protest movements, and hence can be left out of the equation.

The point that I want to make here is not that these movements' concept of representation is more – or, for that matter, less – accurate than Mouffe's. My claim, instead, is that, much as with any term, it is used in rather different ways. In order to appreciate the role that political representation played in the articulation of these protest movements' strategy, we also need to understand what it means in the context of their corresponding discourse. In other words, we cannot simply criticise their dismissal of representation without asking how they used this term. The content of a movement's discourse and the form of its strategy are closely interconnected. If we are to avoid the constructivist paradox, we must not take either for granted, and instead seek to understand how strategy and discourse constitute and correlate with each other.

Discourse and strategy

How, then, are we to approach this interplay between discourse and strategy? How exactly are they interrelated? Let me give an example. In her noteworthy study of American civil rights and student movements in the 1960s, Francesca Polletta explains how anti-segregationist sit-in protesters came to describe their actions as 'spontaneous'. This evinced the movement's wider aspiration to break away from conventional images of political activism. 'In the stories students told,' Polletta argues:

> the 1960 sit-ins were a break with the incomplete engagement and gradualism of adult leaders (spontaneity denoted a moral imperative to act). They were a break with the action-impeding bureaucracy of mainstream civil rights organizations (spontaneity denoted local initiative). And they were a break with the sober asceticism of prior direct action (spontaneity denoted a joy and freedom in action). Narratives of the sit-ins helped make normative a physically dangerous form of activism. (Polletta 2006: 52)

Participants and sympathisers thus viewed these sit-ins as 'immediate, expressive, and powerfully moral – all meanings associated with "spontaneity" – but also as non-political and nonstrategic' (Polletta 2006: 43). Yet it is widely acknowledged that these actions were in fact carefully planned and prepared, its participants often trained, and sometimes even coordinated by formal organisations, such as the Student Nonviolent Coordination Committee (SNCC). Is there not simply a blatant discrepancy, sceptics could suggest, between these movements' self-perception and self-presentation as inherently 'spontaneous' on the one hand, and their 'actual' strategies and organisational structures on the other? Not quite so, Polletta argues. For these activists, the term 'spontaneity' bore specific emotional associations, which corresponded with their own experiences of participating in a sit-in: a sense of courage, strength, calm and determination, but also of fun (Polletta 2006: 41). Within this particular discursive constellation, moreover, 'spontaneity' connoted locality, urgency and moral righteousness (Polletta 2006: 172). These qualities are not logically implied in the concept, nor do they exhaustively grasp its 'meaning'. But rather than other possible associations, such as 'unprepared', 'not carefully planned' or 'pertaining to a lack of formal organisation', in this case 'spontaneity' first and foremost appealed to a movement's self-image as young and daring, locally oriented and morally invested. What is more, this self-articulation translated in a particular strategic repertoire, which prescribed a specific course of action ('direct actions' such as sit-ins), a form and culture of organisation (horizontalist, decentralised and relatively informal, with a focus on coordination rather than partisan discipline) and particular standards or criteria by which political activism could be deemed fulfilling and meaningful (such as a direct experience of democracy and equality) (see Polletta 2002a). The representation that this sit-in movement gave of its own practices, in other words, cannot simply be distinguished from a particular political logic to which it appealed. And this logic had significant consequences for the way in which this movement would assess and appreciate itself. In short, the movement's use of the term 'spontaneous' in its narrative self-presentation was 'both strategically deployed and constitutive of [its] understanding of strategy, interest, and identity' (Polletta 2002b: 48).

I am inclined to approach recent protest movements such as Occupy or the *Indignados*, and their dismissive use of the term 'representation' in a similar manner. For the square occupiers this term bore particular, non-exhaustive associations. One of the term's strongest connotations, it appears, was that political representation inevitably entails the submission of clear-cut, univocal and relatively short-term demands to those illegitimately holding public office. Any attempt to engage with them could only further the experience of a democratic deficit, to which many of the movements' participants appealed. As David Graeber, one of Occupy's initiators, stresses in an interview, for instance, it made perfect sense for his fellow activists not to address any representative institutions with particular demands or grievances:

> If you make demands, you're saying, in a way, that you're asking the people in power and the existing institutions to do something different. And one reason people have been hesitant to do that is they see these institutions as the problem. (Graeber, quoted in Klein 2011)

In his research on the anarchist inspirations and characteristics of *Occupy Wall Street*, Mark Bray suggests that any strategy encouraging 'communication with the elite' – which comprises the articulation of demands or a comprehensive short-term agenda, claiming representative legitimacy and the endorsement of formal leadership – would immediately result in a limitation of the movement's breadth and radicality. The problem with voicing a univocal and narrow set of demands, Bray argues, is that if it 'does not confine itself to [a] discrete sphere of acceptable dissent, it is rendered unintelligible in the media and invalidated entirely' (Bray 2013: 28).

The only alternative, many Occupiers felt, was to refrain from claiming any representative legitimacy, and instead to directly embody or 'prefigure' a different conception of 'democracy' in the movement's practices and forms of organisation. The endorsement of direct, consensus-oriented decision-making procedures (such as facilitation and hand signals), and of general assemblies or spokescouncils as the movements' most important decisional organs, in that sense not only helped the Occupiers to articulate their needs and demands in a radically different way. It also entailed the articulation of a different political repertoire and strategy – which, as a consequence, corresponds with a different, newly articulated conception of 'the political'. Defined in terms such as 'real democracy', 'autonomy', 'protagonism' or 'horizontalism' (Sitrin and Azzellini 2014), this conception thus was counterposed to a *particular* reading of the term 'representation'.

Thus, whether these movements' concept of 'representation' and the underlying political logic to which it contributes are 'accurate' is beside the point. After all, such an alternative understanding of the political also prescribes a specific set of norms and criteria by which the movements' practices could be evaluated and assessed. For example, many insider accounts of Occupy and the *Indignados* movements have stressed their strong experimental and experiential merits (Harvey 2012; Howard and Pratt-Boyden 2013; Juris 2012). The prefigurative experiences with direct democratic organisation not only may have a bearing on the individual worldview of its participants, but they also further contribute to 'a global evolution in tactics' (Gould-Wartofsky 2015: 212). If such aspects indeed grasp best what was at stake during the days of these square occupations, a mere reference to their 'flawed understanding' of politics cannot possibly suffice. The experimental novelty of these movements, the liberatory experiences of their participants and their potential contribution to a new understanding of 'the political' and its underlying logic may – at least for these participants – serve as the main denominators for its success.

If anything, these observations should encourage us to critically rethink not the representative potential of recent protest movements, but first and foremost that of contemporary radical theory. For as much as the contested forms and institutions of representative democracy, this field of research may have turned a blind eye to its subjects' actual needs, grievances and inspirations.

Notes

1. The author would like to thank Lisa Disch and Tim Heysse for their insightful feedback and comments on earlier versions of this chapter.
2. 'Empty' as they may be, Laclau in his later work (Laclau 2005) explicates how and why a signifier with popular – rather than particularist or elitist – aspirations is necessary for the articulation of a *democratic* collective identity. Only under the name of a 'demos' or 'people', an essentially diverse and divided mass comes to recognise itself *as* a 'people'.
3. For a more elaborate discussion of the differences between these concepts of representation, see Alessandro Mulieri's chapter in this volume.

Bibliography

Abizadeh, Arash (2002), 'Does Liberal Democracy Presuppose a Cultural Nation? Four Arguments', *American Political Science Review* 96: 3, pp. 495–509.

Achen, Christopher H. (1975), 'Mass Political Attitudes and the Survey Response', *American Political Science Review* 69: 4, pp. 1218–31.

Achen, Christopher H. and Larry M. Bartels (2016), *Democracy for Realists: Why Elections Do Not Produce Responsive Government*, Princeton, NJ and Oxford: Princeton University Press.

Afary, Janet and Kevin Anderson (2005), *Foucault and the Iranian Revolution*, Chicago, IL: University of Chicago Press.

Ahearn, Laura M. (2001), 'Language and Agency', *Annual Review of Anthropology* 30, pp. 109–37.

Alcoff, Linda (1995), 'The Problem of Speaking for Others', in *Who Can Speak? Authority and Critical Identity*, ed. Judith Roof and Robyn Wigman, Chicago, IL: University of Illinois Press.

Anderson, Benedict [1983] (1991), *Imagined Communities: Reflections on the Origin and Spread of Nationalism* (revised and extended edition), London: Verso.

Ankersmit, F. R. (1996), *Aesthetic Politics: Political Philosophy Beyond Fact and Value*, Stanford, CA: Stanford University Press.

Ankersmit, F.R. (2002), *Political Representation*, Stanford, CA: Stanford University Press.

Balibar, Étienne (2015), *Citizenship*, Cambridge: Polity Press.

Barber, Bemjamin (1984), *Strong Democracy: Participatory Politics for a New Age*, Berkely, CA: University of California Press.

Baron, Hans (1993), *The Crisis of the Early Italian Renaissance: Civic Humanism and Republican Liberty in an Age of Classicism and Tyranny* (revised edition), Princeton, NJ: Princeton University Press.

Barthe, Yannick, Damien de Blic, Jean-Philippe Heurtin, Éric Lagneau, Cyril Lemieux, Dominique Linhardt, Cédric Moreau de Bellaing, Catherine Rémy and Danny Trom (2014), 'Sociologie pragmatique : mode d'emploi', *Politix*, 103, pp. 175–204.

257

Beck, Ulrich (1997), *The Reinvention of Politics*, Cambridge: Polity Press.

Beitz, Charles R. (1989) *Political Equality*, Princeton, NJ: Princeton University Press.

Berger, Peter L. and Thomas Luckmann (1991), *The Social Construction of Reality; a Treatise in the Sociology of Knowledge*, London: Penguin Books.

Bobbio, Norberto (1987), *The Future of Democracy*, trans. Roger Griffin and ed. Richard Bellamy, London: Polity Press.

Bohman, James (2007), *Democracy across Borders: From Dêmos to Dêmoi.* Cambridge, MA: MIT Press.

Boltanski, Luc (2011), *On Critique: a Sociology of Emancipation*, Cambridge and Malden, MA: Polity Press.

Borges, Jorge Luis (1977), *The Book of Sand*, trans. Norman Thomas di Giovanni, New York: E.P. Dutton.

Bose, Sumantra (2002), *Bosnia after Dayton. Nationalist Partition and International Intervention*, London: Hurst & Company.

Bourdieu, Pierre (1979), 'Public Opinion Does Not Exist', *Communication and Class Struggle* 1, pp. 124–30.

Bourdieu, Pierre (1990), 'Social Space and Symbolic Power', in *In Other Words: Essays Towards a Reflexive Sociology*, trans. Matthew Adamson, Stanford: Stanford University Press.

Bourdieu, Pierre (1991a), 'Delegation and Political Fetishism', in *Language and Symbolic Power*, ed. John B. Thompson, Cambridge, MA: Harvard University Press, pp. 203–19.

Bourdieu, Pierre (1991b), 'Political Representation: Elements for a Theory of the Political Field', in *Language and Symbolic Power*, ed. John B. Thompson, Cambridge, MA: Harvard University Press, pp. 171–202.

Bourdieu, Pierre (1991c), 'Social Space and the Genesis of "Classes"', in *Language and Symbolic Power*, ed. John B. Thompson, Cambridge, MA: Harvard University Press, pp. 229–51.

Bray, Mark (2013), *Translating Anarchy: The Anarchism of Occupy Wall Street*, Winchester and Washington: Zero Books.

Breckman, Warren (2005), 'Politics in a Symbolic Key: Pierre Leroux, Romantic Socialism, and the Schelling Affair', *Modern Intellectual History* 2: 1, pp. 61–86.

Breckman, Warren (2013), *Adventures of the Symbolic: Postmarxism and Radical Democracy*, New York: Columbia University Press.

Brennan, Geoffrey and Alan Hamlin (1999), 'On Political Representation'. *British Journal of Political Science* 29: 1, pp. 109–27.

Brito Vieira, Mónica and David Runciman (2008), *Representation*, Cambridge: Polity Press.

Brown, Mark B. (2006), 'Citizen Panels and the Concept of Representation', *Journal of Political Philosophy* 14: 2, pp. 203–25.

Brown, Mark B. (2009), *Science in Democracy: Expertise, Institutions, and Representation*, Cambridge, MA: MIT Press.

Brubaker, Rogers (2004), *Ethnicity without Groups*, Cambridge, MA: Harvard University Press.

Butler, Judith (1995), 'For a Careful Reading', in Seyla Benhabib, Judith Butler, Drucilla Cornel and Nancy Fraser, *Feminist Contentions: A Philosophical Exchange*, London: Routledge, pp. 127–43.

Butters, Humfrey (2010), 'Machiavelli and the Medici', in *The Cambridge Companion to Machiavelli*, ed. John N. Najemy, Cambridge: Cambridge University Press, pp. 64–79.

Cameron, David R. (1974), 'Toward a Theory of Political Mobilization', *Journal of Politics* 36: 1, pp. 138–71.

Carmines, Edward and James Kuklinski (1990), 'Incentives, Opportunities and the Logic of Public Opinion in American Political Representation', in *Information and Democratic Processes*, ed. John A. Ferejohn and James Kuklinski, Urbana, IL: University of Illinois Press.

Castiglione, Dario (2006), 'Accountability', *Encyclopaedia of Governance*, London: Sage.

Castiglione, Dario (2012), 'Giving Pitkin Her Due: What the "Representative Claim" Gets Right, and What It Risks Missing', *Contemporary Political Theory* 11: 1, pp. 118–22.

Castiglione, Dario (2015), 'Trajectories and Transformations of the Democratic Representative System', *Global Policy Journal* 6: 1, pp. 8–16.

Celis, Karen, Sarah Childs, Johanna Kantola and Mona Lena Krook (2014), 'Constituting Women's Interests through Representative Claims', *Politics & Gender* 10: 2, pp. 149–74.

Chambers, Samuel A. (2003), *Untimely Politics*, Edinburgh: Edinburgh University Press.

Chandler, David (2000), *Bosnia. Faking Democracy After Dayton*, London: Pluto Press.

Chartier, Roger (1989), 'Le monde comme représentation', *Annales*, pp. 1505–20.

Chong, Dennis and James Druckman (2007), 'Framing Public Opinion in Competitive Democracies', *American Political Science Review* 101: 4, pp. 637–55.

Christiano, Thomas (1996), *The Rule of the Many: Fundamental Issues in Democratic Theory*, Boulder, CO: Westview Press.

Coby, Patrick (1999), *Machiavelli's Romans: Liberty and Greatness in the Discourses on Livy*, Lanham, MD: Lexington Books.

Cochin, Augustine (1979), *L'esprit du jacobinisme. Une interprétation sociologique de la Révolution française*, Paris: Presses Universitaires de France.

Cohen, Joshua and Charles Sabel (1997), 'Directly-deliberative Polyarchy', *European Law Journal* 3: 4, pp. 313–42.

Colebrook, Claire (1999), *Ethics and Representation: From Kant to Post-Structuralism*, Edinburgh: Edinburgh University Press.

Colliot-Thélène, Catherine (2011), *La démocratie sans demos*, Paris: Presses universitaires de France.

Cowan, Bainard (1981), 'Walter Benjamin's Theory of Allegory', *New German Critique* 22, pp. 109–22.

Crenshaw, Kimberlé (1991), 'Mapping the Margins: Intersectionality, Identity Politics, and Violence against Women of Color', *Stanford Law Review* 43: 6, pp. 1241–99.

Dahl, Robert A. (1996), 'Further Reflections on the Elitist Theory of Democracy', *American Political Science Review* 60: 2, pp. 296–305.

Dahl, Robert (1998), *On Democracy*, New Haven, CT: Yale University Press.

Dastur, Françoise (1993), 'Merleau-Ponty and Thinking from Within', *Merleau-Ponty in Contemporary Perspectives*, ed. Patrick Burke and Jan Van der Veken, London: Kluwer, pp. 25–36.

Davies, Bronwyn (1991), 'The Concept of Agency: A Feminist Poststructuralist Analysis', *Social Analysis: The International Journal of Social and Cultural Practice* 30, pp. 42–53.

Day, Gail (1999), 'Allegory: Between Deconstruction and Dialectics', *Oxford Art Journal*, 22: 1, pp. 103–18.

Decreus, Thomas (2013), 'Beyond Representation? A Critique of the Concept of the Referent', *Representation* 49: 1, pp. 33–43.

Decreus, Thomas, Matthias Lievens and Antoon Braeckman (2014), 'Building Collective Identities: How New Social Movements Try to Overcome Post-Politics', *Parallax* 20: 2, pp. 136–48.

De Man, Paul (1984), *The Rhetoric of Romanticism*, New York: Columbia University Press.

Derrida, Jacques (1973), *Speech and Phenomena and Other Essays on Husserl's Theory of Signs*, trans. David B. Allison and Leonard Lawlor, Evanston, IL: Northwestern University Press.

Derrida, Jacques (1978), *Writing and Difference*, trans. Alan Bass, London: Routledge.

Derrida, Jacques (1982), 'Différance', in *Margins of Philosophy*, trans. Alan Bass, Chicago, IL: University of Chicago Press, pp. 1–28.

Derrida, Jacques (1986), 'Declarations of Independence', *New Political Science* 7: 1, pp. 7–15.

Derrida, Jacques (1988), *Limited Inc.*, trans. Samuel Weber, Jeffrey Mehlman and Alan Bass, Evanston, IL: Northwestern University Press.

Derrida, Jacques (2003), 'Autoimmunity: Real and Symbolic Suicides', in *Philosophy in a Time of Terror: Dialogues with Jürgen Habermas and Jacques Derrida*, ed. Giovanna Borradori, Chicago, IL: University of Chicago Press, pp. 85–136.

Derrida, Jacques (2005), *Rogues: Two Essays on Reason*, trans. Pascale-Anne Brault and Michael Naas, Stanford, CA: Stanford University Press.

Derrida, Jacques (2007a), 'Envois', in *Psyche: Inventions of the Other*, Stanford, CA: Stanford University Press, 1, pp. 94–128.

Derrida, Jacques (2007b), 'A Certain Impossible Possibility of Saying the Event', *Critical Inquiry* 33, pp. 441–61.

Derrida, Jacques (2016), *Of Grammatology*, 40th Anniversary Edition, trans. Gayatri Chakravorty Spivak, Baltimore, MD: Johns Hopkins University Press.

Der Standard (2003), 'Erste Ausbruch aus Dayton-Gefängnis', 16 September.

Devenney, Mark (2011), 'Property, Propriety and Democracy', *Studies in Social Justice* 5: 2, pp. 149–65.

Disch, Lisa (2008), 'The People as "Presupposition" of Representative Democracy: An Essay on the Political Theory of Pierre Rosanvallon, *Redescriptions*', *Political Thought, Conceptual History and Feminist Theory* 12: 1, pp. 47–71.

Disch, Lisa (2011), 'Toward a Mobilization Conception of Democratic Representation', *American Political Science Review* 105: 1, pp. 100–14.

Disch, Lisa (2012), 'Democratic Representation and the Constituency Paradox', *Perspectives on Politics* 10: 2, pp. 599–616.

Disch, Lisa (2014), 'La représentation politique et les "effets de subjectivation"', trans. Rostom Mesli and Benjamin Boudou, *Raisons Politiques* 56: 4, pp. 25–47.

Disch, Lisa (2015), 'The "Constructivist Turn" in Democratic Representation: A Normative Dead-End?', *Constellations* 22: 4, pp. 487–99.

Dovi, Suzanne (2002), 'Preferable Descriptive Representatives: Will Just Any Woman, Black, or Latino Do?', *American Political Science Review* 96: 4, pp. 729–43.

Dovi, Suzanne (2007), *The Good Representative*, Oxford: Blackwell Publishers.

Dowlen, Oliver (2008), *The Political Potential of Sortition: a Study of the Random Selection of Citizens for Public Office*, Charlottesville, VA and Exeter: Imprint Academic.

Druckman, James N. (2004), 'Political Preference Formation: Competition, Deliberation, and the (Ir)relevance of Framing Effects', *American Political Science Review* 98: 4, 671–86.

Druckman, James N. and Lawrence R. Jacobs (2015), *Who Governs? Presidents, Public Opinion, and Manipulation*, Chicago, IL: University of Chicago Press.

Dryzek, John S. and Simon Niemeyer (2008), 'Discursive Representation', *American Political Science Review* 102: 4, pp. 481–493.

Dutoya, Virginie, Samuel Hayat (2016), 'Prétendre représenter', *Revue française de science politique* 66: 1, pp. 7–25.

Ebrahim, Alnoor (2003), *NGOs and Organizational Change: Discourse, Reporting, and Learning*, Cambridge, UK: Cambridge University Press.

Eco, Umberto (1984), *Semiotics and the Philosophy of Language*, Bloomington, IN: Indiana University Press, pp. 143.

Errejón, Iñigo and Chantal Mouffe (2016), *Podemos: In the Name of the People*, trans. Sirio Canós Donnay, London: Lawrence & Wishart.

Fabre, Daniel (1989), 'Symbolisme en questions', *L'Autre et le semblable: Regards sur l'ethnologie des sociétés contemporaines*, ed. Martine Segalen, Paris: Presses du CRNS, p. 61.

Fabre, Daniel (1996), 'Le symbolique, brève histoire d'un objet', *Une école pour les sciences sociales: De la VIᵉ Section à l'École des Hautes Études en Sciences Sociales*, ed. Jacques Revel and Nathan Wachtel, Paris: Les Éditions du CERF, p. 250.

Ferejohn, John (2013), 'Two Views of the City: Republicanism and Law', in *Republican Democracy*, ed. Andreas Niederberger and Philip Schlink, Edinburgh: Edinburgh University Press.

Ferejohn, John (2015), 'Are There Two Cities or One?' unpublished paper delivered at the NYU Law School, 5 November.

Finley, Moses I. (1985), *L'Invention de la politique. Démocratie et politique en Grèce et dans la Rome républicaine*, Paris: Flammarion.

Foucault, Michel (1972), *Power/Knowledge*, ed. Colin Gordon, trans. Colin Gordon, Leo Marshall, John Mepham and Kate Sofer, New York: Pantheon Books.

Foucault, Michel (1977), *Discipline and Punishment*, trans. Alan Sheridan, New York: Pantheon Books.

Foucault, Michel (1978), *History of Sexuality,vol. 1*, trans. Robert Hurley, New York: Pantheon Books.

Foucault, Michel (1982), 'The Subject and Power', *Critical Inquiry* 8: 4, pp. 777–95.

Foucault, Michel (1987), 'Maurice Blanchot: The Thought from Outside', in *Foucault/Blanchot*, trans. Jeffrey Melman and Brian Massumi, New York: Zone Books, pp. 7–60.

Foucault, Michel (2009), *Security, Territory, Population: Lectures at the Collège de France 1977–1978*, ed. Michel Senellart, trans. Graham Burchell, London: Palgrave Macmillan.

Foucault, Michel (2014), *Wrong-Doing and Truth-Telling: The Function of Avowal in Justice*, ed. Fabienne Brion and Bernard E. Harcourt, trans. Stephen W. Sawyer, Chicago, IL: University of Chicago Press.

Fung, Archon (2006), 'Democratizing the Policy Process', in *Oxford Handbook of Public Policy*, ed. Martin Rein, Michael Moran and Robert E. Goodin, Oxford: Oxford University Press, pp. 669–85.

Fung, Archon (2013), 'The Principle of All-Affected Interests: An Interpretation and Defense', *Representation: Elections and Beyond*, ed. Jack H. Nagel and Rogers M. Smith, University Park, PA: Pennsylvania State University Press, pp. 236–68.

Gamson, William A. and Andre Modigliani (1989), 'Media Discourse and Public Opinion on Nuclear Power: A Constructionist Approach', *American Journal of Sociology* 95: 1, pp. 1–37.

Garsten, Bryan (2010), 'Representative Government and Popular Sovereignty', in *Political Representation*, ed. Ian Shapiro, Susan C. Stokes,

Alexander S. Kirshner and Elisabeth Jean Wood, Cambridge: Cambridge University Press, pp. 90–110.

Geenens, Raf (2017), 'Sovereignty as Autonomy', *Law and Philosophy* 36: 5, pp. 495–524.

Geenens, Raf and Helena Rosenblatt (2012), *French Liberalism. From Montesquieu to the Present Day*, Cambridge: Cambridge University Press.

Geenens, Raf, Thomas Decreus, Femmy Thewissen, Antoon Braeckman and Marta Resmini (2015), 'The "Co-Originality" of Constituent Power and Representation', *Constellations* 22: 4, pp. 514–22.

Gerbaudo, Paolo (2017), *The Mask and the Flag: Populism, Citizenism and Protest*, London: Hurst Publishers.

Gilens, Martin and Benjamin I. Page (2014), 'Testing Theories of American Politics: Elites, Interest Groups, and Average Citizens', *Perspectives on Politics* 12: 3, pp. 564–81.

Ginzburg, Carlo (2001), 'Representation: the Word, the Idea, the Thing', in *Wooden Eyes: Nine Reflections on Distance*, New York: Columbia University Press.

Goethe, J. W. von (1898), 'Nachträgliches zu Philostrats Gemälde', in *Werke, Weimarer Ausgabe 1*.

Goethe, J. W. von (1994), 'Maximen und Reflexionen', *Werke. Bd. XII: Schriften zur Kunst. Schriften zur Literatur. Maximen und Reflexionen*, ed. Erich Trunz and Hans Joachim Schrimpf, München: C. H. Beck.

Goodin, Robert E. (2003a), 'Democratic Accountability: The Third Sector and All', Working Paper no. 19, Cambridge, MA: The Hauser Center.

Goodin, Robert E. (2003b), *Reflective Democracy*, Oxford: Oxford University Press.

Goodin, Robert E. (2007), 'Enfranchising All-Affected Interests, and Its Alternatives', *Philosophy and Public Affairs* 35, pp. 40–68.

Goodin, Robert E. and Michael Saward (2005), 'Dog Whistles and Democratic Mandates', *The Political Quarterly* 76: 4, pp. 471–6.

Gould-Wartofsky, Michael (2015), *The Occupiers: The Making of the 99 Percent Movement*, Oxford: Oxford University Press.

Goux, Jean-Joseph (1990), *Symbolic Economies: After Marx and Freud*, trans. Jennifer Curtiss Gage, Ithaca, NY: Cornell University Press.

Graeber, David (2013), *The Democracy Project: a History, a Crisis, a Movement*, London: Allen Lane.

Grant, Ruth and Robert Keohane (2005), 'Accountability and Abuses of Power in World Politics', *American Political Science Review* 99: 1, pp. 29–53.

Guha, Ranajit (1997), *Dominance without Hegemony: History and Power in Colonial India*, Cambridge, MA: Harvard University Press.

Guicciardini, Francesco [1525] (1932), *Dialogo e discorsi del Reggimento di Firenze*, Firenze: Gius Laterza & Figli.

Guicciardini, Francesco [1537–40] (1984), *The History of Italy*, Princeton, NJ: Princeton University Press.

Guicciardini, Francesco [1525] (1998), 'Discorso di Logrono', *Republican Realism in Renaissance Florence: Francesco Giucciardini's Discorso di Logrono*, ed. Athanasios Moulakis, Lanham, MD: Rowman, pp. 117–40.

Guicciardini, Francesco [1529] (2007), 'Considerations of the "Discourses" of Niccolò Machiavelli', in *Sweetness of Power: Machiavelli's Discourses and Guicciardini's Considerations* Dekalb, IL: Northern Illinois University Press.

Guicciardini, Francesco [1525] (1994), *Dialogue on the Government of Florence*, ed. Alison Brown, Cambridge and New York: Cambridge University Press.

Guizot, François [1821] (1988), *Des moyens de gouvernement et d'opposition*, Paris: Belin.

Habermas, Jürgen (1973), *Legitimationsprobleme im Spätkapitalismus*, Frankfurt am Main: Suhrkamp Verlag.

Habermas, Jürgen (1975), *Legitimation Crisis*, trans. Thomas McCarthy, Boston, MA: Beacon Press.

Habermas, Jürgen (1990), *Strukturwandel der Öffentlichkeit – Untersuchungen zu einer Kategorie der bürgerlichen Gesellschaft*, Frankfurt am Main: Suhrkamp Verlag.

Habermas, Jürgen (1992), 'Further Reflections on the Public Sphere', in *Habermas and the Public Sphere*, ed. Graig Calhoun, Cambridge, MA: MIT Press, pp. 421–61.

Habermas, Jürgen (1996), *Between Facts and Norms: Contributions to a Discourse Theory of Law and Democracy*, trans. William Rehg, Cambridge, MA: MIT Press.

Hachez, Nicolas and Jan Wouters (2011), 'A Glimpse at the Democratic Legitimacy of Private Standards: Assessing the Public Accountability of GLOBALG. AP', *Journal of International Economic Law* 14: 3, pp. 677–710.

Hacking, Ian (1992), 'The Self-Vindication of the Laboratory Sciences', in *Science as Practice and Culture*, ed. Andrew Pickering, Chicago, IL and London: University of Chicago Press, pp. 29–64.

Hankins, James (2004), *Renaissance Civic Humanism: Reappraisals and Reflections*, Cambridge: Cambridge University Press.

Hankinson, R. J. (2008), 'Philosophy of Nature', *The Cambridge Companion to Galen*, New York: Cambridge University Press, pp. 210–41.

Hardt, Michael and Antonio Negri (2000), *Empire*, Cambridge, MA: Harvard University Press.

Hardt, Michael and Antonio Negri (2009), *Commonwealth*, Cambridge, MA: Belknap/Harvard University Press.

Hardt, Michael and Antonio Negri (2011), 'Arabs are Democracy's New Pioneers', *The Guardian*, 24 February.

Hardt, Michael and Antonio Negri (2012), *Declaration*, New York: Argo Navis Author Services.

Harvey, Ryan (2012), 'Occupy before and beyond', in *We Are Many: Reflections on Movement Strategy. From Occupation to Liberation*, ed. Kate Khatib, Margaret Killjoy and Mike McGuire, Oakland, CA and Edinburgh: AK Press, pp. 123–33.

Hatherell, Michael (2014), 'Repertoires of Representation and an Application to Indonesia's Jokowi', *Representation* 50: 4, pp. 439–51.

Hayat, Samuel (2013), 'La représentation inclusive', *Raisons Politiques* 50, pp. 115–35.

Hayat, Samuel (2014), *Quand la République était révolutionnaire. Citoyenneté et représentation en 1848*, Paris: Seuil.

Hayat, Samuel (2015), 'The Revolution of 1848 in the History of French Republicanism', *History of Political Thought* 36: 2, pp. 331–53.

Hayat, Samuel (2018), 'Varieties of Inclusive Representation', in *Creating Political Presence. The New Politics of Democratic Representation*, ed. Dario Castiglione and Johannes Pollak, Chicago, IL: Chicago University Press, pp. 141–61.

Held, David (1996), *Models of Democracy*, Stanford, CA: Stanford University Press.

Held, David and Mathias Koenig-Archibugi (2005), *Global Governance and Public Accountability*, Oxford: Blackwell Publishing.

Hénaff, Marcel (1998), *Claude Lévi-Strauss and the Making of Structural Anthropology*, trans. Mary Baker, Minneapolis, MN: University of Minnesota Press, 6.

Hirschman, Albert O. (1970), *Exit, Voice, and Loyalty: Responses to Decline in Firms, Organizations, and States*, Cambridge, MA: Harvard University Press.

Hobbes, Thomas [1651] (1909), *Hobbes's Leviathan: Reprinted from the Edition of 1651*, Oxford: Clarendon Press.

Hofmann, Hasso (1974), *Repräsentation: Studien zur Wort-und Begriffsgeschichte von der Antike bis ins 19. Jahrhundert*, Berlin: Duncker & Humblot.

Hofmann, Hasso (2013), 'Le Concept de représentation: un problème allemand?', trans. Gaëtan Pégny, rev. Yves Sintomer, *Raisons politiques*, 50: 2, pp. 79–96.

Homer (1991), *The Iliad*, trans. Robert Fagles, introduction and notes Robert Knox, New York: Penguin Books.

Honig, Bonnie (2016), *Public Things: Democracy in Disrepair*, New York: Fordham University Press.

hooks, bell [1981] (2015), *Ain't I a Woman: Black Women and Feminism*, New York: Routledge.

Howard, Neil and Keira Pratt-Boyden (2013), 'Occupy London as prefigurative action', *Development in Practice* 23: 5–6, pp. 729–41.

Ihalainen, Pasi, Cornelia Ilie and Kari Palonen (2016), 'Parliament as a Conceptual Nexus', in *Parliament and Parliamentarism: A Comparative History of A European Concept*, New York: Berghahn, pp. 1–16.

Inston, Kevin (2010), *Rousseau and Radical Democracy*, London: Continuum.

Joerges, Christian and Jürgen Neyer (1997), 'From Intergovernmental Bargaining to Deliberative Political Processes: The Constitutionalisation of Comitology', *European Law Journal* 3: 3, pp. 273–99.

Jurdjevic, M. (2007), 'Machiavelli's Hybrid Republicanism', *The English Historical Review* CXXII: 499, pp. 1228–57.

Juris, Jeffrey (2012), 'Reflections on Occupy Everywhere', *American Ethnologist* 39: 2, pp. 259–79.

Kaiser, David Aram (1993), '"The Perfection of Reason": Coleridge and the Ancient Constitution', *Studies in Romanticism* 32, p. 47.

Kaldor, Mary and Sabine Selchow (2013), 'The "Bubbling Up" of Subterranean Politics in Europe', *Journal of Civil Society* 9: 1, pp. 78–99.

Kantorowicz, Ernst H. (1997), *The King's Two Bodies: A Study in Mediaeval Political Theology*, Princeton, NJ: Princeton University Press.

Kateb, George (1981), 'The Moral Distinctiveness of Representative Democracy', *Ethics* 91: 3, pp. 357–74.

Kelly, Duncan (2004), 'Carl Schmitt's Political Theory of Representation', *Journal of the History of Ideas* 65: 1, pp. 113–34.

Kelsen, Hans [1929] (2013), *On the Worth and Values of Democracy*, ed. Nadia Urbinati and Carlo Invernizzi Accetti, trans. Brian Graf, Lanham, MD: Rowman & Littlefield.

Key, V. O. (1942), *Politics, Parties, and Pressure Groups*, New York: Crowell.

Kirshner, Alexander S. (2014), *A Theory of Militant Democracy: The Ethics of Combating Political Extremism*, New Haven, CT: Yale University Press.

Kishlansky, Mark A. (1986), *Parliamentary Selection: Social and Political Choice in Early Modern England*, Cambridge: Cambridge University Press.

Klein, Ezra (2011), 'You're Creating a Vision of the Sort of Society You Want to Have in Miniature', *The Washington Post*, 3 October.

Kröger, Sandra (2014), *Political Representation in the European Union: Still Democratic in Times of Crisis?*, New York: Routledge.

Laclau (1985), 'Theory, Democracy and Socialism', *New Reflections on the Revolution of Our Time*, London: Verso Books, pp. 219–29.

Laclau, Ernesto (1996), *Emancipation(s)*, London and New York: Verso.

Laclau, Ernesto (2000), 'Structure, History, and the Political', in *Contingency, Hegemony, Universality: Contemporary Dialogues on the Left*, ed. Judith Butler, Ernesto Laclau, and Slavoj Žižek, London: Verso, pp.182–212.

Laclau, Ernesto (2005), *On Populist Reason*, London and New York: Verso.

Laclau, Ernesto (2014), *The Rhetorical Foundations of Society*, London and New York: Verso.

Laclau, Ernesto and Chantal Mouffe (1985), *Hegemony and Socialist Strategy*, London and New York: Verso.

Laclau, Ernesto and Chantal Mouffe (1990), 'Post-Marxism without Apologies', in *New Reflections on The Revolution of Our Time*, ed. Ernesto Laclau, London and New York: Verso, pp. 97–132.

Laclau, Ernesto and Chantal Mouffe (2001), *Hegemony and Socialist Strategy: Towards a Radical Democratic Politics*, 2nd edn, London and New York: Verso.

Landemore, Hélène (2008), 'Is Representative Democracy Really Democratic?', *La Vie des Idées* 31: 3.

Latour, Bruno (2003), 'What If We Talked Politics a Little?', *Contemporary Political Theory* 2: 2, pp. 143–64.

Lefort, Claude (1951), 'L'Échange et la lutte des hommes', *Les Temps Modernes* 6: 64, pp. 1400–17.

Lefort, Claude (1972), *Le Travail de l'œuvre Machiavel*, Paris: Gallimard.

Lefort, Claude (1988), *Democracy and Political Theory*, trans. David Macey, Cambridge: Polity Press.

Lefort, Claude (1992), *Ecrire. A l'épreuve du politique*, Paris: Calmann-Lévy.

Lefort, Claude (2007), 'Démocratie et représentation', in *Le temps présent*, Paris: Éditions Belin, pp. 611–24.

Lefort, Claude (2012), *Machiavelli in the Making*, trans. Michael B. Smith, Evanston, IL: Northwestern University Press.

Leibovici, Martine (2002), 'From Fight to Debate: Machiavelli and the Revolt of the Ciompi', *Philosophy and Social Criticism* 28: 6, pp. 647–60.

Lemieux, Cyril (2013), 'Peut-on ne pas être constructiviste?', *Politix* 100: 4, pp. 169–87.

Levy, David N. (2014), *Wily Elites and Spirited Peoples in Machiavelli's Republicanism*, London: Lexington Books.

Lilla, Mark (2006), *The Reckless Mind: Intellectuals in Politics*, New York: New York Review of Books.

Lindahl, Hans (2003), 'Acquiring a Community: The *Acquis* and the Institution of European Legal Order', *European Law Journal* 9: 4, pp. 433–50.

Loewenstein, Karl (1937), 'Militant Democracy and Fundamental Rights, I', *American Political Science Review* 31: 3, pp. 417–32.

Lupia, Arthur (1992), 'Busy Voters, Agenda Control, and the Power of Information', *American Political Science Review* 86: 2, pp. 390–403.

Lupia, Arthur (1994), 'Shortcuts versus Encyclopedias: Information and Voting Behavior in California Insurance Reform Elections', *American Political Science Review* 88: 1, pp. 63–76.

Lupia, Arthur and Mathew D. McCubbins (1998), *The Democratic Dilemma: Can Citizens Learn What They Need to Know?* New York: Cambridge University Press.

Lütticken, Sven (2008), 'Attending to Abstract Things', *New Left Review*, 54, p. 113.

McCormick, John P. (2003), 'Machiavelli against Republicanism: On Cambridge School's "Guicciardinian Moments"', *Political Theory* 31: 5, pp. 615–43.

McCormick, John P. (2006), 'Contain the Wealthy and Patrol the Magistrates: Restoring Elite Accountability to Popular Government', *American Political Science Review* 100: 2.

McCormick, John P. (2011), *Machiavellian Democracy*, New York: Cambridge University Press.

Machiavelli, Niccolò (1999), 'Discourse on Remodelling the Government of Florence', *The Chief Works and Others*, vol. 1, Durham, NC: Duke University Press.

Machiavelli, Niccolò [1517] (1995), *Discourses on Livy*, Chicago, IL: University of Chicago Press.

Machiavelli, Niccolò [1532] (1990), *Florentine Histories*, Princeton, NJ: Princeton University Press.

Machiavelli, Niccolò [1532] (2005), *The Prince*, New York: Oxford University Press.

Magni, Beatrice (2012), *Conflitto e libertà: saggio su Machiavelli*, Pisa: Edizioni ETS.

Manent, Pierre (2006), *A World Beyond Politics? A Defense of the Nation-State*, Princeton, NJ: Princeton University Press.

Manin, Bernard (1987), 'On Legitimacy and Political Deliberation', *Political Theory* 15, pp. 338–68.

Manin, Bernard (1997), *The Principles of Representative Government*, New York: Cambridge University Press.

Mansbridge, Jane (1999), 'Should Blacks Represent Blacks and Women Represent Women? A Contingent "Yes"?', *Journal of Politics* 61, pp. 628–57.

Mansbridge, Jane (2003), 'Rethinking Representation', *American Political Science Review* 97: 4, pp. 515–28.

Mansbridge, Jane (2004), 'Representation Revisited: Introduction to the Case Against Electoral Accountability', *Democracy and Society* 2: 1, pp. 12–13.

Mansbridge, Jane (2009), 'A "Selection Model" of Political Representation', *Journal of Political Philosophy* 17: 4, pp. 369–98.

Mansbridge, Jane (2011), 'Clarifying the Concept of Representation', *American Political Science Review* 105: 3, pp. 621–30.

Marchart, Oliver (2007), *Post-Foundational Political Thought. Political Difference in Nancy, Lefort, Badiou and Laclau*, Edinburgh: Edinburgh University Press.

Marchart, Oliver (2015), 'Wrestling with the Cheating Gene: a Post-Foundational Approach to Ideology Critique', in *Ends of Critique* (Global Dialogues 10), ed. Pol Bargués-Pedreny, Kai Koddenbrock,

Jessica Schmidt and Mario Schmidt, Duisburg: Käte Hamburger Kolleg/Centre for Global Cooperation Research, pp. 44–51.

Marx, Karl [1844] (1984), 'On the Jewish Question', in *Early Writings*, trans. Rodney Livingstone and Gregor Benton, London: Penguin, pp. 211–41.

Mbembe, Achille (2017), *Critique of Black Reason*, trans. Lauren Dubois, Durham, NC: Duke University Press.

Medearis, John (2005), 'Labour, Democracy, Utility and Mill's Critique of Private Property', *American Journal of Political Science* 49: 1, pp. 135–49.

Merleau-Ponty, Maurice (1962), *The Phenomenology of Perception*, trans. Colin Smith, New York: Humanities Press.

Merleau-Ponty, Maurice (1968), *The Visible and the Invisible*, trans. Alphonso Lingis, Evanston, IL: Northwestern University Press.

Miller, David (1995), *On Nationality*, Oxford: Clarendon Press.

Miller, Warren E. and Donald E. Stokes (1963), 'Constituency Influence in Congress', *American Political Science Review* 57: 1, pp. 45–56.

Mineur, Didier (2010), *Archéologie de la représentation politique: structure et fondement d'une crise*, Paris: Presses de la Fondation Nationale des Sciences Politiques.

Montanaro, Laura (2012), 'The Democratic Legitimacy of "Self-Appointed" Representatives', *Journal of Politics* 74: 4, pp. 1094–107.

Mouffe, Chantal [1993] (2005a), *The Return of the Political*, London: Verso.

Mouffe, Chantal (2005b), *On the Political*, London: Verso.

Mouffe, Chantal [2005] (2009), *The Democratic Paradox*, London; New York: Verso.

Mouffe, Chantal (2013), *Agonistics: Thinking the World Politically*, London: Verso.

Moussa, Hélène (1992), *The Social Construction of Women Refugees: A Journey of Discontinuities and Continuities*, PhD thesis, University of Toronto.

Mulieri, Alessandro (2013), 'Beyond Electoral Democracy? A Critical Assessment of Constructivist Representation in the Global Arena', *Representation* 49: 4, pp. 515–27.

Mulieri, Alessandro (2014), 'Political Representation: A Historical and Conceptual Investigation into its Polysemy', PhD thesis, KU Leuven.

Mulieri, Alessandro (2016), 'Hasso Hofmann and the Polysemy of Representation', *Redescriptions, Political Thought, Conceptual History and Feminist Theory* 19: 2, pp. 127–45.

Müller, Jan-Werner (2012), 'A "Practical Dilemma Which Philosophy Alone Cannot Resolve"? Rethinking Militant Democracy: An Introduction', *Constellations* 19: 4, pp. 536–9.

Najemy, John M. (1982), 'Machiavelli and the Medici: The Lessons of Florentine History', *Renaissance Quarterly* 35: 4, pp. 551–76.

Najemy, John M. (2008), *A History of Florence 1200–1575*, Oxford: Wiley-Blackwell.

Näsström, Sofia (2006), 'Representative Democracy as Tautology. Ankersmit and Lefort on Representation', *European Journal of Political Theory* 5: 3, pp. 321–42.

Näsström, Sofia (2015), 'Democratic Representation Beyond Elections', *Constellations* 22: 1, pp. 1–12.

Neyer, Jürgen (2000), 'Justifying Comitology: The Promise of Deliberation', in *European Integration After Amsterdam. Institutional Dynamics and Prospects for Democracy*, ed. Karlheinz Neunreither and Antje Wiener, Oxford: Oxford University Press, pp. 112–28.

Ober, Josiah (2008), 'The Original Meaning of "Democracy": Capacity to do Things, not Majority Rule', *Constellations* 15: 1, pp. 3–9.

Ochoa, Paulina Espejo (2011), *The Time of Popular Sovereignty: Process and the Democratic State*, University Park, PA: Pennsylvania State University Press.

Offe, Claus (1996), *Modernity and the State: East, West*. Cambridge, MA: MIT Press.

Oksala, Johanna (2012), *Foucault, Politics and Violence*, Evanston, IL: Northwestern University Press.

Ostrogorski, Moisey (1902), *Democracy and the Organization of Political Parties*, trans. Frederick Clarke. London: Macmillan.

Parel, Anthony (1992), *The Machiavellian Cosmos*, New Haven, CT: Yale University Press.

Pasquino, Pasquale (1998), *Sieyès et l'invention de la constitution en France*, Paris: O. Jacob.

Pettit, Philip (2012), *On The People's Terms: A Republican Theory and Model of Democracy*, Cambridge: Cambridge University Press.

Phillips, Anne (1995), *The Politics of Presence*, Oxford: Oxford University Press.

Pierce, Roy and Phillip E. Converse (1986), *Political Representation in France*, Cambridge, MA: Harvard University Press.

Pitkin, Hanna Fenichel (1967), *The Concept of Representation*, Berkeley, CA: University of California Press.

Pitkin, Hanna Fenichel (2004), 'Representation and Democracy: Uneasy Alliance', *Scandinavian Political Studies* 27: 3, pp. 335–42.

Plotke, David (1997), 'Representation is Democracy', *Constellations* 4: 1, pp. 19–34.

Pocock, John G. A. (1975), *The Machiavellian Moment: Florentine Political Thought and the Atlantic Republican Tradition*, Princeton, NJ: Princeton University Press.

Podlech, A. (2004), 'Repräsentation', in *Geschictliche Grundbegriffe. Historisches Lexikon zur politisch-sozialen Prache in Deutschland*, ed. Reinhart Koselleck, Werner Conze and Otto Bruner, Stuttgart: Ernst Klett, 5, pp. 509–47.

Polletta, Francesca (2002a), *Freedom is an Endless Meeting: Democracy in American Social Movements*, Chicago, IL: University of Chicago Press.

Polletta, Francesca (2002b), 'Plotting Protest: Mobilizing Stories in the 1960s Student Sin-Ins', in *Stories of Change: Narrative and Social Movements*, ed. Joseph Davis, Albany, NY: State University of New York Press.

Polletta, Francesca (2006), *It Was Like a Fever: Storytelling in Protest and Politics*, Chicago, IL: University of Chicago Press

Przeworski, Adam (1999), 'Minimalist Conception of Democracy: A Defense', in *Democracy's Value*, ed. Ian Shapiro and Casiano Hacker-Cordón, Cambridge: Cambridge University Press, pp. 23–55.

Rancière, Jacques (1999), *Disagreement: Politics and Philosophy*, trans. Julie Rose, Minneapolis, MN: University of Minnesota Press.

Rancière, Jacques (2011), 'Democracies Without Democracy: An Interview with Eric Hazan', in *Democracy in What State?*, trans. William McCuaig, New York: Columbia University Press, pp. 76–81.

Rehfeld, Andrew (2005), *The Concept of Constituency: Political Representation, Democratic Legitimacy and Institutional Design*, Cambridge: Cambridge University Press.

Rehfeld, Andrew (2006), 'Towards a General Theory of Political Representation', *Journal of Politics* 68: 1, pp. 1–21.

Rehfeld, Andrew (2009), 'Representation Rethought: On Trustees, Delegates, and Gyroscopes in the Study of Political Representation and Democracy', *American Political Science Review* 103: 2, pp. 214–30.

Rehfeld, Andrew (2011), 'The Concepts of Representation', *American Political Science Review* 105: 3, pp. 631–41.

Rosanvallon, Pierre (1998), *Le Peuple introuvable. Histoire de la répresentation démocratique en France*, Paris: Gallimard.

Rosanvallon, Pierre (2006), *La contre-démocratie. La politique à l'âge de la defiance*, Paris: Seuil.

Rosanvallon, Pierre (2008), *Counter-Democracy: Politics in an Age of Distrust*, Cambridge: Cambridge University Press.

Rosanvallon, Pierre (2011), *Democratic Legitimacy: Impartiality, Reflexivity, Proximity*, Princeton, NJ: Princeton University Press.

Rosanvallon, Pierre (2015), *Le bon gouvernement*, Paris: Seuil.

Rousseau, Jean-Jacques and Gita May (2002), *The Social Contract: And, the First and Second Discourses*, New Haven, CT: Yale University Press.

Runciman, David (2007), 'The Paradox of Political Representation', *Journal of Political Philosophy* 15: 1, pp. 93–114.

Saffon, Maria Paula and Nadia Urbinati (2013), 'Procedural Democracy: the Bulwark of Political Equality', *Political Theory* 41, pp. 441–81.

Saussure, Ferdinand de [1916] (2013), *Course in General Linguistics*, trans. Roy Harris, London: Bloomsbury Academic.

Saward, Michael (2006), 'The Representative Claim', *Contemporary Political Theory* 5, pp. 297–318.

Saward, Michael (2009), 'Authorisation and Authenticity: Representation and the Unelected', *Journal of Political Philosophy* 17: 1, pp. 1–22.

Saward, Michael (2010), *The Representative Claim*, Oxford: Oxford University Press.

Saward, Michael (2012), 'Claims and Constructions', *Contemporary Political Theory* 11: 1, pp. 123–7.

Saward, Michael (2014), 'Shape-Shifting Representation', *American Political Science Review*, 108: 4, pp. 723–36.

Saward, Michael (2016), 'Fragments of Equality in Representative Politics', *Critical Review of International Social and Political Philosophy* 19: 3, pp. 245–62.

Schelling, Friedrich (1856), *Sämmtliche Werke* vol. 5, Stuttgart/Augsburg: J. G. Cotta.

Schlegel, Friedrich (1957), 'Fragmente zur Literatur und Poesie I', *Literary Notebooks 1797–1801*, ed. Hans Eichner, Toronto: University of Toronto Press.

Schlegel, Friedrich (1967), 'Gespräch über die Poesie', *Kritische Friedrich-Schlegel-Ausgabe, 2, Charakteristiken und Kritiken I (1797–1801)*, ed. Ernst Behler, München: Verlag Ferdinand Schönigh.

Schlegel, Friedrich (1996), 'Essay on the Concept of Republicanism occasioned by the Kantian Tract "Perpetual Peace"', *The Early Political Writings of the German Romantics*, ed. Frederick C. Beiser, Cambridge: Cambridge University Press.

Schlögl, Rudolf (2004), 'Symbole in der Kommunikation. Zur Einführung', *Die Wirklichkeit der Symbole: Grundlagen der Kommunikation in historischen und gegenwärtigen Gesellschaften*, ed. Rudolf Schlögl, Bernhard Giesen and Jürgen Osterhammel, Konstanz: UVK Verlagsgesellschaft, p. 13.

Schmitt, Carl (2003), *Nomos of the Earth*, trans. G. L. Ulmen, New York: Telos Press.

Schumpeter, Joseph Alois (1976), *Capitalism, Socialism and Democracy*, New York: Harper Torchbooks.

Schürmann, Reiner (1987), *Heidegger on Being and Acting: From Principles to Anarchy*, Bloomington, IN: Indiana University Press.

Severs, Eline (2010), 'Representation as Claims-Making. Quid Responsiveness?', *Representation* 46: 4, pp. 411–23.

Severs, Eline (2012), 'Substantive Representation Through a Claims-Making Lens: A Strategy for the Identification and Analysis of Substantive Claims', *Representation* 48: 2, pp. 169–81.

Sewell, William Hamilton (1980), *Work and Revolution in France: The Language of Labor from the Old Regime to 1848*, Cambridge and New York: Cambridge University Press.

Silvano, Giovanni (1990), 'Florentine Republicanism in the Early Sixteenth Century', in *Machiavelli and Republicanism*, ed. Gisela Bock, Quentin

Skinner and Maurizio Viroli, Cambridge: Cambridge University Press, pp. 41–70.

Sintomer, Yves (2009), *Il potere al popolo: giurie cittadine, sorteggio e domocrazia partecipativa*, Bari: Edizioni Dedalo.

Sintomer, Yves (2010), 'Random Selection, Republican Self-Government, and Deliberative Democracy', *Constellations* 17: 3, pp. 472–87.

Sintomer, Yves (2011), *Petite histoire de l'expérimentation démocratique: tirage au sort et politique d'Athènes à nos jours*, Paris: la Découverte.

Sintomer, Yves (2013), 'Les sens de la représentation politique: usages et mésusages d'une notion', *Raisons politiques*, 50: 2, pp. 13–34.

Sitrin, Marina and Dario Azzellini (2014), *They Can't Represent Us! Reinventing Democracy from Greece to Occupy*, London: Verso.

Skinner, Quentin (2000), *Machiavelli*, Oxford: Oxford University Press.

Skinner, Quentin (2004), 'Republican Virtues in an Age of Princes', in *Visions of Politics, volume II: Renaissance Virtues*, Cambridge: Cambridge University Press, pp. 118–59.

Sniderman, Paul M. (2000), 'Taking Sides: A Fixed Choice Theory of Political Reasoning', in *Elements of Reason: Cognition, Choice, and the Bounds of Rationality*, ed. Arthur Lupia, Mathew D. McCubbins and Samuel L. Popkin. NY: Cambridge University Press.

Sniderman, Paul M. and Sean M. Theriault (2004), 'The Structure of Political Argument and the Logic of Issue Framing', in *Studies in Public Opinion*, ed. Willem E. Saris and Paul M. Sniderman, Princeton, NJ: Princeton University Press.

Sørensen, Eva (2002), 'Democratic Theory and Network Governance', *Administrative Theory & Praxis* 24: 4, pp. 693–720.

Spivak, Gayatri Chakravorty (1988), 'Can the Subaltern Speak?', in *Marxism and the Interpretation of Culture*, ed. Cary Nelson and Lawrence Grossberg, Champaign, IL: University of Illinois Press, pp. 271–314.

Squires, Judith (2008), 'The Constitutive Representation of Gender: Extra-Parliamentary Re-Presentations of Gender Relations', *Representation*, 44: 2, pp. 187–204.

Stavrakakis, Yannis (1999), *Lacan and the Political*, London: Routledge.

Tanasescu, Mihnea (2014), 'Rethinking Representation: The Challenge of Non-Humans', *Australian Journal of Political Science* 49: 1, pp. 40–53.

Taylor, Charles (1971), 'Interpretation and the Sciences of Man', *Review of Metaphysics* 25: 1, pp. 3–51.

Taylor, Charles (1994), *Multiculturalism: Examining the Politics of Recognition*, Princeton, NJ: Princeton University Press.

Thiel, Markus (2013), 'Introduction', *The 'Militant Democracy' Principle in Modern Democracies*, Farnham: Ashgate Publishing.

Thomassen, Lasse (2007), 'Beyond Representation?', *Parliamentary Affairs* 60: 1, pp. 111–26.

Thomassen, Lasse (2010), 'Deconstruction as Method in Political Theory', Österreichische Zeitschrift für Politikwissenschaft 39: 1, pp. 41–53.

Thomassen, Lasse (2011), 'Deliberative Democracy and Provisionality', Contemporary Political Theory 10: 4, pp. 423–43.

Thomassen, Lasse (2017), British Multiculturalism and the Politics of Representation, Edinburgh: Edinburgh University Press.

Thompson, Dennis F. (2004), 'Election Time: Normative Implications of Temporal Properties of the Electoral Process in the United States', American Political Science Review 98, pp. 51–63.

Thompson, Simon (2012), 'Making Representations: Comments on Michael Saward's The Representative Claim', Contemporary Political Theory, 11: 1, pp. 111–14.

Tocqueville, Alexis de (1992), De la démocratie en Amérique II. In Œuvres. Tome II, Paris: Gallimard.

Tormey, Simon (2015), The End of Representative Politics, Cambridge: Polity Press.

Urbinati, Nadia (2000), 'Representation as Advocacy: A Study of Democratic Deliberation', Political Theory 28: 6, pp. 758–86.

Urbinati, Nadia (2006), Representative Democracy: Principles and Genealogy, Chicago, IL: University of Chicago Press.

Urbinati, Nadia (2010), 'Unpolitical Democracy', Political Theory, 38: 1, pp. 65–92.

Urbinati, Nadia (2013), Democrazia in diretta: le nuove sfide alla rappresentanza, Milano: Feltrinelli.

Urbinati, Nadia (2014), Democracy Disfigured: Opinion, Truth, and the People, Cambridge, MA: Harvard University Press.

Urbinati, Nadia (2016), 'Reflections on the Meaning of the "Crisis of Democracy"', Democratic Theory 3: 1, pp. 6–31.

Urbinati, Nadia and M. E. Warren (2008), 'The Concept of Representation in Contemporary Democratic Theory', Annual Review of Political Science, 11, pp. 387–412.

Ursino, Carmelo and Antonio Cantaro (1993), 'L'antiparlamentarismo tecnocratico', Democrazia e diritto 33: 3, pp. 219–230.

Van de Sande, Mathijs (2015), 'Fighting with Tools: Prefiguration and Radical Politics in the 21st Century', Rethinking Marxism 27: 2, pp. 177–94.

Violante, Piero (1982), Lo spazio della rappresentanza: Francia 1788–89, Palermo, Ila Plama.

Virno, Paolo (1996), 'Virtuosity and Revolution: The Political Theory of Exodus', in Radical Thought in Italy – A Potential Politics, ed. Michael Hardt and Paolo Virno, Minneapolis, MN: University of Minnesota Press, pp. 189–209.

Virno, Paolo (2004), A Grammar of the Multitude: For an Analysis of Contemporary Forms of Life, trans. Isabella Bertoletti, James Casciato and Andrea Casson, Los Angeles, CA: Semiotext(e).

Viroli, Maurizio (2005), *From Politics to Reason of the State: the Acquisition and Transformation of the Language of Politics, 1250–1600*, Cambridge: Cambridge University Press.

Walker, Jack L. (1996), 'A Critique of the Elitist Theory of Democracy', *American Political Science Review* 60: 2, pp. 285–95.

Warren, Mark E. (2001), *Democracy and Association*, Princeton, NJ: Princeton University Press.

Warren, Mark E. (2002), 'What Can Democratic Participation Mean Today?', *Political Theory* 30, pp. 678–702.

Warren, Mark E. (2006a), 'Democracy and Deceit: Regulating Appearances of Corruption', *American Journal of Political Science* 50, pp. 160–74.

Warren, Mark E. (2006b), 'Democracy and the State', *Oxford Handbook of Political Theory*, ed. John S. Dryzek, Bonnie Honig and Anne Phillips, Oxford: Oxford University Press, pp. 382–99.

Warren, Mark E. (2008), 'Citizen Representatives', in *Designing Deliberative Democracy: The British Columbia Citizens' Assembly*, ed. Mark Warren and Hilary Pearse, Cambridge: Cambridge University Press, pp. 50–69.

Warren, Mark E. (2016), 'What Kinds of Trust Does a Democracy Need? Trust from the Perspective of Democratic Theory', in *The Handbook of Political Trust*, ed. Sonja Zmerli and Tom W. G. van der Meer, Cheltenham: Edward Elgar Publishing.

White, Jonathan and Lea Ypi (2016), *The Meaning of Partisanship*, Oxford: Oxford University Press.

Williams, Melissa S. (1998), *Voice, Trust, and Memory: Marginalized Groups and Failings of Liberal Representation*, Princeton, NJ: Princeton University Press.

Young, Iris Marion (1990), *Justice and the Politics of Difference*, Princeton, NJ: Princeton University Press.

Young, Iris Marion (1997), 'Deferring Group Representation', in *Ethnicity and Group Rights. Nomos XXXIX*, ed. Ian Shapiro and Will Kymlicka, New York: New York University Press, pp. 349–76.

Young, Iris Marion (2000), *Inclusion and Democracy*, Oxford: Oxford University Press.

Žižek, Slavoj (1989), *The Sublime Object of Ideology*, London and New York: Verso.

Žižek, Slavoj (1999a), *Sehr innig und nicht zu rasch: Zwei Essays über sexuelle Differenz als philosophische Kategorie*, trans. Erik M. Vogt, Wien: Turia & Kant.

Žižek, Slavoj (1999b), *The Ticklish Subject, The Absent Centre of Political Ontology*, London: Verso.

Žižek, Slavoj (2000a), 'Class Struggle or Postmodernism? Yes, Please!', in *Contingency, Hegemony, Universality: Contemporary Dialogues on the Left*, ed. Judith Butler, Ernesto Laclau and Slavoj Žižek, London: Verso, pp. 90–135.

Žižek, Slavoj (2000b), 'Holding the Place', in *Contingency, Hegemony, Universality: Contemporary Dialogues on the Left*, ed. Judith Butler, Ernesto Laclau and Slavoj Žižek, London: Verso, pp. 308–29.

Žižek, Slavoj (2001), *On Belief*, New York: Routledge.

Zolo, Danilo (1992). *Democracy and Complexity: A Realist Approach*, University Park, PA: Pennsylvania State University Press.

Index

EU representative:
Easy Access System Europe
Mustamäe tee 50, 10621 Tallinn, Estonia
Gpsr.requests@easproject.com

www.ingramcontent.com/pod-product-compliance
Lightning Source LLC
Chambersburg PA
CBHW051954270326
41929CB00015B/2653